SPORTS IN AMERICA
RECREATION, BUSINESS, EDUCATION, AND CONTROVERSY

ISSN 1557-5535

SPORTS IN AMERICA

RECREATION, BUSINESS, EDUCATION, AND CONTROVERSY

Bob Jacobson

INFORMATION PLUS® REFERENCE SERIES
Formerly published by Information Plus, Wylie, Texas

GALE
CENGAGE Learning™

Detroit • New York • San Francisco • New Haven, Conn • Waterville, Maine • London

GALE
CENGAGE Learning™

Sports in America: Recreation, Business, Education, and Controversy

Bob Jacobson
Paula Kepos, Series Editor

Project Editors: Kathleen J. Edgar, Elizabeth Manar

Permissions: Barb McNeil, Aja Perales

Composition and Electronic Capture: Evi Abou-El-Seoud

Manufacturing: Cynde Bishop

For product information and technology assistance, contact us at
Gale Customer Support, 1-800-877-4253.
For permission to use material from this text or product, submit all requests online at **www.cengage.com/permissions**.
Further permissions questions can be e-mailed to
permissionrequest@cengage.com

Cover photograph reproduced by permission of Corbis/Wally McNamee (picture of closing ceremony of the Summer Olympics, Los Angeles, 1984).

Gale
27500 Drake Rd.
Farmington Hills, MI 48331-3535

ISBN-13: 978-0-7876-5103-9 (set)   ISBN-10: 0-7876-5103-6 (set)
ISBN-13: 978-1-4144-3168-0   ISBN-10: 1-4144-3168-6

ISSN 1557-5535

This title is also available as an e-book.
ISBN-13: 978-1-4144-3828-3 (set)
ISBN-10: 1-4144-3828-1 (set)
Contact your Gale sales representative for ordering information.

Printed in the United States of America
1 2 3 4 5 6 7 12 11 10 09 08

TABLE OF CONTENTS

problems that have plagued Major League Baseball and professional cycling.

Americans like to bet on sports almost as much as they like to play them. Sports gambling is a huge business in the United States, and most of it is underground. From pari-mutuel betting on horse races, to legal sports bookmaking in Nevada, to the office Super Bowl pool, to offshore Internet betting operations, this chapter surveys the scope of sports gambling in the United States. It also considers the problems sports gambling sometimes creates.

PREFACE

Sports in America: Recreation, Business, Education, and Controversy is part of the *Information Plus Reference Series*. The purpose of each volume of the series is to present the latest facts on a topic of pressing concern in modern American life. These topics include today's most controversial and most studied social issues: abortion, capital punishment, care for the elderly, crime, the environment, health care, immigration, minorities, national security, social welfare, women, youth, and many more. Although written especially for the high school and undergraduate student, this series is an excellent resource for anyone in need of factual information on current affairs.

By presenting the facts, it is the intention of Gale, a part of Cengage Learning, to provide its readers with everything they need to reach an informed opinion on current issues. To that end, there is a particular emphasis in this series on the presentation of scientific studies, surveys, and statistics. These data are generally presented in the form of tables, charts, and other graphics placed within the text of each book. Every graphic is directly referred to and carefully explained in the text. The source of each graphic is presented within the graphic itself. The data used in these graphics are drawn from the most reputable and reliable sources, in particular from the various branches of the U.S. government and from major independent polling organizations. Every effort has been made to secure the most recent information available. The reader should bear in mind that many major studies take years to conduct, and that additional years often pass before the data from these studies are made available to the public. Therefore, in many cases the most recent information available in 2008 dated from 2005 or 2006. Older statistics are sometimes presented as well, if they are of particular interest and no more-recent information exists.

Although statistics are a major focus of the *Information Plus Reference Series*, they are by no means its only

content. Each book also presents the widely held positions and important ideas that shape how the book's subject is discussed in the United States. These positions are explained in detail and, where possible, in the words of their proponents. Some of the other material to be found in these books includes: historical background; descriptions of major events related to the subject; relevant laws and court cases; and examples of how these issues play out in American life. Some books also feature primary documents or have pro and con debate sections giving the words and opinions of prominent Americans on both sides of a controversial topic. All material is presented in an even-handed and unbiased manner; the reader will never be encouraged to accept one view of an issue over another.

HOW TO USE THIS BOOK

Sports have an enormous presence in American life. Most Americans engage in sporting activities of one type or another and enjoy watching sports in person or on television. The American passion for sports has made it a major industry worth billions of dollars. It has also brought with it a host of problems. Illegal sports gambling is commonplace. Athletes at all levels have been caught using performance-enhancing drugs. Professional athletes and their teams squabble over their shares of the profits to the dismay of fans. The lure of money has also had a corrupting influence on major college sports and encouraged student athletes to quit school and turn professional at an increasingly young age. Meanwhile, less popular sports, including many women's sports, struggle for attention and funds.

Sports in America: Recreation, Business, Education, and Controversy consists of ten chapters and three appendixes. Each of the chapters examines a particular aspect of sports and American society. For a summary of the information covered in each chapter, please see the synopses provided in the Table of Contents at the front of the book. Chapters generally begin with an overview of the basic facts and background information on the chapter's topic, then proceed to examine subtopics of particular interest. For example, Chapter 9: Performance-Enhancing Drugs begins with a history of the use of drugs to increase strength, stamina, and other athletic traits. Particular attention is paid to recent scandals in American sports. This is followed by a description of the major types of performance-enhancing drugs and their effects. The serious, long-term health consequences of the drugs are also examined. Next, the chapter gives an overview of what is known about drug use within youth, college, and professional sports. The final section discusses steroids and the law and outlines the efforts undertaken by the U.S. government and the World Anti-Doping Agency to combat performance-enhancing-drug use. Readers can find their way through a chapter by looking for the section and subsection headings, which are clearly set off from the text. They can also refer to the book's extensive Index if they already know what they are looking for.

Statistical Information

The tables and figures featured throughout *Sports in America: Recreation, Business, Education, and Controversy* will be of particular use to the reader in learning about this issue. These tables and figures represent an extensive collection of the most recent and important statistics on sports and their role in American society— for example, graphics in the book cover the earnings of professional sports leagues, the percentage of college students who gamble on sports, the number of Americans who participate in various sports, spending on athletic scholarships by gender, and racial and ethnic differences in TV audiences for sports. Gale believes that making this information available to the reader is the most important way in which we fulfill the goal of this book: to help readers understand the issues and controversies surrounding sports in the United States and to reach their own conclusions.

Each table or figure has a unique identifier appearing above it for ease of identification and reference. Titles for the tables and figures explain their purpose. At the end of each table or figure, the original source of the data is provided.

In order to help readers understand these often complicated statistics, all tables and figures are explained in the text. References in the text direct the reader to the relevant statistics. Furthermore, the contents of all tables and figures are fully indexed. Please see the opening section of the Index at the back of this volume for a description of how to find tables and figures within it.

Appendixes

In addition to the main body text and images, *Sports in America: Recreation, Business, Education, and Controversy* has three appendixes. The first is the Important Names and Addresses directory. Here the reader will find contact information for a number of government and private organizations that can provide further information on sports and related issues. The second appendix is the Resources section, which can also assist the reader in conducting his or her own research. In this section, the author and editors of *Sports in America: Recreation, Business, Education, and Controversy* describe some of the sources that were most useful during the compilation of this book. The final appendix is the detailed Index, which facilitates reader access to specific topics in this book.

ADVISORY BOARD CONTRIBUTIONS

The staff of Information Plus would like to extend their heartfelt appreciation to the Information Plus Advisory Board. This dedicated group of media professionals provides feedback on the series on an ongoing basis. Their comments allow the editorial staff who work on the project to make the series better and more user-friendly. Our top priority is to produce the highest-quality and most useful books possible, and the Advisory Board's contributions to this process are invaluable.

The members of the Information Plus Advisory Board are:

- Kathleen R. Bonn, Librarian, Newbury Park High School, Newbury Park, California
- Madelyn Garner, Librarian, San Jacinto College–North Campus, Houston, Texas
- Anne Oxenrider, Media Specialist, Dundee High School, Dundee, Michigan
- Charles R. Rodgers, Director of Libraries, Pasco-Hernando Community College, Dade City, Florida
- James N. Zitzelsberger, Library Media Department Chairman, Oshkosh West High School, Oshkosh, Wisconsin

COMMENTS AND SUGGESTIONS

The editors of the *Information Plus Reference Series* welcome your feedback on *Sports in America: Recreation, Business, Education, and Controversy*. Please direct all correspondence to:

Editors
Information Plus Reference Series
27500 Drake Rd.
Farmington Hills, MI 48331-3535

CHAPTER 1
AMERICA'S SPORTS OBSESSION

WHAT ARE SPORTS?

A sport is a physical activity that people engage in for recreation, usually according to a set of rules, and often in competition with each other. However, such a simple definition does not capture the passion many Americans feel for their favorite sports. Sports are the recreational activity of choice for a huge portion of the U.S. population, both as spectators and as participants in sporting competitions. When enthusiasts are not participating in sports, they are flocking to the nation's arenas and stadiums to watch their favorite athletes play or tuning in to see games and matches broadcast on television. Table 1.1 gives a sport-by-sport view of spectator interest in the United States, based on polling data from the Gallup Organization examining percentages of the population identifying themselves as at least "somewhat" of a fan of each sport.

There are two broad categories of sports: professional and amateur. A professional athlete is paid to participate; an amateur athlete is one who participates merely as a pastime, not for pay. The word *amateur* comes from the Latin word for "love," suggesting that an amateur athlete plays simply because he or she loves the game.

SPORTS PARTICIPATION

Sports participation is difficult to measure because there are many different levels of participation, from backyard games to organized leagues, but analysts continue to refine research methods. The most direct approach is through surveys. One of the most extensive regular surveys is the *Superstudy of Sports Participation* (http://www.amer icansportsdata.com/ss_participation1.asp), which is conducted annually by American Sports Data Inc. (ASD). The information collected by ASD is analyzed by organizations such as the Sporting Goods Manufacturers Association (SGMA). Chapter 2 contains detailed information

from the *Superstudy* as well as from other surveys of sports participation.

Table 1.2 ranks sports by total participation. According to the National Sporting Goods Association (NSGA; 2007, http://www.nsga.org/public/pages/index.cfm?pageid=150), the trade association for sporting goods retailers, more Americans played basketball than any other team sport in 2006. The NSGA estimates that 26.7 million people aged seven and over played basketball in 2006. Other popular team sports included baseball (14.6 million participants), soccer (14 million), softball (12.4 million), tackle football (11.9 million), and volleyball (11.1 million). Even though participation in cross-country skiing experienced a dramatic 36.7% increase, most team sports showed a decline from 2005 to 2006. Participation in basketball, soccer, softball, and volleyball all declined, whereas hockey participation grew by 6% and tackle football participation increased by 19.7% from 2005 to 2006.

Americans love to participate in individual sports as well. The NSGA estimates that 44.8 million Americans went bowling in 2006, making it the most popular of all competitive sports nationally. (See Table 1.2.) In *2007 Sports & Fitness Participation Report* (2007, http://www.sgma.com/associations/5119/files/topline07.pdf), the SGMA also identifies bowling as the most popular competitive sport and estimates the number of participants even higher, at about 54.3 million Americans in 2006. Billiards is also exceedingly popular as a recreational sport, though its appeal has decreased in recent years. According to the NSGA, 31.8 million people shot pool in the United States in 2006, which was a 9.8% decline from 2005. (See Table 1.2.) Proprietors of bowling and billiards facilities are attempting to overcome a seedy reputation to draw in a new generation of enthusiasts.

The SGMA notes in *2007 Sports & Fitness Participation Report* that 28.7 million Americans went golfing

TABLE 1.1

Poll respondents who are fans of various sports, 2004–07

FOR EACH OF THE FOLLOWING, PLEASE SAY WHETHER YOU ARE A FAN OF THAT SPORT OR NOT. FIRST—[RANDOM ORDER]?

Sport	Percentage of Americans who are fans
Professional football (Dec. 2005)	59
College football (July 2006)	45
Professional baseball (Dec. 2006)	41
Figure skating (Dec. 2004)	41
Professional basketball (Dec. 2004)	38
Professional golf (January 2007)	36
College basketball (April 2006)	35
Auto racing (July 2006)	31
Professional tennis (Dec. 2004)	24
Professional ice hockey (Dec. 2004)	23
Professional or college soccer (June 2006)	19
Professional wrestling (Dec. 2004)	10

SOURCE: Adapted from "For each of the following, please say whether you are a fan of that sport or not. First—[RANDOM ORDER]?" in *Sports*, The Gallup Organization, July 2, 2007, http://www.galluppoll.com/content/?ci=4735&pg=1 (accessed July 23, 2007). Copyright © 2007 by The Gallup Organization. Reproduced by permission of The Gallup Organization.

TABLE 1.2

Sports participation, by total participation, 2006

[In millions. Respondents seven years of age or older who participated more than once.]

Sport	Total	Percent change
Exercise walking	87.5	1.70%
Swimming	56.5	−2.60%
Exercising with equipment	52.4	−3.40%
Camping (vacation/overnite)	48.6	5.70%
Bowling	44.8	−1.30%
Fishing	40.6	−2.50%
Workout at club	36.9	6.50%
Bicycle riding	35.6	−13.30%
Aerobic exercising	33.7	0.00%
Weight lifting	32.9	−1.90%
Billiards/pool	31.8	−9.80%
Hiking	31	4.00%
Boating, motor/power	29.3	6.20%
Running/jogging	28.8	−1.60%
Basketball	26.7	−7.40%
Golf	24.4	−1%
Hunting with firearms	17.8	−8.30%
Target shooting	17.1	−14.10%
Baseball	14.6	0.10%
Soccer	14	−0.80%
Backpack/wilderness camp	13.3	0.40%
Softball	12.4	−5.00%
Football (tackle)	11.9	19.70%
Volleyball	11.1	−9.30%
In-line roller skating	10.5	−20.00%
Tennis	10.4	−6.90%
Skateboarding	9.7	−19.20%
Scooter riding	9.5	−8.50%
Mountain biking (off road)	8.5	−7.20%
Paintball games	8	−0.20%
Canoeing	7.1	na
Skiing (alpine)	6.4	−7.30%
Water skiing	6.3	−6.60%
Hunting with bow & arrow	5.9	−11.60%
Target shooting—airgun	5.6	−15.70%
Snowboarding	5.2	−13.10%
Racquetball	4	na
Cheerleading	3.8	15.60%
Wrestling	3.8	na
Muzzle loading	3.7	−8.70%
Skiing (cross country)	2.6	36.70%
Hockey (ice)	2.6	6.00%

Note: Percent change is from 2005.
na=Not surveyed in 2004.

SOURCE: 2006 Participation—Ranked by Total Participation, National Sporting Goods Association, 2007, http://www.nsga.org/public/pages/index.cfm?pageid=150 (accessed July 23, 2007)

in 2006. Most golf rounds were played by a core of 17.2 million adults who golfed at least eight times per year. Tennis, while less popular now than at its peak in the late 1980s, has been enjoying a comeback in the 2000s. In 2006 about 14.6 million people got out on U.S. tennis courts.

An interesting transition is taking place in youth sports participation. Generally, participation among youth in traditional team sports has been declining for several years. One exception is soccer, which is becoming a major sport in the United States. An increasing number of young Americans are also opting for extreme sports such as snowboarding. Golf has also enjoyed an increase in participation among youth since the mid-1990s, as has lacrosse, a modern game derived from a Native American competition that became popular among French pioneers in Canada. U.S. Lacrosse reports in the *U.S. Lacrosse Participation Survey 2006* (2007, http://www.lacrosse.org/pdf/06 participationsurvey.pdf) that 426,022 people played lacrosse in 2006, compared with 253,931 in 2001, and that over the previous decade the number of people playing lacrosse nationally had increased more than 10% per year.

Another way to gauge interest in sports is by examining how much money people spend on equipment. According to the NSGA, U.S. consumers spent more than $24 billion on sporting goods in 2006. Table 1.3 shows consumer purchases of sporting goods broken down by sport.

SPORTS ATTENDANCE

Besides participation, another measure of interest in sports is the number of people who attend games in person. Sports attendance in the United States is dominated by the four major team sports: baseball, football, basketball, and hockey. In professional team sports, attendance is affected by two main factors: the size of the market in which the team plays and the team's current success. Big-city teams and winning teams typically draw bigger crowds than small-town teams and losing teams.

Major League Baseball (MLB) reports in the press release "Major League Baseball's Record Attendance Tops 76 Million" (October 2, 2006, http://mlb.mlb.com/news/press_releases/) that just over seventy-six million people attended MLB games during the 2006 regular season, setting a new all-time high for the third straight year. Average attendance at an MLB game was nearly

TABLE 1.3

Consumer sports equipment purchases, by sport, 2005 and 2006

[In millions]

	2006	2005
Archery	$ 398.3	$ 372.1
Baseball & softball	$ 402.0	$ 372.4
Basketball	$ 312.3	$ 309.3
Billiards & indoor games	$ 570.9	$ 572.3
Bowling	$ 181.5	$ 183.5
Camping	$ 1,534.6	$ 1,446.5
Exercise	$ 5,226.4	$ 5,176.6
Fishing tackle	$ 2,218.9	$ 2,138.9
Football	$ 101.3	$ 95.2
Golf	$ 3,662.0	$ 3,465.5
Helmets, sport protective	$ 159.1	$ 153.3
Hockey & ice skates	$ 142.2	$ 138.5
Hunting & firearms	$ 3,708.7	$ 3,563.4
Optics	$ 1,013.9	$ 886.9
Racquetball	$ 40.9	$ 45.4
Skin diving & scuba gear	$ 369.0	$ 358.3
Snow skiing	$ 615.0	$ 642.7
Snowboarding	$ 278.4	$ 301.0
Soccer balls	$ 74.3	$ 66.5
Tennis	$ 419.8	$ 397.1
Volleyball & badminton sets	$ 30.8	$ 32.1
Water skis	$ 43.5	$ 42.2
Wheel sports	$ 411.3	$ 407.7
Athletic goods team sales	$ 2,618.9	$ 2,567.5
Total equipment	**$24,472.0**	**$23,688.1**

SOURCE: Adapted from "2006 Consumer Equipment Purchases by Sport," National Sporting Goods Association, 2007, http://www.nsga.org/public/pages/index.cfm?pageid=162 (accessed July 23, 2007)

thirty-one thousand. According to the press release "NBA Sets All-Time Attendance Records" (April 19, 2007, http://www.nba.com/news/attendance_070419.html), the National Basketball Association (NBA) also set a new season attendance record during the 2006–07 regular season, drawing 21.8 million spectators to its arenas, for an average of 17,757 per game. Professional football set a new record for the 2006 regular season as well. The Entertainment and Sports Programming Network (ESPN) indicates in "NFL Attendance Report—2006" (2006, http: //sports .espn.go.com/nfl/attendance?year=2006) that the total paid attendance for the National Football League (NFL) was 17.6 million, with an average paid attendance of 68,773 per game. The National Hockey League (NHL) has rebounded since its 2004–05 season was canceled due to a labor dispute. ESPN reports in "NHL Attendance Report—2007" (2007, http://sports.espn.go.com/nhl/attendance?year =2007) that attendance in 2006–07 was 20.8 million, for an average of 16,956 per game, a new league record.

The other big sports draw in the United States is auto racing. The National Association for Stock Car Auto Racing (NASCAR), the nation's major stock car racing circuit, has experienced substantial growth in attendance over the last decade, though data from ESPN suggest that there was a drop-off in both attendance and television ratings for NASCAR races in 2006. Chapter 2 presents

more detailed discussion of major sports attendance in the United States.

PROFESSIONAL SPORTS
Team Sports

Throughout most of the twentieth century professional team sports in the United States meant baseball, football, basketball, and hockey. However, since the 1990s soccer has been gaining popularity and is often included in discussions of professional sports in the United States. Detailed information on professional team sports is provided in Chapter 4.

MLB has long been considered "America's national pastime." MLB, according to their Web site (2007, http://mlb.mlb.com/index.jsp), consists of thirty teams, divided into the sixteen-team National League and the fourteen-team American League. Each league is in turn divided into three divisions. The MLB season consists of 162 games, running from early April through late September, followed by playoffs and finally the championship series known as the World Series. According to Plunkett Research, in "Sports Industry Overview" (2007, http://www.plunkettresearch.com/Industries/Sports/SportsStatistics/tabid/273/Default.aspx), MLB was a $5.2 billion industry in 2006.

The premier professional football league in the United States is the NFL. Plunkett Research reports in "Sports Industry Overview" that the NFL generated league-wide revenue of $5.9 billion during the 2006–07 season, making it the richest of the major sports. There are thirty-two teams in the NFL (2007, http://www.nfl.com/), divided into two conferences: the National Football Conference (NFC) and the American Football Conference (AFC). The NFC and AFC are each divided into four divisions. NFL teams play a sixteen-game season, which begins around Labor Day. It ends with a single-elimination playoff series, culminating in the Super Bowl in early February. The Super Bowl is the biggest sporting event in the country in terms of viewing audience. The NFL reports in "Colts-Bears Draws No. 3 Audience of All-Time" (August 7, 2007, http://www.nfl.com/news/story?id=09000d5d800226d0&template=with-video&confirm=true) that 93.2 million viewers tuned in to the 2007 Super Bowl, making it the third-most-watched television show of all time, behind only the 1996 Super Bowl and the final episode of the sitcom *M*A*S*H*.

The NBA (2007, http://www.nba.com/), the top professional basketball league in the country, consists of thirty teams split into the Eastern and Western Conferences. Each conference has three divisions within it. The NBA season, which lasts for eighty-two regular-season games, begins in early November. The regular season is followed by the NBA playoffs, which begin in April. In "Sports Industry Overview," Plunkett Research notes that the NBA generated $3.1 billion in revenue during the 2006–07 season, placing it behind both football and baseball. Unlike football and baseball, however, basketball has a women's professional league, the Women's National Basketball Association (WNBA). There are thirteen teams in the WNBA. They play a thirty-four-game regular season, after which the top four teams in each conference compete in the championship playoffs. Thomas Heath notes in "A Matter of Value Instead of Profit" (*Washington Post*, July 12, 2006) that unlike any of the major men's professional sports, the WNBA loses money, though league officials expressed hope that the league would turn its first profit in 2007.

The top professional hockey league in North America is the NHL, which actually encompasses two countries, the United States and Canada, and is arguably more popular in the latter. The NHL (2007, http://www.nhl.com/) consists of thirty teams, divided into Eastern and Western Conferences. These conferences are in turn broken into three divisions each. The NHL season, like that of the NBA, is eighty-two games long. It is followed by the Stanley Cup playoffs, which ultimately determine the NHL champion. The NHL has struggled for more than a decade. Even before the entire 2004–05 season was canceled due to a labor strike, the league's popularity was in decline. In the two seasons since the strike, interest in the NHL has rebounded some. According to Plunkett Research, in "Sports Industry Overview," league-wide revenue was about $2.2 billion in the 2006–07 season, considerably less than any of the other major team sports.

Even though only hockey has experienced a labor dispute that resulted in cancellation of an entire season, each of these sports is occasionally subject to disputes that threaten their continuity and that sometimes result in cancellation of part of a season. Labor disagreements in professional sports often pit the league, which represents the interests of the team owners, against the players, who are represented by a labor union.

Individual Sports

Team sports get most of the media attention in the United States, but professional sports that feature individual competitors are also of considerable interest.

The premier golf tour in the United States and in the world is the PGA Tour (2007, http://www.pgatour.com/r/schedule/), which in 2007 consisted of forty-four official events offering more than $280 million in total prize money. The PGA Tour organization also runs a developmental tour called the Nationwide Tour and a tour for senior players called the Champions Tour. There are several other prominent regional professional golf tours based in other countries. Women's professional golf has a similar structure. The most prominent women's tour is the LPGA Tour, which is operated by the Ladies Profes-

sional Golf Association, and there are several other regional women's tours around the world.

Men's professional tennis is coordinated primarily by two organizations: the Association of Tennis Professionals (ATP), which operates the worldwide ATP Tour; and the International Tennis Federation, which coordinates the four international events that make up the Grand Slam of tennis. The 2007 ATP Tour (2007, http://www.atptennis.com) included sixty-four tournaments in thirty-one countries. Women's professional tennis is organized by the Women's Tennis Association, which runs the premier women's tour, currently sponsored by Sony Ericsson. According to the tour's official Web site (2007, http://www.sonyericssonwtatour.com/1/), the 2007 Sony Ericsson Tour included sixty-two events in thirty-five countries, in which fourteen hundred players representing seventy-five nations competed for $62 million in total prize money.

Auto racing has enjoyed a huge surge in popularity in the United States since the mid-1990s. The most important racing circuit for stock cars—which resemble ordinary cars externally—is NASCAR. NASCAR (2007, http://www.nascar.com/races/cup/2007/data/schedule.html) sanctions more than fifteen hundred races per year at more than one hundred tracks in thirty-eight states, plus Canada and Mexico.

The other major type of race car is the open-wheeled racer. There are two main open-wheeled racing circuits in the United States: the Indy Racing League (IndyCar) and the Champ Car Series. The 2007 IndyCar Series (2007, http://www.indycar.com/schedule/) featured seventeen races between March and September, most in the United States with one in Japan; the 2007 Champ Car Series (2007, http://www.champcarworldseries.com/Event/EventSchedule.asp?Year=2007) included seventeen races in the United States, Australia, Canada, Mexico, Europe, and China.

Boxing is unique among professional sports in that it has no single commission that regulates or monitors it nationwide. A number of organizations sanction professional boxing matches, including the World Boxing Association, the World Boxing Council, the World Boxing Organization, and the International Boxing Federation. Each follows its own set of regulations, employs its own officials, and acknowledges its own champions. A fighter can be recognized as champion by more than one organization simultaneously. Professional boxing in the United States has been plagued by corruption over the years, including tainted judging and fixed fights. Nevertheless, devoted fans tune in regularly to watch boxing on pay cable networks, and gamblers wager millions on the outcomes of boxing contests, injecting huge sums of money into the industry.

SPORTS AND THE MEDIA

For American sports enthusiasts, it is hard to separate the sports from the media industry that surrounds all aspects of professional and elite amateur sports. Leagues, teams, promoters, organizations, and schools make money through lucrative media contracts that give television networks the rights to broadcast sporting events over the public airwaves. For a full discussion of the intersection of sports and media, see Chapter 3.

The History of Sports on Television

The history of sports on television began with the 1939 broadcast of a college baseball game between Columbia and Princeton universities. Five years later the *Gillette Cavalcade of Sports* televised by the National Broadcasting Corporation (NBC) became the first network-wide television sports show. When single-company sponsorship became too expensive during the mid-1960s, sports programming developed a new model in which different companies bought advertising spots throughout the program.

The amount of sports programming and the amount of money in televised sports has continued to grow quickly since then. In "Sports and Television" (2004, http://www.museum.tv/archives/etv/S/htmlS/sportsandte/sportsandte.htm), the Museum of Broadcast Communications states that in 1970 the networks paid $50 million for the rights to broadcast NFL games, $18 million for MLB games, and $2 million for NBA games. By 1985 these totals had grown to $450 million, $160 million, and $45 million, respectively. In the 1980s the addition of cable television outlets extended the reach of televised sports even further. However, television ratings for the four major team sports generally declined during the 1990s as competition for the same audience arose from other viewing options.

Major Sports on Television

In the 1950s baseball was the most popular televised sport. Since then, however, it has lost a large share of its audience to other sports, particularly football. Even though television ratings for World Series broadcasts declined for several years, they rebounded after 2002, but sank again after peaking in 2004. In "The Cardinals Won? Series Averages Record-Low Ratings" (October 29, 2006, http://sports.espn.go.com/mlb/playoffs2006/news/story?id=2642964), ESPN notes that the 2006 World Series had a 10.1 rating (meaning 10.1% of all households were tuned in) and 17.0 share (meaning 17% of those watching something were watching the World Series). In *Sports Business Resource Guide & Fact Book* (2007, http://www.sportsbusinessjournal.com/images/random/resource2006_E-116,117.pdf), the *SportsBusiness Journal* indicates that MLB has a $2.4 billion broadcast contract with ESPN that runs through the 2013 season.

TABLE 1.4

Latest NFL TV contracts, by network or satellite provider

ESPN

Monday night
- 8 years, 2006–13
- $1.1 billion per year
- No Super Bowls

NBC

Sunday night
- 6 years, 2006–11
- $600 million per year
- Super Bowls in 2009 and 2012

Fox

Sunday afternoon NFC (National Football Conference)
- 6 years, 2006–11
- $712.5 million per year
- Super Bowls in 2008 and one other year during deal

CBS

Sunday afternoon AFC (American Football Conference)
- 6 years, 2006–11
- $622.5 million per year
- Super Bowls in 2007 and one other year during deal

DirecTV

Sunday Ticket satellite
- 5 years, 2006–10
- $700 million per year
- No Super Bowls

SOURCE: Created by Robert Jacobson for The Gale Group, 2007

Well before the close of the twentieth century, football had supplanted baseball as the reigning king of televised sports. In *2001 ESPN Information Please Sports Almanac* (2000), Gerry Brown and Michael Morrison state that, as of the turn of the century, five of the ten top-rated television shows of all time had been sports programs, and four of those were Super Bowls. Several more Super Bowl broadcasts were in the top twenty. As mentioned previously, Super Bowl XLI of 2007 became the third-most-watched program of all time, and Paul R. La Monica reports in "CBS Scores with Super Bowl Ratings" (CNNMoney.com, February 5, 2007) that Super Bowl XLI drew a 42.0 rating. The NFL signed a new round of television deals in April 2005, the most lucrative being a $1.1 billion contract resulting in the move of *Monday Night Football* from American Broadcasting Company (ABC) to ESPN beginning in 2006. (See Table 1.4.) The NFL received hundreds of millions of additional dollars from Fox, Columbia Broadcasting System (CBS), and NBC for various subsets of the NFL schedule.

Regular-season NBA basketball has never drawn as big a viewing audience as the NFL has—probably because there are so many more games—but viewership expands significantly during the playoffs. Of the major sports, the NHL is struggling the most to maintain its television audience. Even at its peak, hockey drew far fewer viewers than the other major sports, and the cancellation of the 2004–05 season hurt the NHL further. At the other extreme, NASCAR has enjoyed a surge in its television audience in the 2000s, including an increased female audience and broader viewership in the Pacific Northwest and other regions of the country that have not traditionally favored auto racing.

AMATEUR SPORTS
College Sports

Most college sports take place under the auspices of the National Collegiate Athletic Association (NCAA). In *Composition & Sport Sponsorship of the NCAA* (March 1, 2007, http://www1.ncaa.org/membership/membership_svcs/membership_breakdown.html), the NCAA explains that it is a voluntary association with a membership of about 1,250 colleges, college athletic conferences, and other organizations and individuals. The NCAA is divided into Divisions I, II, and III based on size, athletic budget, and related variables. Division I is further divided into three subdivisions, I-A, I-AA, and I-AAA. I-AAA includes schools that have substantial sports programs but do not field a football team. Within the NCAA many major sports colleges are grouped into conferences, which function like the divisions and leagues in professional sports.

According to the NCAA's annual *Sports Sponsorship and Participation Rates Report* (May 2007, http://www.ncaa.org/library/research/participation_rates/1982-2006/1982_2006_participation_rates.pdf), more than 393,000 student-athletes participated in championship sports at NCAA member schools during the 2005–06 season. The average NCAA institution had about 375 athletes—214 men and 161 women. However, women's teams actually outnumbered men's teams. Among men, the sport with the greatest number of Division I teams in 2005–06 was basketball. However, in terms of number of players, football was the leader. Among women, outdoor track and field had the most participants in 2003–04, but more colleges had women's basketball teams than had women's track and field teams.

For most of the twentieth century, men's college teams and athletes far outnumbered women's teams and athletes, and far more money went into men's sports. However, the gap has been closing, largely because of the passage in 1972 of Title IX, a law mandating gender equity in federally funded education programs. Under Title IX, girls' sports were to be funded at the same rate as sports programs for boys. Since Title IX's mandatory compliance date of 1978, women's collegiate sports have experienced explosive growth.

Much to the discomfort of some in the academic world, college sports have become big business in the United States. Spending on sports programs has been rising at a faster rate than overall institutional spending across the NCAA. Even though college sports generate substantial revenue, this revenue does not cover the cost of running the entire athletic program at the vast majority of schools, largely because only a few sports—often only football and men's basketball programs—are actually profitable. The NCAA notes in *2002–03 NCAA Revenues and Expenses of Divisions I and II Intercollegiate Athletics Programs Report* (February 2005, http://www.ncaa.org/library/research/i_ii_rev_exp/2003/2002-03_d1_d2_rev_exp.pdf) that the average Division I-A athletic program had total revenues of $29.4 million and expenses of $27.2 million in 2003. Football and basketball accounted for a huge share of both revenues and expenses. A new edition of this report featuring data from 2003–04 through 2005–06 was scheduled for publication in the fall of 2007.

High School Sports

The National Federation of State High School Associations (NFHS) conducts a detailed survey of high school sports participation each year. NFHS (2007, http://www.nfhs.org/core/contentmanager/uploads/2005_06NFHSparticipationsurvey.pdf) data show that 7.1 million students participated in high school sports in the 2005–06 season. This total was a record high. Participation among boys was 4.2 million, whereas 2.9 million girls participated.

For years, football has been the most popular high school sport for boys. According to the 2005–06 NFHS High School Athletics Participation Survey, a little over one million boys played high school football during the 2005–06 season. Basketball was second, with 546,335 participants. Among girls, basketball was the most popular high school sport, with 452,929 participants, followed by outdoor track and field with 439,200 participants.

Analysis by the research group Child Trends of data from Lloyd D. Johnston et al.'s *Monitoring the Future, National Results on Adolescent Drug Use:Overview of Key Findings, 2006* (May 2007, http://www.monitoringthefuture.org/pubs/monographs/overview2006.pdf) indicates that kids who participated in high school sports between 1991 and 2004 were less likely to engage in risky behavior and more likely to do well in school. By contrast, there is also evidence that the corrupting influence of money in big-time sports is beginning to trickle down to the high school level, including a series of reports in the *New York Times* in late 2005 of athletes buying diplomas and passing grades from bogus correspondence schools. The NCAA took measures in 2006 to crack down on these so-called diploma mills.

The Olympics

The concept behind the Olympic movement is to bring the world together through sports, in the spirit of

TABLE 1.5

Olympic sports

Summer games		Winter games
Aquatics	Hockey	Biathlon
Archery	Judo	Bobsleigh
Athletics	Modern pentathlon	Curling
Badminton	Rowing	Ice hockey
Baseball	Sailing	Luge
Basketball	Shooting	Skating
Boxing	Softball	Skiing
Canoe/kayak	Table tennis	
Cycling	Taekwondo	
Equestrian	Tennis	
Fencing	Triathlon	
Soccer	Volleyball	
Gymnastics	Weight lifting	
Handball	Wrestling	

SOURCE: Created by Robert Jacobson for The Gale Group, 2007. Data from the International Olympic Committee, http://www.olympic.org/uk/sports/index_uk.asp.

common understanding and noble competition. The Olympic games are based on an athletic festival that took place in ancient Greece from about 776 BC until AD 393. The Olympics were revived in their modern form in 1896. The Summer Olympics take place every four years, the same years in which February has twenty-nine days. According to the International Olympic Committee (IOC; 2007, http://www.olympic.org/uk/games/past/index_uk.asp?OLGT=1&OLGY=2004), 10,625 athletes from 201 countries competed in the 2004 Summer Olympics held in Athens, Greece, and medals were awarded in 28 sports that encompassed 301 events.

The Winter Olympics also take place every four years, halfway between the summer games. The winter games are smaller than the summer games. The IOC (2007, http://www.olympic.org/uk/games/past/index_uk.asp?OLGT=2&OLGY=2006) notes that the 2006 Winter Olympics in Turin, Italy, featured 2,508 athletes from 80 countries, competing in 7 sports that encompassed 84 events. Table 1.5 lists the sports that currently make up the Summer and Winter Olympic games.

The founder of the modern Olympics was the French historian and educator Pierre de Coubertin (1862–1937). Coubertin believed that war could be averted if nations participated together in friendly athletic competition. His ideas have not proved true, but the Olympic movement has thrived anyway. The inaugural Olympic games took place in 1896 in Athens, Greece, where 241 athletes from 14 countries competed in what was the largest international sporting event in history at the time.

The winter games arose initially as an outgrowth of the summer games. A handful of winter sports were included in early versions of the Olympics. The Winter Olympics finally became their own event in 1924. Until 1992 the winter games took place the same year as the summer

games; beginning in 1994 they have been held in the years halfway between the Summer Olympics.

Politics have frequently disrupted, or even canceled, the Olympics. The 1916 games were canceled because of World War I (1914–1918), and World War II (1939–1945) caused the cancellation of the 1940 and 1944 Olympics. Boycotts have also diminished the scope of the games. The U.S. team, along with sixty-four other Western nations, boycotted the 1980 Olympics in Moscow in protest of the Soviet invasion of Afghanistan. In 1984 the Soviet Union and fourteen of its allies boycotted the Olympics in Los Angeles, ostensibly because of security concerns but more realistically as a response to the Moscow boycott. Scandals related to doping—such as the BALCO affair described in detail in Chapter 9—and bribery—including the implication of the organizing committee for the 2002 Winter Games in Salt Lake City—have also marred the idealistic image of international cooperation and amateur athleticism on which the Olympics were founded.

The International Olympic Committee (IOC) is the worldwide governing body for the Olympics. Each participating country has its own national Olympic committee (NOC), whose role is to support that nation's Olympic team and to coordinate bids by cities within their country to host the Olympics. The U.S. Olympic Committee, headquartered in Colorado Springs, Colorado, is the NOC in the United States.

Individual sports are governed worldwide by International Federations, which make the rules for the events within their portfolio. On the national level, there are corresponding organizations called national governing bodies (NGBs). Some of the NGBs in the United States include USA Gymnastics, USA Swimming, and USA Track and Field. These organizations are in charge of choosing which athletes will represent the United States in that sport. In the host country the Olympic games are planned by an Organizing Committee for the Olympic games, which takes care of the logistical preparations for the Olympics.

The Olympics generates billions of dollars through a handful of marketing programs. The biggest source of money is television broadcast revenue. Other sources include corporate sponsorships, ticket sales, and sales of licensed merchandise. Chapter 7 contains detailed information about Olympic revenue. It also includes descriptions of other Olympic-style meets, such as the Special Olympics, Paralympics, and Deaflympics.

SPORTS AND HEALTH

Participation in sports yields great health benefits. Many health benefits of physical activity have been well documented. Physical activity builds and maintains bones and muscles, reduces fat, reduces blood pressure, and decreases the risk of obesity and heart attacks. There is also substantial evidence that physical activity improves mental health and may help fend off depression. A number of studies, including a massive 2001 survey conducted by researchers at the University of Florida (http://news.ufl.edu/2001/03/07/body-image/), link sports participation with a better self-image and a healthier attitude toward one's own body. Sports participation by youth has been shown to reduce the likelihood of engaging in risky behavior, though some studies, such as "Sports Participation, Delinquency, and Substance Use among Rural African-American Girls" (August 25, 2001, http://www.apa.org/releases/sportinvolvement.html) by Matthew J. Taylor of the University of Wisconsin, LaCrosse, have been more ambiguous on this point.

These benefits do not come without risk, however. Every year, millions of people injure themselves participating in sports. The most common sports injuries are muscle sprains and strains, ligament and tendon tears, dislocated joints, and bone fractures. The University of Chicago Medical Center indicates in "Sports Injuries" (2007, http://www.uchospitals.edu/online-library/content=P00725) that soft tissue injuries, such as bruises, sprains, and tendonitis, account for about 95% of all sports injuries. Injuries that happen suddenly during an activity, such as those resulting from a fall, are called acute injuries, whereas injuries that occur through repeated overuse are called chronic injuries.

According to the National Center for Health Statistics' *Monthly Statistical E-Letter* (March 2007, http://www.cdc.gov/nchs/pressroom/data/mnh_0307.htm), there were about 5.4 million sports injuries in the United States serious enough to require medical consultation in 2005. Bjorn Carey notes in "The Most Dangerous Sports in America" (Livescience.com, June 14, 2006) that in 2005 basketball, cycling, and football were the sports responsible for the greatest number of sports injuries requiring a trip to the emergency room.

Sports participation brings special hazards for children and youth. Children who are placed under severe pressure to succeed by parents, coaches, and other adults are at risk of psychological damage. The stress of ultra-competitive sports participation leads to high rates of burnout among young athletes. Pressure to perform also puts children and youth at elevated risk of physical injury, as demands are put on young bodies not yet developed enough to withstand the strain. Chapter 8 explores both the health benefits and health risks of athletic participation.

Doping

The use of prohibited substances to give an athlete an unfair advantage over other competitors is called doping. Doping has been around almost as long as sports have. Historical writings suggest that athletes were using concoctions made of herbs or psychoactive mushrooms to give themselves a competitive edge as early as the ancient Olympics.

The modern era of doping began in 1935, when injectable testosterone was first developed by scientists in Nazi Germany. Testosterone is a male hormone that occurs naturally in the body. Boosting its levels in the blood is thought to increase strength and aggressiveness.

Several decades later, anabolic steroids—chemical variants of testosterone—were developed. John Ziegler (1917–2000), the team physician for the U.S. weightlifting squad, learned about steroids from his Soviet counterparts, and soon steroids were in wide use in the United States. By the late 1960s the IOC had compiled a list of officially banned substances, but it had no effective way to monitor steroid use.

Steroids soon spread to professional football and other sports requiring extreme strength and bulk. Professional and Olympic sports eventually developed into a kind of cat-and-mouse game between developers of performance-enhancing drugs and the governing bodies of sports that prohibited their use. The latter would invent a way to detect the latest drugs, only to discover that the former had invented a new method for avoiding detection. The issue of doping in elite athletics still remains.

One of the biggest doping scandals to date, the BALCO scandal, has been unfolding since 2003. BALCO, the Bay Area Laboratory Co-Operative, was a California-based drug distributor. The scandal erupted in the summer of 2003, when Trevor Graham, a disgruntled track coach, provided authorities with a syringe containing a previously unknown steroid called THG. Authorities raided BALCO facilities and uncovered not only large amounts of steroids but also documents implicating a number of high-profile athletes and trainers in football, baseball, and track and field. The scandal continued to dog baseball superstar Barry Bonds (1964–) in the 2007 season as he approached the all-time home-run record long held by Hank Aaron (1934–). Fan reaction to the prospect of Bonds holding the record was decidedly mixed, as suspicion lingered that Bonds had gotten much of the way toward this landmark with the aid of illicit substances. Professional cycling has also been hit hard by steroid scandal. Floyd Landis (1975–), a 2006 Tour de France champion, tested positive for steroids, raising questions about the legitimacy of his victory. Then, just when the Tour needed to display its cleanliness the most, several more top Tour contenders failed drug tests in 2007, throwing the sport into chaos. In September 2007 Landis was stripped of his 2006 Tour title.

Steroid use has been linked to many potentially serious health problems, including liver and kidney tumors, high blood pressure, elevated cholesterol, severe acne, and in men, shrunken testicles. Steroid use is also associated with emotional disturbances, including violent mood swings popularly known as "roid rage."

Besides steroids, athletes turned to a number of other substances to gain an advantage before each was banned from sports. These include erythropoietin, a hormone that increases oxygen in the blood, which was at the center of a 1998 doping scandal in cycling; androstenedione, which stimulates testosterone production and was made famous by the home-run leader Mark McGwire (1963–); and ephedra, an herbal stimulant that has been used in Chinese medicine for centuries.

Steroid use in youth sports has tapered off recently, after a period of explosive growth during the late 1990s and early 2000s. (See Figure 1.1.) Approximately 1.8% of twelfth graders in 2006 reported having used steroids in the previous year. The National Institute on Drug Abuse reports in "NIDA InfoFacts: Steroids (Anabolic-Androgenic)" (March 2007, http://www.drugabuse.gov/Infofacts/Steroids.html) that the number of high school seniors who perceived steroids as being harmful increased from 56.8% in 2005 to 60.2% in 2006.

Chapter 9 includes more detailed information on the variety of anabolic steroids and other performance-enhancing substances that have been used over the years.

SPORTS AND GAMBLING

For millions of sports fans, the pleasure of watching a sporting event is enhanced by betting on its outcome. Even though gambling on sports (not including horse- and greyhound racing) is technically legal only in Nevada, Americans nevertheless find ways to engage in sports wagering in huge numbers, whether through small-scale office pools or via offshore Internet gambling sites of questionable legality.

Legal Sports Betting

In Nevada legal sports betting is practiced through legitimate bookmaking operations, which are often affiliated with and located in a casino. Bookmakers set the line (margin) of victory required to win the bet for each game. Football is the biggest betting draw among the major team sports. The Nevada Gaming Control Board (February 6, 2007, http://www.gaming.nv.gov/documents/pdf/pr_2007superbowl.pdf) reports that more than $93 million was bet legally on the Super Bowl alone in 2007, a slight decrease from the $94.5 million wagered the previous year, but higher than in any other year.

While most sports gambling remains illegal, polls show that many Americans are perfectly comfortable with sports gambling, even though a relatively small percentage actually participate. According to the Pew Research Center, in *Gambling: As the Take Rises, So Does Public Concern* (May 23, 2006, http://pewresearch.org/assets/social/pdf/Gambling.pdf), in 2006, 42% of respond-

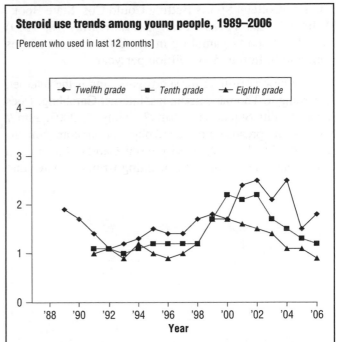

FIGURE 1.1

Steroid use trends among young people, 1989–2006

[Percent who used in last 12 months]

SOURCE: Adapted from Lloyd D. Johnston et al., "Steroids: Trends in Annual Use, Risk, Disapproval, and Availability, Eighth, Tenth, and Twelfth Graders," in *Monitoring the Future, National Results on Adolescent Drug Use: Overview of Key Findings, 2006*, National Institute on Drug Abuse, May 2007, http://www.monitoringthefuture.org/pubs/monographs/overview2006.pdf (accessed July 23, 2007)

ents approved of legalized gambling on professional sports. However, only 14% had actually bet on professional sports in 2006.

Gambling on horse racing, dog racing, and jai alai (a handball-like sport popular in Florida) uses what is called the pari-mutuel system. In this type of betting, all the wagers go into a single pool, which is then split among the winners, with management taking a small share off the top. In the fact sheet "Gaming Revenue: Current-Year Data" (October 2006, http://www.americangaming.org/Industry/factsheets/statistics_detail.cfv?id=7), the American Gaming Association (AGA) estimates that total revenue from pari-mutuel gambling in the United States was nearly $3.7 billion in 2005.

Illegal Sports Betting

In spite of these impressive dollar amounts for both Nevada sports books and pari-mutuel gambling, these sums represent just the tip of the sports betting iceberg. Legal gambling in the United States is utterly dwarfed by illegal gambling. The AGA estimates in the fact sheet "Sports Wagering" (March 12, 2007, http://www.americangaming.org/Industry/factsheets/issues_detail.cfv?id=16) that Nevada sports books account for less than 1% of all sports gambling nationwide in a typical year. It is almost impossible to gauge how much money is bet on sports when illegal bets are included. Robert Macy estimates in "Ban on College Sports Betting Could Cost State Books Millions" (*Las Vegas Review-Journal*, May 18, 1999) that illegal sports gambling in the United States ranges from $80 billion to $380 billion per year.

The newest frontier for sports gambling is the Internet. According to Thomas Jensen, in "Internet Gambling: Does America Still Stand for Liberty?" (July 4, 2007, http://www.point-spreads.com/index2.php?option=com_content&do_pdf=1&id=2157), Christiansen Capital Advisors, a gaming and entertainment consulting firm, estimates that about twenty-three million people—eight million of them in the United States—bet $5.9 billion over the Internet in 2005. There is still a fair amount of disagreement as to the legal status of online gambling, because most operations are not based in the United States. In 2006 Congress passed the Unlawful Internet Gambling Enforcement Act, which made it difficult for financial institutions to transfer funds to and from online gambling operations. Even though the full impact of the act remains to be seen, it will likely result in a reduction in sports wagering taking place over the Internet.

CHAPTER 2
SPORTS PARTICIPATION AND ATTENDANCE

For when the One Great Scorer comes

to write against your name,

He marks—not that you won or lost—

But how you played the game.

—Grantland Rice (1880–1954)

People have been playing games in one form or another ever since the first time a pair of humans decided to start grappling for fun rather than over food. The number and variety of sports in which people have participated through the ages is impossible to calculate. In North America, Native Americans were playing lacrosse and many other organized sports before Europeans settled permanently on the continent. In addition, one need only think of gladiators doing battle at the Colosseum in ancient Rome to realize that people have been gathering to watch other people play sports for centuries as well. The following is a summary of sports participation and sports attendance in the United States, drawing information from government and industry publications.

SPORTS PARTICIPATION

There is no shortage of data available on sports participation in the United States. Participation is measured by market research firms, coordinating bodies of individual sports, and government agencies, among others. Sports participation is nevertheless a difficult thing to measure, and nobody has yet figured out how to measure it perfectly. People who go for a casual walk or swim at the beach may not think of themselves as engaging in a sport, but those interested in selling walking shoes or studying the health benefits of physical activity might disagree. Then there is the matter of defining the word *participation*—does it mean a person plays the sport once per year, once per month, or only those who play almost every day? Besides determining who qualifies as a sports participant, the reliability of self-reported data presents additional problems. For example, can an individual accurately report that he played touch football with his friends twelve months ago rather than fifteen months ago? Distortion is inevitable, especially with regard to recreational activities that participants tend to engage in less frequently, such as scuba diving. There is also a tendency when responding to this kind of survey to want to receive credit for having participated in a sport, especially a glamorous one such as rock climbing, even if the respondent has not undertaken the activity in several years. Another way to assess participation is through sales of sports equipment. However, this approach also has its perils. As Harvey Lauer, the president of American Sports Data (ASD), observes in "Sports Participation Research: Not Yet a Science" (2006, http://www.americansportsdata.com/pr-participantsportmethodology.asp), "80% of all athletic/sports shoes are never sweated in."

Participation *Superstudy*

Each year ASD, a leader in sports participation and fitness research, conducts a massive nationwide survey called the *Superstudy of Sports Participation* (http://www.americansportsdata.com/ss_participation1.asp). The Sporting Goods Manufacturers Association (SGMA) analyzes data from the *Superstudy* and publishes reports on various aspects of sports participation in the United States. The SGMA's annual *Sports Participation Topline Report* (2006, http://www.sgma.com/associations/5119/files/Sports%20Participation%20Topline-2006.pdf) outlines major trends in every category of sports participation. Table 2.1 shows trends in sports participation over the last two decades.

TEAM SPORTS. Table 2.2 shows the total number of people participating by sport in 2006. Basketball was the most popular team sport in which to engage. About 24.7 million Americans aged six and over reported that they played basketball at least once in 2006. Even though

TABLE 2.1

Sports participation trends, selected years, 1987–2005

[In thousands. U.S. population, 6 years of age or older, who participated at least once per year.]

	1987 benchmark	1990	1993	1998	2000	2004	2005	1 year % change (2004–2005)	7 year % change (1998–2005)	18 year % change (1987–2005)
Team sports										
Baseball	15,098	15,454	15,586	12,318	10,881	9,694	10,255	+5.8	−16.7	−32.1
Basketball	35,737	39,808	42,138	42,417	37,552	34,223	31,963	−6.6	−24.6	−10.6
Cheerleading	na	3,039	3,257	3,266	3,377	4,131	4,154	+0.6	+27.2	+36.7[a]
Ice hockey	2,393	2,762	3,204	2,915	2,761	1,998	2,585	+29.4	−11.3	+8.0
Field hockey	na	na	na	1,375	1,349	na	na	na	na	na
Football (touch)	20,292	20,894	21,241	17,382	15,456	12,993	14,083	+8.4	−19.0	−30.6
Football (tackle)	na	na	na	na	5,673	5,440	5,794	+6.5	na	na
Football (net)	na	na	na	na	18,285	16,436	18,179	+10.6	na	na
Lacrosse	na	na	na	926	751	914	1,622	+77.5	+75.2	na
Rugby	na	na	na	546	na	na	na	na	na	na
Soccer (indoor)	na	na	na	na	na	4,349	5,024	+15.5	na	na
Soccer (outdoor)	na	na	na	na	na	14,608	15,786	+8.1	na	na
Soccer (net)	15,388	15,945	16,365	18,176	17,734	15,900	17,009	+7.0	−6.4	+10.5
Softball (regular)	na	na	na	19,407	17,585	14,267	12,859	−9.9	−33.7	na
Softball (fast-pitch)	na	na	na	3,702	3,795	4,042	3,519	−12.9	−4.9	na
Softball (net)	na	na	na	21,352	19,668	16,941	15,144	−10.6	−29.1	na
Volleyball (hard surface)	na	na	na	na	na	11,762	12,371	+5.2	na	na
Volleyball (grass)	na	na	na	na	na	9,163	7,314	−20.2	na	na
Volleyball (beach)	na	11,560	13,509	10,572	8,763	7,741	6,884	−11.1	−34.9	−40.4[a]
Volleyball (net)	35,984	39,633	37,757	26,637	22,876	22,216	20,918	−5.8	−21.5	−41.9
Racquet sports										
Badminton	14,793	13,559	11,908	9,936	8,490	6,432	6,186	−3.8	−37.7	−58.2
Racquetball	10,395	9,213	7,412	5,853	5,155	5,533	4,909	−11.3	−16.1	−52.8
Squash	na	na	na	289	364	290	na	na	na	na
Tennis	21,147	21,742	19,346	16,937	16,598	18,346	18,305	−0.2	+8.1	−13.4
Personal contact sports										
Boxing	na	na	na	na	1,085	1,140	602	−47.2	na	+4.5
Martial arts	na	na	na	5,368	5,722	6,898	6,028	−12.6	+12.3	+28.2
Wrestling	na	na	na	na	2,405	2,303	2,211	−4.0	na	−28.5
Indoor sports										
Billiards/pool	35,297	38,862	40,254	39,654	37,483	36,356	35,164	−3.3	−11.3	−0.4
Bowling	47,823	53,537	49,022	50,593	53,844	53,603	53,514	−0.2	+5.8	+11.9
Darts	na	na	na	21,792	18,484	na	18,753	na	−13.9	na
Table tennis	na	20,089	17,689	14,999	13,797	14,286	14,119	−1.2	−5.9	−29.7[a]
Wheel sports										
Roller hockey	na	na	2,323	3,876	3,287	1,788	2,094	+17.1	−46.0	−9.9[b]
Roller skating (2×2 wheels)	na	27,101	24,223	14,752	10,834	11,103	10,554	−4.9	−28.5	−61.1[a]
Roller skating (inline wheels)	na	4,695	13,689	32,010	29,024	17,348	16,490	−4.9	−48.5	+251.2[a]
Scooter riding (non-motorized)	na	na	na	na	13,881	10,196	9,606	−5.8	na	na
Skateboarding	10,888	9,267	5,388	7,190	11,649	10,592	11,382	+7.5	+58.3	+4.5
Other sports/activities										
Bicycling (BMX)	na	na	na	na	3,977	2,642	2,480	−6.1	na	na
Bicycling (recreational)	na	na	na	54,575	53,006	52,021	51,431	−1.1	−5.8	na
Golf	26,261	28,945	28,610	29,961	30,365	27,314	25,709	0.0	−14.2	−2.1
Gymnastics	na	na	na	6,224	6,689	5,273	5,917	+12.2	−4.9	na
Swimming (recreational)	na	na	na	94,371	93,976	95,268	91,314	−4.2	−3.2	na
Walking (recreational)	na	na	na	80,864	82,561	92,677	87,628	−5.4	+8.4	na
Outdoors activities										
Camping (tent)	35,232	36,915	34,772	42,677	42,241	41,561	38,602	−7.1	−9.5	+9.6
Camping (recreational vehicle)	22,655	20,764	22,187	18,188	19,035	17,424	18,214	+4.5	0.0	−19.6
Camping (net)	50,386	50,537	49,858	50,650	51,606	49,412	47,623	−3.6	−6.0	−5.5
Hiking (day)	na	na	na	38,629	39,015	39,334	36,623	−6.9	−5.2	na
Hiking (overnight)	na	na	na	6,821	6,750	6,396	6,268	−2.0	−8.1	na
Hiking (net)	na	na	na	40,117	40,133	40,713	38,006	−6.6	−5.3	na
Horseback riding	na	na	na	16,522	16,988	14,695	na	na	na	na
Mountain biking	1,512	4,146	7,408	8,611	7,854	5,334	6,466	+21.2	−24.9	+327.6
Mountain/rock climbing	na	na	na	2,004	1,947	2,161	2,299	+6.4	+14.7	na
Artificial wall climbing	na	na	na	4,696	6,117	7,659	8,869	+15.8	+88.9	na
Trail running	na	na	na	5,249	5,232	6,486	6,167	−4.9	+17.5	na

basketball still enjoyed a comfortable lead over all other team sports, this figure represented a 9.7% drop since 2000. Football (almost 21 million, including both tackle and touch), baseball (16.1 million), and outdoor soccer (14.7 million) were the other team sports with the most participants in 2006. Like basketball, participation in

TABLE 2.1

Sports participation trends, selected years, 1987–2005 [CONTINUED]

[In thousands. U.S. population, 6 years of age or older, who participated at least once per year.]

	1987 benchmark	1990	1993	1998	2000	2004	2005	1 year % change (2004–2005)	7 year % change (1998–2005)	18 year % change (1987–2005)
Shooting sports										
Archery	8,558	9,252	8,648	7,109	6,047	6,756	6,633	−1.8	−6.7	−22.5
Hunting (shotgun/rifle)	25,241	23,220	23,189	16,684	16,481	15,196	*17,972	*na	*na	*na
Hunting (bow)	na	na	na	4,719	4,120	3,661	3,802	+3.9	−19.4	na
Paintball	na	na	na	5,923	7,121	9,640	10,357	+7.4	+74.9	na
Shooting (sport clays)	na	2,932	3,100	2,734	2,843	3,222	2,964	−8.0	+8.4	+1.1a
Shooting (trap/skeet)	5,073	na	na	3,800	3,827	4,059	4,046	−0.3	+6.5	−20.2
Target shooting (rifle)	na	na	na	14,042	12,984	14,057	13,795	−1.9	−1.8	na
Target shooting (hand gun)c	na	na	na	na	na	11,932	10,650	−10.7	na	na
Target shooting (net)c	18,947	21,840	23,498	18,330	16,293	18,037	16,900	−6.3	−7.8	−10.8
Fishing										
Fishing (fly)	11,359	8,039	6,598	7,269	6,581	4,623	6,546	+41.6	−9.9	−42.4
Fishing (freshwater-other)	50,500	53,207	50,198	45,807	44,050	39,433	42,123	+6.8	−8.0	−16.6
Fishing (saltwater)	19,646	19,087	18,490	15,671	14,710	13,453	13,055	−3.0	−16.7	−33.5
Fishing (net)	58,402	58,816	55,442	55,488	53,846	47,906	50,943	+6.3	−8.2	−12.8
Winter sports										
Ice skating	na	na	na	18,710	17,496	14,692	14,581	−0.8	−22.1	na
Skiing (cross-country)	8,344	7,292	6,489	4,728	4,613	4,007	2,701	−32.6	−42.9	−67.6
Skiing (downhill)	17,676	18,209	17,567	14,836	14,749	11,971	12,047	−0.6	−18.8	−31.8
Snowboarding	na	2,116	2,567	5,461	7,151	7,110	7,304	+2.7	+33.7	+245.2a
Snowmobiling	na	na	na	6,492	7,032	4,688	4,780	+2.0	−26.4	na
Snowshoeing	na	na	na	1,721	1,970	2,302	1,920	−16.6	+11.6	na
Water sports										
Boardsailing/windsurfing	1,145	1,025	835	1,075	655	418	535	+28.0	−50.2	−53.3
Canoeing	na	na	na	13,615	13,134	11,449	11,783	+2.9	−13.5	na
Kayaking	na	na	na	3,501	4,137	6,147	6,962	+13.3	+98.9	na
Rafting	na	na	na	5,570	4,941	4,209	4,505	+7.0	−19.1	na
Jet skiing	na	na	na	11,203	10,835	7,972	9,129	+14.5	−18.5	na
Sailing	6,368	5,981	3,918	5,902	5,271	4,307	4,680	+8.7	−20.7	−26.5
Scuba diving	2,433	2,615	2,306	3,448	2,901	3,430	2,900	−15.4	−15.9	+19.2
Snorkeling	na	na	na	10,575	10,526	11,112	9,392	−15.5	−11.2	na
Surfing	1,459	1,224	na	1,395	2,180	1,936	2,658	+37.3	+90.5	+82.2
Wakeboarding	na	na	na	2,253	3,581	2,843	2,697	−5.1	+19.7	na
Water skiing	19,902	19,314	16,626	10,161	10,335	6,835	7,282	+6.5	−28.3	−63.4

na=not applicable

aFifteen-year change.

bTwelve-year change.

c2003 figure is elevated due to change in category definition from "pistol" to "handgun."

*2005 measurement elevated due to addition of "hunting-handgun" category.

SOURCE: Adapted from "SGMA Sports Participation Trends," in *SGMA Sports Participation Topline Report 2006*, Sporting Goods Manufacturers Association, 2006, http://www.sgma.com/associations/5119/files/Sports%20Participation%20Topline-2006.pdf (accessed July 24, 2007)

---

each of these sports has been trending downward in recent years. The *Superstudy* defines core participants as those who engage in the sport over a given number of times per year, varying from sport to sport. In terms of percentage of core participants, the leading team sports are basketball, baseball, and slow-pitch softball. (See Table 2.3.)

Even though *Topline Report* data suggest that soccer participation has leveled off, there is ample evidence that soccer's emergence as a major sport in the United States continues. For example, the SGMA notes in *Manufacturers Sales by Category Report—2007 Edition* (August 6, 2007, http://www.sgma.com/associations/5119/files/Mfg_ Sales_Category07.pdf) that sales of soccer balls

and equipment rose from $280 million in 2005 to $300 million in 2006, an increase of 7%. Soccer is clearly a youth movement, which bodes well for the future of the sport. The SGMA reports in *State of the Industry Report* (2005) that as of 2004, 70% of all soccer players were between the ages of six and seventeen, and another 25% were aged eighteen to forty-four; the remaining 5% included both those under six years old and those aged forty-five and older.

INDIVIDUAL SPORTS. Bowling, golf, and tennis remain quite popular pastimes among the American public. In the *2007 Sports & Fitness Participation Report* (2007, http://www.sgma.com/associations/5119/files/topline07.pdf), the SGMA indicates that 54.3 million Americans bowled in 2006, making it the most popular

TABLE 2.2

Sports participation, 2006 vs. 2000

[Numbers in thousands. U.S. population, 6 years of age or older, who participated at least once per year.]

	Total participants			
	2006	2000	1 year change (2005 to 2006)	6 year change (2000 to 2006)
Individual sports				
Adventure racing	809			
Archery	7,497	6,531	4.7%	14.8%
Billiards/pool	46,990	45,405	10.3%	3.5%
Bowling	54,305	51,828	5.4%	4.8%
Boxing	2,072		−10.0%	
Darts	22,195		10.1%	
Golf on a 9/18 hole course	28,743	28,083	−2.0%	2.4%
Horseback riding	11,576		−12.8%	
Ice skating	10,578	12,969	−2.1%	−18.4%
Martial arts	6,270	6,440	−7.6%	−2.6%
Roller skating (2 × 2 wheels)	8,147	8,355	0.1%	−2.5%
Roller skating (inline wheels)	13,069	23,256	−1.1%	−43.8%
Scooter riding (non-motorized)	8,495	11,064	10.9%	−23.2%
Skateboarding	11,083	10,787	5.2%	2.7%
Trail running	4,436			
Triathlon (non-traditional/off road)	390			
Triathlon (traditional/road)	692			
Racquet sports				
Badminton	6,323	9,271	−6.4%	−31.8%
Racquetball	3,476	4,371	−16.5%	−20.5%
Squash	569			
Table tennis	15,107	12,726	16.0%	18.7%
Tennis	14,665	13,065	1.8%	12.2%
Team sports				
Baseball	16,114	17,508	−2.3%	−8.0%
Basketball	24,665	27,305	6.1%	−9.7%
Cheerleading	3,125	2,809	−9.6%	11.3%
Field hockey	943			
Football (tackle)	9,016	8,829	0.0%	2.1%
Football (touch)	11,974	11,686	12.5%	2.5%
Gymnastics	4,552	6,114	−15.8%	−25.5%
Ice hockey	1,849	2,619		−29.4%
Lacrosse	1,153	686		68.1%
Paintball	4,960	3,944		25.8%
Roller hockey	1,289	3,624		−64.4%
Rugby	683			
Soccer (indoor)	4,811			
Soccer (outdoor)	14,665		0.9%	
Softball (fast pitch)	1,897	2,904		−34.7%
Softball (slow-pitch)	8,640	12,324	−4.1%	−29.9%
Track and field	4,638		−2.9%	
Ultimate frisbee	4,073		−4.1%	
Volleyball (beach)	3,072	4,863	−19.6%	−36.8%
Volleyball (court)	6,005		−5.2%	
Volleyball (grass)	4,328		−8.6%	
Wrestling	3,326	4,272	−15.3%	−22.1%

TABLE 2.2

Sports participation, 2006 vs. 2000 [CONTINUED]

[Numbers in thousands. U.S. population, 6 years of age or older, who participated at least once per year.]

	Total participants			
	2006	2000	1 year change (2005 to 2006)	6 year change (2000 to 2006)
Outdoor sports				
Backpacking overnight - more than 1/4 mile from vehicle/home	7,084			
Bicycling-BMX	2,144	4,163	−17.4%	−48.5%
Bicycling (mountain/non-paved surface)	6,978		−4.1%	
Bicycling (road/paved surface)	39,398		9.1%	
Birdwatching more than 1/4 mile from home/vehicle	11,183			
Camping (recreational vehicle)	17,328	18,296	−1.0%	−5.3%
Camping within 1/4 mile of vehicle/home	36,107		2.1%	
Climbing (sport/indoor/boulder)	5,215			
Climbing (Traditional/ice/mountaineering)	1,897			
Fishing (fly)	6,121	6,772	−9.1%	−9.6%
Fishing (freshwater-other)	44,597	45,214	3.1%	−1.4%
Fishing (saltwater)	12,684	14,997	−4.7%	−15.4%
Hiking (day)	29,406			
Hunting (bow)	4,053	4,846	−9.4%	−16.4%
Hunting (handgun)	2,611		−14.8%	
Hunting (rifle)	11,271		0.3%	
Hunting (shotgun)	9,091		1.3%	
Shooting (sport clays)	3,670	4,009	−12.2%	−8.5%
Shooting (trap/skeet)	2,934	3,326	−16.6%	−11.8%
Snowmobiling	2,989	5,926	−25.8%	−49.6%
Target shooting (handgun)	9,773		0.5%	
Target shooting (rifle)	11,911	10,114	10.8%	17.8%
Wildlife viewing more than 1/4 mile from home/vehicle	20,451			
Water sports				
Boardsailing/windsurfing	1,116			
Canoeing	9,633			
Jet skiing	6,749	9,244	−13.3%	−27.0%
Kayaking (recreational)	4,371			
Kayaking (sea/touring)	1,236			
Kayaking (white water)	1,007			
Rafting	3,791			
Sailing	3,570	4,639	−13.3%	−23.0%
Scuba diving	2,912			
Snorkeling	8,416	10,328	−8.7%	−18.5%
Surfing	2,280			
Wakeboarding	3,511	5,254	−11.3%	−33.2%
Water skiing	5,110	8,494	−14.6%	−39.8%

SOURCE: Adapted from *SGMA 2007 Sports and Fitness Participation Report*, Sporting Goods Manufacturers Association, 2007, http://www.sgma.com/associations/5119/files/topline07.pdf (accessed July 24, 2007)

of all competitive sports in the United States. This figure represented an increase of nearly three million after several stable years. Bowling has been undergoing a transformation in the form that participation takes. In the past a large percentage of bowlers played on a team affiliated with a bowling league. The SGMA estimates that in the 1980s about two-thirds of all bowling was done by league bowlers; in the 2000s about one-third of all bowling takes place under the auspices of a league. The decline in the number of league bowlers has been compensated for by the addition of a great number of young, individual

bowlers. However, these bowlers are less serious about the sport than league players. Only 26% of bowlers in 2006 were core bowlers, meaning they bowled at least thirteen times. As a result of this shift, sales of bowling equipment have stagnated in spite of strong numbers of people who can be counted as participants.

The U.S. Bowling Congress notes that another challenge facing bowling is that the number of places to bowl has been decreasing for the last several years. This trend is partly the result of consolidation, as older, smaller bowling centers are replaced by larger, state-of-the-art facilities, many of which feature upscale decor and good food service, in contrast to the stereotypical grimy, beer-

TABLE 2.3

Team sports participation, 2006

Rank/sport	Core participants	Total participation	% of core participants
Basketball	18,761,000 (13+ days)	24,665,000	76.1%
Baseball	12,175,000 (13+ days)	16,114,000	75.6%
Slow-pitch softball	5,665,000 (13+ days)	8,640,000	65.6%

SOURCE: "Leading Team Sports Based on Percentage of Core Participants," in *Core Participants: The Focus of SGMA's New Sports Participation Study*, Sporting Goods Manufacturers Association, May 14, 2007, http://www.sgma .com/displayindustryarticle.cfm?articlenbr=33686&searchcriteria= participation&securetype=All&startrec=1 (accessed July 24, 2007)

splashed dens of the mid-twentieth century. Newer bowling centers usually offer modern, automated scoring, as well as better in-house balls and shoes. Some are megacenters offering other activities as well, including golf driving ranges, skating, or even basketball. Efforts to lure a younger crowd back to bowling alleys also include special events such as "Rock 'n' Bowl," or "Cosmic Bowling," which features glow-in-the-dark pins and discotheque or ultraviolet lighting.

As in the bowling industry, proprietors of billiards halls are attempting to shed the game's rough image in an effort to attract to the sport new players who may have previously been put off by pool's unsavory reputation. According to the National Sporting Goods Association (NSGA; 2007, http://www.nsga.org/public/pages/index.cfm?pageid=150), 31.8 million people shot pool or billiards in 2006, which was a decline of 9.8% from the previous year. The SGMA states that the profile of the typical billiards player has changed over the past few decades. Pool halls were once frequented primarily by older men, but in the twenty-first century pool is becoming a sport played increasingly by women and young people. Since the 1980s many facilities have upgraded their traditional low-budget style, and most no longer resemble the no-nonsense rooms immortalized in movies such as *The Hustler* (1961). New and refurbished billiards rooms, similar to contemporary bowling centers, are well lit, clean, and frequently part of multi-activity facilities offering many recreation options.

The *2007 Sports & Fitness Participation Report* shows that golf's popularity has remained fairly constant since 2000, when 28 million people hit the links. In 2006 the sport had 28.7 million participants. Tennis has been enjoying an upswing in popularity in recent years. In 2000 just over 13 million tennis enthusiasts hoisted a racket. By 2006 the total had grown by 12.2%, to 14.6 million. One factor in the resurgence of tennis is a conscious effort to democratize the sport. Once played primarily by the wealthy at country clubs, tennis is now available to people at all socioeconomic levels. The U.S. Tennis Association (USTA; 2007, http://www.usta.com/ home/default.sps) has helped this trend along by inves-

ting heavily in programs aimed at growing the sport, including a $50-million initiative launched in 1997 called the USA Tennis Plan for Growth, which offered free lessons around the country; the USTA also has a Diversity Plan aimed at encouraging multicultural participation in a sport that has long been dominated by white players, coaches, and officials. Gains in minority participation have received a boost from the success and popularity of such African-American stars as Serena Williams (1981–), Venus Williams (1980–), and James Blake (1979–). The *2007 Sports & Fitness Participation Report* indicates that in 2006 other widely played racquet sports included table tennis (15.1 million participants), badminton (6.3 million), and racquetball (3.4 million).

National Sporting Goods Association Survey

The NSGA also conducts a broad nationwide survey on sports participation. The following are a few highlights from the 2006 NSGA survey.

Table 1.2 in Chapter 1 ranks sports and other physical activities by total participation and provides a useful snapshot of what Americans choose to do when they want to move their bodies.

Table 2.4 provides a sport-by-sport glance at trends in participation since 1996. According to NSGA data, basketball participation has declined over the past ten years, whereas football has enjoyed recent growth. Baseball and soccer have remained fairly stable. It is interesting to note that as participation in cycling has dropped off, skateboarding has attracted more participants. Similarly, the decrease in alpine skiing over the past ten years has been offset by growth in snowboarding.

YOUTH SPORTS. The National Alliance for Youth Sports cites in "Sports Participation Key to Character Building, Study Finds" (2003, http://www.nays.org/Int Main_News.cfm?Cat=6&Story=221) a 2004 survey sponsored by Velocity Sports Performance, an independent training program for athletes of all ages and skill levels. According to the survey, American adults believe it is important for children to participate in sports. For example, 36% of respondents believed that sports participation has the greatest impact on a youth's character, ranking ahead of such activities as after-school programs, travel, and summer camp. This sentiment was even more prevalent among the affluent, those with full-time jobs, and those under the age of fifty-five.

However, according to the NSGA, youth participation in team sports is on the decline. The population of seven- to seventeen-year-olds grew 9.5% between 1997 and 2006. (See Table 2.5.) Therefore, a sport that grows in participation any less than that among youths is not keeping up with population growth. According to NSGA data, youth baseball participation grew by just 3.5%. Basketball participation shrank by 12.8% during this

TABLE 2.4

Ten-year history of selected sports participation, selected years, 1996–2006

[In millions. Respondents seven years of age or older who participated more than once.]

Sport	2006	2004	2002	2000	1998	1996
Aerobic exercising	33.7	29.5	29	28.6	25.8	24.1
Backpack/wilderness camp	13.3	15.3	14.8	15.4	14.6	11.5
Baseball	14.6	15.9	15.6	15.6	15.9	14.8
Basketball	26.7	27.8	28.9	27.1	29.4	31.8
Bicycle riding	35.6	40.3	39.7	43.1	43.5	53.3
Billiards/pool	31.8	34.2	33.1	32.5	32.3	34.5
Boating, motor/power	29.3	22.8	26.6	24.2	25.7	28.8
Bowling	44.8	43.8	42.4	43.1	40.1	42.9
Camping (vacation/overnite)	48.6	55.3	55.4	49.9	46.5	44.7
Canoeing	7.1	7.5	7.6	6.2	7.1	8.4
Cheerleading	3.8	3.8	na	na	3.1	na
Exercise walking	87.5	84.7	82.2	86.3	77.6	73.3
Exercising with equipment	52.4	52.2	46.8	44.8	46.1	47.8
Fishing	40.6	41.2	44.2	49.3	43.6	45.6
Football (tackle)	11.9	8.6	7.8	7.5	7.4	9
Golf	24.4	24.5	27.1	26.4	27.5	23.1
Hiking	31	28.3	27.2	24.3	27.2	26.5
Hockey (ice)	2.6	2.4	2.1	1.9	2.1	2.1
Hunting with bow & arrow	5.9	5.8	4.6	4.7	5.6	5.5
Hunting with firearms	17.8	17.7	19.5	19.1	17.3	18.3
In-line roller skating	10.5	11.7	18.8	21.8	27	25.5
Mountain biking (off road)	8.5	8	7.8	7.1	8.6	7.3
Muzzleloading	3.7	3.8	3.6	2.9	3.1	3.2
Paintball games	8	9.4	6.9	5.3	na	na
Running/jogging	28.8	26.7	24.7	22.8	22.5	22.2
Scooter riding	9.5	12.9	13.4	11.6	na	na
Skateboarding	9.7	10.3	9.7	9.1	5.8	4.7
Skiing (alpine)	6.4	6.3	7.4	7.4	7.7	10.5
Skiing (cross country)	2.6	2.4	2.2	2.3	2.6	3.4
Snowboarding	5.2	6.6	5.6	4.3	3.6	3.1
Soccer	14	13.3	13.7	12.9	13.2	13.9
Softball	12.4	12.5	13.6	14	15.6	19.9
Swimming	56.5	53.4	53.1	60.7	58.2	60.2
Target shooting	17.1	19.2	18.9	14.8	12.8	14.7
Tennis	10.4	9.6	11	10	11.2	11.5
Volleyball	11.1	11.8	11.5	12.3	14.8	18.5
Water skiing	6.3	5.3	6.9	5.9	7.2	7.4
Weight lifting	32.9	26.2	25.1	24.8	na	na
Workout at club	36.9	31.8	28.9	24.1	26.5	22.5
Wrestling	3.8	na	na	na	na	na

SOURCE: "Ten-Year History of Selected Sports Participation," National Sporting Goods Association, 2007, http://www.nsga.org/public/pages/index.cfm?pageid=153 (accessed July 24, 2007)

period. Even soccer, which is generally perceived as an emerging sport, saw participation growth among youth of only 2.7%. Hockey, football, skateboarding, and snowboarding all saw strong increases in youth participation between 1997 and 2006.

SPORTS PARTICIPATION AND GENDER. According to NSGA survey data, the sports that drew the greatest number of female participants in 2006 (excluding exercise and recreational activities such as walking, aerobics, and camping) were swimming (31.1 million), bowling (22.1 million), and bicycling (16.1 million). (See Table 2.6.) Basketball, at 8.8 million participants, topped the list among team sports, with softball (6.8 million participants) and volleyball (6.6 million participants) not far behind. Golf, soccer, and tennis were also high on the list. Women represent a greater share of participants in some sports than in others. For example, 59.6% of the nation's

volleyball players and 48.9% of tennis players in 2006 were female. Table 2.7 shows changes in participation among women between 2001 and 2006. Few sports experienced significant shifts in participation among women between these two years.

Emerging Sports

EXTREME SPORTS. As participation in traditional team sports such as baseball and basketball stagnates, especially among youth and young adults, a generation of sports participants is turning instead to a class of activities collectively known as extreme sports. Even though there is no consensus on exactly which sports qualify as extreme, their binding characteristic can be loosely identified as pointing to sports that result in a so-called adrenaline rush, or a degree of risk-taking not associated with old-school sports. Most lists include

TABLE 2.5

Youth sports participation, 2006 vs. 1997

[In thousands. Respondents seven years of age or older who participated more than once.]

	Year	Total	Change vs. 1997	Total 7–11	Change vs. 1997	Total 12–17	Change vs. 1997
Total U.S.	1997	240,325		19,466		23,071	
Total U.S.	2006	263,138	9.50%	19,472	0.00%	25,261	9.50%
Sport							
Baseball							
Baseball	1997	14,146		4,739		3,678	
Baseball	2006	14,646	3.50%	3,691	−22.10%	3,910	6.30%
Basketball							
Basketball	1997	30,660		6,837		7,880	
Basketball	2006	26,735	−12.80%	5,427	−20.60%	7,218	−8.40%
Bicycle riding							
Bicycle riding	1997	45,119		11,190		8,482	
Bicycle riding	2006	35,621	−21.10%	7,872	−29.60%	6,341	−25.30%
Bowling							
Bowling	1997	44,770		5,731		7,118	
Bowling	2006	44,779	0.00%	5,060	−11.70%	7,612	6.90%
Fishing (fresh water)							
Fishing (fresh water)	1997	38,956		4,831		5,025	
Fishing (fresh water)	2006	36,637	−6.00%	4,470	−7.50%	4,067	−19.10%
Football (tackle)							
Football (tackle)	1997	8,219		1,841		2,983	
Football (tackle)	2006	11,888	44.60%	2,199	19.50%	4,149	39.10%
Golf							
Golf	1997	26,216		1,049		2,255	
Golf	2006	24,428	−6.80%	879	−16.10%	2,150	−4.70%
Ice hockey							
Ice hockey	1997	1,925		304		406	
Ice hockey	2006	2,559	32.90%	430	41.30%	335	−17.50%
In-line skating							
In-line skating	1997	26,550		9,152		7,163	
In-line skating	2006	10,497	−60.50%	3,103	−66.10%	3,054	−57.40%
Mountain biking (off road)							
Mountain biking (off road)	1997	8,109		997		1,192	
Mountain biking (off road)	2006	8,543	5.40%	863	−13.50%	1,000	−16.10%
Skateboarding							
Skateboarding	1997	6,334		2,654		2,401	
Skateboarding	2006	9,731	53.60%	2,910	9.60%	4,437	84.80%
Skiing (alpine)							
Skiing (alpine)	1997	8,866		913		1,321	
Skiing (alpine)	2006	6,394	−27.90%	422	−53.80%	882	−33.20%
Snowboarding							
Snowboarding	1997	2,816		476		1,093	
Snowboarding	2006	5,205	84.80%	859	80.50%	1,686	54.30%
Soccer							
Soccer	1997	13,651		5,624		4,109	
Soccer	2006	14,024	2.70%	4,796	−14.70%	4,095	−0.30%
Softball							
Softball	1997	16,339		2,385		3,431	
Softball	2006	12,442	−23.90%	2,339	−1.90%	2,824	−17.70%
Tennis							
Tennis	1997	11,106		1,022		1,766	
Tennis	2006	10,356	−6.80%	787	−23.00%	2,216	25.50%
Volleyball							
Volleyball	1997	17,836		1,801		4,869	
Volleyball	2006	11,062	−38.00%	1,095	−39.20%	3,971	−18.40%

SOURCE: "2006 Youth Participation in Selected Sports with Comparisons to 1997," National Sporting Goods Association, 2007, http://www.nsga.org/public/pages/index.cfm?pageid=158 (accessed July 24, 2007)

skateboarding, rock climbing, snowboarding, mountain biking, BMX bicycling, and windsurfing. The boldest of extreme sportspeople will engage in such daredevilry as riding a motorcycle off of a ski jump. Many of these sports, according to *Superstudy* data, are among the fastest growing in the country.

Inline skating is by far the most popular extreme sport. (See Table 2.8.) In 2006, 16.5 million people aged six and over donned inline skates. Skateboarding was second, with 11.4 million participants. The SGMA notes in *Extreme Sports: Forever Popular* (July 6, 2006, http://www.sgma.com/) that in 2006 most of these skateboarders

TABLE 2.6

Sports participation among women, by total participation, 2006

[In millions. Respondents seven years of age or older who participated more than once.]

Sport	Total	Percent female
Exercise walking	52.4	59.90%
Swimming	31.1	55.10%
Exercising with equipment	26.9	51.30%
Aerobic exercising	23.9	71.10%
Camping (vacation/overnite)	23.8	49.00%
Bowling	22.1	48.60%
Workout at club	20.5	56.30%
Bicycle riding	16.1	45.30%
Hiking	15.2	49.20%
Running/jogging	13.7	47.80%
Fishing	13.6	33.40%
Boating, motor/power	12.7	43.30%
Billiards/pool	12.1	38.10%
Weight lifting	11.6	35.20%
Basketball	8.8	32.90%
Softball	6.8	54.90%
Volleyball	6.6	59.60%
Soccer	6.3	44.90%
Golf	5.9	24.10%
Backpack/wilderness camp	5.6	42.30%
In-line roller skating	5.5	52.50%
Tennis	5.1	48.90%
Scooter riding	4.1	43.20%
Cheerleading	3.6	93.60%
Target shooting	3.5	20.50%
Baseball	3.2	21.80%
Canoeing	3.2	44.70%
Mountain biking (off road)	3	35.70%
Water skiing	2.7	42.50%
Hunting with firearms	2.4	13.30%
Skateboarding	2.3	23.80%
Skiing (alpine)	2.3	36.20%
Paintball games	1.7	21.30%
Football (tackle)	1.6	13.70%
Racquetball	1.5	36.80%
Snowboarding	1.4	27.20%
Skiing (cross country)	1.3	49.30%
Hunting with bow & arrow	0.7	12.70%
Wrestling	0.7	17.80%
Hockey (ice)	0.6	21.40%
Muzzleloading	0.2	6.30%

SOURCE: "2006 Women's Participation—Ranked by Total Female Participation," National Sporting Goods Association, 2007, http://www.nsga.org/public/pages/index.cfm?pageid=154 (accessed July 24, 2007)

were a young group: 81% of them were between the ages of six and seventeen. However, the sheer number of people participating indicates that skateboarding and other extreme sports are not just the domain of the young. The numbers suggest that as this youthful core group ages, these sports may outgrow their "alternative" status and become mainstream.

The mark of extreme sports can be found across the entire sports spectrum. For example, as noted earlier, participation in snowboarding has soared, whereas skiing has not. It is no coincidence that nearly three-quarters of all snowboarders are under the age of twenty-four, according to the SGMA. Artificial wall-climbing, another popular extreme sport, with 8.9 million participants in 2006 (see Table 2.8), likewise illustrates the new demographics of sports: 54% of participants are female, according to the SGMA, and the average age of all climbers is 16.9. Climbing on real mountains and rocks is growing fast as well; participation grew by 21% between 2000 and 2006.

LACROSSE. Among the fastest-growing team sports in the United States is lacrosse. Lacrosse is similar in form to hockey or soccer. It is played on a field by two teams of ten players. Players use netted sticks to throw and catch a small rubber ball and, ultimately, to propel the ball into the opponents' goal, which resembles a hockey goal. Lacrosse may be the oldest sport in North America. It originated among Native Americans and has been played in one form or another for at least five hundred years.

U.S. Lacrosse, the organization that coordinates lacrosse activity nationwide, estimates that there were 426,022 active lacrosse players in the United States in 2006, up from 253,931 in 2001. (See Table 2.9.) According to U.S. Lacrosse's most recent nationwide survey, about half of current players are in the youth category (220,797 in 2006). (See Table 2.10.) Another 169,625 played high school lacrosse, and 26,651 played at the collegiate level. Lacrosse has long been popular in the Northeast and in the mid-Atlantic states, but in the 2000s it has been surging in popularity in many parts of the country, including the Pacific Northwest and the Rocky Mountain states.

SOCCER. Soccer is the only well-established team sport that does not appear to be losing players, largely because of its growing popularity among young people. The organization U.S. Youth Soccer (2007, http://www.usyouthsoccer.org/) reports the registration of 3.2 million players between the ages of five and nineteen— an impressive number when compared with the 100,000 registered members the organization had in 1974, the year it was founded. Moreover, two other smaller nationwide youth soccer agencies—the American Youth Soccer Organization (2007, http://soccer.org/) and the Soccer Association for Youth (2007, http://www.saysoccer.org/)—have a combined 1.5 million members. The presence of these young soccer players on U.S. soccer fields, as well as the growing populations of people from places such as Latin America, where soccer has long reigned supreme among sports, is likely to lift soccer into prominence among adults in the coming years.

CONSUMER PURCHASES OF SPORTING GOODS

Besides asking individuals about their sports participation, the NSGA also tracks nationwide retail sales of sporting goods. Americans spent $90.5 billion on sports-related items in 2006 and were projected to spend slightly more in 2007. (See Table 2.11.) Of this total, $38.4 billion was spent on what the NSGA calls "recreational transport," a category that includes bicycles, pleasure boats, recreational vehicles, and snowmobiles. The other $52 billion was spent on what most people consider

TABLE 2.7

Female sports participation, 2006 vs. 2001

[In millions. Respondents seven years of age or older who participated more than once.]

Sport	Total	2006 total female	2006 percent female	2001 total female	2001 percent female	Percent difference
Aerobic exercising	33.7	23.9	71.10%	17.8	73.20%	−2.10%
Backpack/wilderness camp	13.3	5.6	42.30%	5.7	39.50%	2.80%
Baseball	14.6	3.2	21.80%	3.3	22.30%	−0.50%
Basketball	26.7	8.8	32.90%	9.1	32.40%	0.50%
Bicycle riding	35.6	16.1	45.30%	17.2	44.00%	1.30%
Billiards/pool	31.8	12.1	38.10%	12.8	39.10%	−1.00%
Boating, motor/power	29.3	12.7	43.30%	9.5	42.00%	1.30%
Bowling	45.4	22.1	48.60%	19.1	47.30%	1.30%
Camping (vacation/overnite)	48.6	23.8	49.00%	21.4	47.00%	2.00%
Canoeing	7.1	3.2	44.70%	3	43.70%	1.10%
Cheerleading	3.8	3.6	93.60%	3.4	90.70%	2.90%
Exercise walking	87.5	52.4	59.90%	44.8	62.90%	−3.00%
Exercising with equipment	52.4	26.9	51.30%	22.5	52.30%	−1.00%
Fishing	40.6	13.6	33.40%	11.9	26.80%	6.60%
Football (tackle)	11.9	1.6	13.70%	0.8	9.00%	4.70%
Golf	24.4	5.9	24.10%	5.3	19.90%	4.20%
Hiking	31	15.2	49.20%	12.4	47.50%	1.70%
Hockey (ice)	2.6	0.6	21.40%	0.4	19.10%	2.30%
Hunting with bow & arrow	5.9	0.7	12.70%	0.4	8.40%	4.40%
Hunting with firearms	17.8	2.4	13.30%	2.4	12.70%	0.50%
In-line roller skating	10.5	5.5	52.50%	10.1	52.50%	0.00%
Mountain biking (off road)	8.5	3	35.70%	2	31.50%	4.20%
Muzzleloading	3.7	0.2	6.30%	0.3	9.70%	−3.50%
Paintball games	8	1.7	21.30%	0.8	14.70%	6.60%
Racquetball	4	1.5	36.80%	1	30.00%	6.80%
Running/jogging	28.8	13.7	47.80%	11.1	45.30%	2.50%
Scooter riding	9.5	4.1	43.20%	5.6	43.80%	−0.60%
Skateboarding	9.7	2.3	23.80%	1.9	20.00%	3.80%
Skiing (alpine)	6.4	2.3	36.20%	3	39.80%	−3.50%
Skiing (cross country)	2.6	1.3	49.30%	1.2	50.00%	−0.70%
Snowboarding	5.2	1.4	27.20%	1.5	27.60%	−0.40%
Soccer	14	6.3	44.90%	5.9	42.10%	2.80%
Softball	12.4	6.8	54.90%	6.4	48.70%	6.20%
Swimming	56.5	31.1	55.10%	29.6	54.00%	1.10%
Target shooting	17.1	3.5	20.50%	3.3	21.00%	−0.50%
Tennis	10.4	5.1	48.90%	5.5	50.60%	−1.80%
Volleyball	11.1	6.6	59.60%	6.5	53.80%	5.80%
Water skiing	6.3	2.7	42.50%	2.3	42.30%	0.20%
Weight lifting	32.9	11.6	35.20%	7.2	33.70%	1.50%
Workout at club	36.4	20.5	56.30%	13.945	52.70%	3.60%
Wrestling	3.8	0.7	17.80%	0.5	15.50%	2.30%

SOURCE: "Female Sports Participation: 2006 vs. 2001," National Sporting Goods Association, 2007, http://www.nsga.org/public/pages/index.cfm?pageid=156 (accessed July 24, 2007)

TABLE 2.8

Extreme sports participation, 2006

[U.S. population; 6 years of age or older]

1. Inline skating: 16,490,000
2. Skateboarding: 11,382,000
3. Paintball: 10,357,000
4. Artificial wall climbing: 8,869,000
5. Snowboarding: 7,304,000
6. Mountain biking: 6,466,000
7. Trail running: 6,167,000
8. Wakeboarding: 2,697,000
9. BMX bicycling: 2,480,000
10. Mountain/rock climbing: 2,299,000
11. Roller hockey: 2,094,000
12. Boardsailing/windsurfing: 535,000

SOURCE: "Most Popular Extreme Sports in the USA," in *Extreme Sports: Forever Popular*, Sporting Goods Manufacturers Association, July 6, 2006, http://www.sgma.com/displayindustryarticle.cfm?articlenbr=30713&searchcriteria=extreme%20sports&securetype=All&startrec=1 (accessed July 24, 2007)

"sporting goods," including specialized equipment, footwear, and clothing. Footwear accounted for $16.9 billion of this spending and clothing for $10.7 billion.

Excluding apparel, footwear, and exercise equipment, hunting and firearms and golf equipment accounted for the largest shares of sports equipment purchased by Americans in 2006. (See Table 1.3 in Chapter 1.) Consumer purchases of golf gear tallied nearly $3.7 billion. According to the National Golf Foundation (2007, http://www.ngf.org/cgi/home.asp), avid golfers (those who play at least twenty-five rounds per year) account for nearly two-thirds of the spending, even though they make up less than a quarter of the nation's golfers. Hunting and firearms, one of the fastest-growing categories of consumer purchases, has now eclipsed golf, registering $3.7 billion in equipment sales in 2006.

TABLE 2.9

Lacrosse participation, 2001–06

2001	253,931
2002	288,104
2003	301,560
2004	351,852
2005	381,568
2006	426,022

SOURCE: "US Lacrosse Estimate on Number of Lacrosse Players Nationally," in *US Lacrosse Participation Study 2006*, US Lacrosse, 2007, http://www.uslacrosse.org/pdf/06participationsurvey.pdf (accessed July 24, 2007)

TABLE 2.10

Lacrosse participation at various levels, 2006

Youth (non-high school, age 15 and under)	220,797
High School	169,625
College	26,651
Post-Collegiate Club	8,649
Professional	300
Total	**426,022**

SOURCE: "US Lacrosse Estimate on Number of Lacrosse Players in 2006," in *US Lacrosse Participation Study 2006*, US Lacrosse, 2007, http://www.uslacrosse.org/pdf/06participationsurvey.pdf (accessed July 24, 2007)

SPORTS FANS

Since 2000 the Gallup Organization has been asking Americans whether or not they are sports fans. A majority has said yes each year, though the 54% answering positively in June 2007 was the lowest yet recorded, well below the high of 66% in March 2003. (See Table 2.12.) Table 1.1 in Chapter 1 ranks each sport according to the percentage of people who say they are fans. Gallup data show that there are gender and generational differences in sports preference. Even though football was the top choice of both men (50%) and women (36%) in 2006, men were much more likely to name football as their favorite sport to watch. (See Table 2.13.) Women were four times as likely to name figure skating as their favorite. In 2006 adults between the ages of eighteen and thirty-four were more likely than older adults to call football their favorite sport, whereas more older adults made baseball their top choice. (See Table 2.14.)

Even though baseball has long been called the national pastime, as of December 2006 only 35% of the population considered themselves fans of the professional version of the sport. (See Table 2.15.) A much greater percentage of the population, 50%, considered themselves football fans as of December 2005. (See Table 2.16.) Even though basketball has surpassed baseball as a favorite sport for Americans to watch, college basketball has declined in popularity somewhat in recent years. In April 2006, 29% of respondents called themselves college basketball fans, compared with 38% five years earlier. (See Table 2.17.)

Race

Gallup polls have shown over the years a general shift among American sports fans away from baseball and toward basketball and football, but the pace of this shift has been even more pronounced among African-Americans. In "The Disappearing Black Baseball Fan" (July 15, 2003, http://www.galluppoll.com/), Jeffrey M. Jones of the Gallup Organization states that 43% of African-Americans named baseball as their favorite sport in 1960, compared with 33% of the overall American public. This strong preference among African-Americans may have been the result of the integration of professional baseball over the previous decade, beginning with Jackie Robinson (1919–1972) crossing baseball's "color line" in 1947, followed by the emergence of African-American stars such as Willie Mays (1931–), Hank Aaron (1934–), Ernie Banks (1931–), and Frank Robinson (1935–).

Jones notes that a Gallup analysis found that by 1985 the percentage of African-Americans calling baseball

TABLE 2.11

Sales of sporting goods, by category, 2000–07

[In millions]

	2000	2001	2002	2003	2004	2005	2006	2007[a]	Change 06 vs 05
Equipment	21,603	21,599	21,699	22,394	23,328	23,688	24,472	25,195	3%
Footwear	13,026	13,814	14,144	14,446	14,752	15,719	16,902	17,497	8%
Clothing	11,030	10,217	9,801	10,543	11,201	10,898	10,699	12,292	−2%
Subtotal	45,659	45,630	45,644	47,382	49,280	50,305	52,073	53,682	4%
Recreational transport[b]	28,779	28,712	32,106	32,396	36,531	38,082	38,389	37,035	1%
Total	**74,438**	**74,342**	**77,750**	**79,778**	**85,811**	**88,387**	**90,462**	**90,717**	**2%**

[a]Projected.
[b]Bicycles, pleasure boats, RVs and snowmobiles; projections provided by other associations.

SOURCE: "2006 Consumer Purchases by Category," National Sporting Goods Association, 2007, http://www.nsga.org/public/pages/index.cfm?pageid=161 (accessed July 24, 2007)

TABLE 2.12

Poll respondents who described themselves as sports fans, 2000–07

IN GENERAL, WOULD YOU DESCRIBE YOURSELF AS A SPORTS FAN, OR NOT?

	Yes, sports fan	No, not a fan
	%	%
2007 Jun 1–3	54	45
2006 May 5–7	56	44
2005 Feb 25–27	63	37
2005 Feb 4–6	58	42
2005 Jan 7–9	56	44
2004 Dec 17–19	57	43
2004 Jan 9–11	62	38
2003 Aug 4–6	56	44
2003 Jul 25–27	63	37
2003 Jun 27–29	57	42
2003 Apr 22–23	61	39
2003 Mar 14–15	66	34
2003 Feb 24–26	61	39
2003 Jan 3–5	62	38
2002 Dec 9–10	62	38
2001 Aug 24–26	57	42
2001 Jan 15–16	58	42
2000 Apr 28–30	62	37

SOURCE: "In general, would you describe yourself as a sports fan, or not?" in *Sports*, The Gallup Organization, July 2, 2007, http://www.galluppoll.com/content/?ci=4735&pg=1 (accessed July 24, 2007). Copyright © 2007 by The Gallup Organization. Reproduced by permission of The Gallup Organization.

TABLE 2.13

Poll respondents' rating of their favorite sport to watch, by gender, December 11–14, 2006

	Men	Women
	%	%
Football	50	36
Basketball	9	14
Baseball	11	11
Auto racing	5	3
Golf	3	2
Ice/figure skating	1	4
Soccer	3	2
Ice hockey	2	3
Boxing	2	1
Tennis	*	2
Gymnastics	*	1
Other	3	2
None	7	16

*Less than 0.5%.

SOURCE: Joseph Carroll, "Favorite Sport to Watch, by Gender," in *Football Reaches Historic Popularity Levels in Gallup Poll*, The Gallup Organization, January 19, 2007, http://www.galluppoll.com/content/?ci=26188&pg=1 (accessed July 24, 2007). Copyright © 2007 by The Gallup Organization. Reproduced by permission of The Gallup Organization.

TABLE 2.14

Poll respondents' rating of their favorite sport to watch, by age, December 11–14, 2006

	18 to 34	35 to 49	50+
	%	%	%
Football	49	43	39
Basketball	15	9	12
Baseball	7	10	14
Auto racing	2	7	3
Golf	—	3	5
Ice/figure skating	2	3	3
Soccer	5	3	*
Ice hockey	1	4	2
Boxing	2	1	2
Tennis	*	1	1
Gymnastics	—	1	1
Other	5	2	2
None	11	10	13

*Less than 0.5%.

SOURCE: Joseph Carroll, "Favorite Sport to Watch, by Age," in *Football Reaches Historic Popularity Levels in Gallup Poll*, The Gallup Organization, January 19, 2007, http://www.galluppoll.com/content/?ci=26188&pg=1 (accessed July 24, 2007). Copyright © 2007 by The Gallup Organization. Reproduced by permission of The Gallup Organization.

their favorite support had fallen to just 17%, a drop that far outpaced the decline among white fans, from 32% to 19%. Combined polls from 2000 to 2002 demonstrate a continuation of the decline of baseball's popularity among African-Americans. By this time, only 5% said baseball was their favorite sport. Meanwhile, both basketball and football had gained substantial popularity among African-American sports fans: Football was the favorite of 31%, and basketball was the favorite of 37%.

The contrast between the sports preferences of white and African-American fans is striking. Jones combines the Gallup data from 2002 and 2003 and shows that when asked simply whether they are baseball fans and whether they are basketball fans, white respondents gave baseball an edge over basketball, 39% to 28%. Nearly twice as many African-American respondents said they were basketball fans (60%) as said they were baseball fans (33%). Jones's analysis of these results suggests two possible reasons for the differences:

- The dominance of professional basketball by African-American players

- The relative lack of baseball facilities and programs in urban areas with predominantly African-American populations

Geography

In December 2006 football was the favorite sport to watch in every region of the country, ranging from 48% in the South to 38% in the West. Many of those westerners who did not choose football as their favorite opted to watch basketball; nearly twice as many in the West (19%) called basketball their favorite sport than in any other region. Interestingly, auto racing, a sport with deep roots in the South, was the favorite sport to watch by people in the East (5%) than in the South (4%). (See Table 2.18.)

Figure 2.1 shows that 68.4% of American adults were professional football fans in 2006, by far the biggest fan

TABLE 2.15

Poll respondents who are or are not professional baseball fans, by percentage, 1996–2006

FOR EACH OF THE FOLLOWING, PLEASE SAY WHETHER YOU ARE A FAN OF THAT SPORT OR NOT. FIRST – PROFESSIONAL BASEBALL [RANDOM ORDER]?

	Yes, a fan	Somewhat of a fan (vol.)	No, not a fan
	%	%	%
2006 Dec 8–10	35	6	59
2006 Sep 15–17	37	9	54
2006 Jul 21–23	40	12	48
2006 Jun 9–11	47	9	43
2006 Apr 7–9	33	8	58
2006 Mar 10–12	37	10	53
2005 Dec 9–11	36	11	53
2005 Aug 5–7	37	10	53
2005 Mar 18–20	39	9	52
2005 Jan 14–16	41	7	52
2004 Dec 5–8	43	9	48
2004 Mar 26–28	36	9	55
2003 Oct 24–26	44	11	45
2003 Oct 10–12	42	8	50
2003 Jun 27–29	36	10	54
2003 Jun 9–10	39	11	50
2002 Nov 8–10	38	13	49
2002 Aug 19–21	37	8	54
2002 Jul 26–28	37	10	53
2002 Jun 7–8	35	16	48
2002 Mar 22–24	44	10	46
2002 Jan 11–14	36	11	53
2001 Nov 26–27	38	10	52
2001 Nov 2–4	45	11	44
2001 Jun 8–10	35	14	51
2001 Mar 26–28	46	10	44
2000 May 5–7	35	11	54
2000 Apr 28–30	40	12	48
2000 Mar 30–Apr 2	45	10	45
1999 Nov 18–21	45	16	39
1999 Oct 21–24	37	10	53
1999 Jul 13–14	40	19	41
1999 Mar 19–21	34	15	51
1998 Oct 9–12	47	14	39
1998 Sep 14–15	45	18	37
1998 Jun 22–23	34	10	56
1996 Mar 15–17	38	10	52

SOURCE: Adapted from "For each of the following, please say whether you are a fan of that sport or not. First—...Professional Baseball?" in *Sports*, The Gallup Organization, July 2, 2007, http://www.galluppoll.com/content/?ci=4735&pg=1 (accessed July 23, 2007). Copyright © 2007 by The Gallup Organization. Reproduced by permission of The Gallup Organization.

TABLE 2.16

Poll respondents who are or are not professional football fans, by percentage, 1998–2005

FOR EACH OF THE FOLLOWING, PLEASE SAY WHETHER YOU ARE A FAN OF THAT SPORT OR NOT. PROFESSIONAL FOOTBALL [RANDOM ORDER]?

	Yes, a fan	Somewhat of a fan (vol.)	No, not a fan
	%	%	%
2005 Dec 9–11	50	9	41
2004 Dec 5–8	58	6	36
2003 Jan 23–25	50	9	41
2001 Mar 26–28	54	9	37
2001 Mar 9–11	48	14	38
2001 Jan 15–16	44	14	42
2000 Aug 24–27	42	12	46
1999 Mar 5–7	47	9	44
1999 Jan 22–24	51	10	39
1998 Jan 16–18	45	11	43

SOURCE: Adapted from "For each of the following, please say whether you are a fan of that sport or not. First—[RANDOM ORDER]: Professional Football?" in *Sports*, The Gallup Organization, July 2, 2007, http://www.galluppoll.com/content/?ci=4735&pg=1 (accessed July 23, 2007). Copyright © 2007 by The Gallup Organization. Reproduced by permission of The Gallup Organization.

TABLE 2.17

Poll respondents who are or are not college basketball fans, by percentage, 2001–06

FOR EACH OF THE FOLLOWING, PLEASE SAY WHETHER YOU ARE A FAN OF THAT SPORT OR NOT. COLLEGE BASKETBALL [RANDOM ORDER]?

	Yes, a fan	Somewhat of a fan (vol.)	No, not a fan
	%	%	%
2006 Apr 7–9	29	6	65
2004 Dec 5–8	35	6	59
2004 Mar 26–28	32	6	62
2002 Mar 18–20	37	5	58
2001 Mar 26–28	38	9	52

SOURCE: Adapted from "For each of the following, please say whether you are a fan of that sport or not. First—[RANDOM ORDER]: College Basketball?" in *Sports*, The Gallup Organization, July 2, 2007, http://www.galluppoll.com/content/?ci=4735&pg=1 (accessed July 23, 2007). Copyright © 2007 by The Gallup Organization. Reproduced by permission of The Gallup Organization.

base among all sports. Major League Baseball (59.1%) and college football (58.2%) had the next biggest fan bases. Table 2.19 tracks the fan bases of major sports since 2001. It shows that the fan base for football, both professional and college, has grown in recent years, whereas the professional basketball and hockey fan bases have shrunk slightly. Baseball has remained relatively stable. The National Association for Stock Car Auto Racing (NASCAR) fan base, which experienced explosive growth during the 1990s, has tapered off since 2001.

SPORTS ATTENDANCE

Attendance trends vary considerably from one sport to another, and in general one sport's loss, whether because of scandal or declining interest, translates into another sport's gain. Professional sports teams rely on revenue from ticket sales to cover much of the cost of the huge salaries they pay their players. At the college level, ticket sales are a big part of what keeps university athletic programs solvent.

Major Sports

BASEBALL. Even though the national pastime seems to have lost some of its luster in terms of participation and self-identified fan base over the decades, the public is still taking itself out to the ball game. According to the

TABLE 2.18

Poll respondents' rating of their favorite sport to watch, by region, December 11–14, 2006

	East	Midwest	South	West
	%	%	%	%
Football	40	42	48	38
Basketball	8	10	11	19
Baseball	18	11	8	10
Auto racing	5	4	4	3
Golf	3	3	3	3
Ice/figure skating	2	1	4	2
Soccer	2	4	1	3
Ice hockey	4	2	1	2
Boxing	*	1	3	2
Tennis	1	—	1	2
Gymnastics	2	*	—	*
Other	3	2	3	2
None	12	15	10	10

*Less than 0.5%.

SOURCE: Favorite Sport to Watch, by Region, in *Football Reaches Historic Popularity Levels in Gallup Poll*, The Gallup Organization, January 19, 2007, http://www.galluppoll.com/content/?ci=26188&pg=1 (accessed July 24, 2007). Copyright © 2007 by The Gallup Organization. Reproduced by permission of The Gallup Organization.

Entertainment and Sports Programming Network (ESPN), approximately 75.9 million fans attended Major League Baseball (MLB) games during the 2006 regular season, a new record. Average attendance at MLB games for the year was 31,419. Eight different teams topped the three-million mark for home games. One team, the New York Yankees, drew 4.2 million fans during the season for the second year in a row, also averaging more than fifty-one thousand paid attendees for the second straight season. No other team has achieved a higher season total or per-game average since 1993. Only three teams—the Kansas City Royals, the Tampa Bay Devil Rays, and the Florida Marlins—drew fewer than twenty thousand fans per game to the stadium.

BASKETBALL. Professional basketball is enjoying strong ticket sales in the 2000s. Attendance at National Basketball Association (NBA) games during the 2006–07 regular season reached 21.8 million, breaking the league's all-time record. The Chicago Bulls led the pack in home attendance for the season, drawing a total home-court crowd of 908,600, or an average of 22,160 over the course of their forty-one home games. The Bulls were followed closely by the Detroit Pistons, Cleveland Cavaliers, and Dallas Mavericks, each enjoying average home-game attendance of more than twenty thousand. The Memphis Grizzlies finished at the bottom of the league in attendance numbers. Memphis crowds averaged 14,654 per game, for a season total of 600,836.

On a team-by-team basis, attendance in the NBA has a lot to do with the success of the team and the size of the city. It is not difficult to predict that a winning team in a large city is likely to sell more tickets than a lousy team

FIGURE 2.1

Fan bases of selected sports, 2006

[Sample size=24,215. 18 years of age and older.]

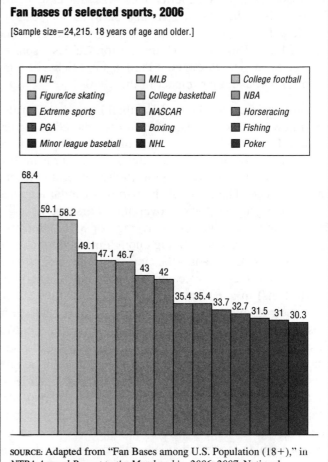

SOURCE: Adapted from "Fan Bases among U.S. Population (18+)," in *NTRA Annual Report to the Membership, 2006–2007*, National Thoroughbred Racing Association, 2007, http://www.ntra.com/content/NTRAAnnualReport2007.pdf (accessed July 31, 2007)

TABLE 2.19

Fan bases of major sports, 2001–06

[Sample size=24,215. 18 years of age and older.]

League:	2001	2002	2003	2004	2005	2006
NFL	65.8	66.1	66.2	67.5	67.8	68.4
MLB	59.4	58.7	58.7	60.1	59.7	59.1
NBA	48.8	48.1	48.3	48.3	47.2	46.7
NHL	34.0	34.0	34.1	32.7	28.0	31.0
College football	54.7	54.9	55.8	56.1	56.2	58.2
College basketball	46.0	44.9	45.6	46.3	46.4	47.1
NASCAR	44.9	44.7	43.2	43.4	43.3	42.0

SOURCE: Adapted from "Horseracing Fan Base Growth Compared to Major Leagues (18+)," in *NTRA Annual Report to the Membership, 2006–2007*, National Thoroughbred Racing Association, 2007, http://www.ntra.com/content/NTRAAnnualReport2007.pdf (accessed July 31, 2007)

in a small market. Perhaps more than any other sport, however, professional basketball attendance is influenced by personalities. The acquisition of a truly high-profile player—such as Shaquille O'Neal (1972–) or Kevin Garnett (1976–)—can lead to a spike in ticket sales for the star's new team. Periodically, a player or set of players emerges with such charisma that the entire league's attendance numbers benefit. This was the case in the 1980s, when the ongoing rivalry between the team of Magic Johnson (1959–)—the Los Angeles Lakers—and that of Larry Bird (1956–)—the Boston Celtics—spurred a surge of interest throughout the league. Michael Jordan (1963–) had a similar impact in the 1990s.

FOOTBALL. The National Football League (NFL) also set a new overall attendance record for the 2006 regular season. League-wide, an average of 68,773 fans attended NFL games, for a total paid attendance of 17.6 million for the season. The Washington Redskins led the league in attendance. The pride of the nation's capital attracted 701,049 paying customers over the course of its eight home games in 2006, for an average of 87,631 fans per game. New York City is a big enough market not only to have two NFL squads—the Jets and the Giants—but also to have these two teams place second (Giants) and fourth (Jets) in attendance. (Both the Jets and the Giants play their home games at the Meadowlands stadium in East Rutherford, New Jersey, just across the Hudson River from New York City.) As with all spectator sports, one of the most important factors in an NFL team's attendance—along with market size and personalities—is team performance. However, in 2006 market size clearly trumped performance: The Indianapolis Colts, the eventual champs of the 2007 Super Bowl, had the lowest regular-season attendance in the league, drawing paid attendance of 57,144 per game, for a regular-season total of 457,154 fans.

The Super Bowl, which determines the NFL champion from between the champions of its two conferences, is much more about television viewing than about live attendance. Its paid attendees are limited by the size of the venue, which changes each year. For example, the NFL (2007, http://www.nfl.com/superbowl/history/ringandticket/sbxli) notes that Super Bowl XLI brought 74,512 ticket-holders to Dolphin Stadium in Miami, Florida, on February 4, 2007, to see the Indianapolis Colts defeat the Chicago Bears. This was nowhere near record attendance for a Super Bowl; according to the NFL (2007, http://www.nfl.com/superbowl/history/ringandticket/sbxiv), in 1980, 103,985 spectators packed the Rose Bowl in Pasadena, California, to watch the Pittsburgh Steelers beat the Los Angeles Rams in Super Bowl XIV.

HOCKEY. National Hockey League attendance for the 2006–07 season was nearly twenty-one million, a new record. ESPN (http://sports.espn.go.com/nhl/attendance?year=2006) notes that this represented a small increase over the previous record set a season earlier, when the league's games drew 20.8 million in paid attendance. It represented a much larger increase over the 2004–05 season, when attendance was zero; that entire season was canceled because of labor turmoil. The top draw in

2006–07 was the Montreal Canadiens, with 872,193 spectators over the course of the season, for an average of 21,273 per home game. The only other team to attract more than twenty thousand fans per game was the Detroit Red Wings, a perennial powerhouse. The Red Wings' total paid attendance for the season was 822,706. The St. Louis Blues had the poorest turnout for the season, with total attendance of 513,345.

SOCCER. Even as soccer emerges as a major sport in the United States, attendance at Major League Soccer (MLS) games has stagnated over the last several years. According to the MLS (2007, http://ww2.mlsnet.com/about/), MLS games drew an average of 15,504 fans during the 2006 regular season. The MLS (November 18, 2004, http://www.mlsnet.com/history/archive.jsp?year=2004&conten*equals;stats_league) states that this figure fell short of the 15,559 league average in 2004. The MLS further reports (October 30, 2006, http://web.mlsnet.com/stats/?club=mls&year=2006) that the top drawing team in 2006 was the Los Angeles Galaxy, whose home game averaged twenty-one thousand per game. The Galaxy expected to boost attendance further in 2007 with the signing of the British megastar David Beckham (1975–).

AUTO RACING. Auto racing has enjoyed a surge in popularity during the 2000s. The most prominent auto racing event in the United States is the Indianapolis 500 (Indy 500), which is held on Memorial Day weekend each year at Indianapolis Motor Speedway. The 2007 race was the ninety-first Indy 500. The Indy 500 does not release official attendance figures, but according to Curt Cavin, in "Busch Makes Amends, Finishes 4th at Brickyard" (*Indianapolis Star*, July 30, 2007), NASCAR estimated that more than 270,000 fans packed the grandstand for the 2007 event.

However, the Indy Racing League (IndyCar) is only one faction of the broader auto racing scene. There is also NASCAR, which has become such a phenomenon that its followers (also know as NASCAR dads) are now viewed by political analysts as a powerful voting bloc alongside so-called "soccer moms." The Super Bowl of the NASCAR circuit is the Daytona 500, which is held in February at the Daytona International Speedway in Florida. Like the Indy 500, exact attendance figures for Daytona are not released, but David Caraviello reports in "Martin Finds Himself Odd Man out ... Again" (February 20, 2007, http://www.nascar.com/2007/news/opinion/02/18/mmartin.daytona/story_single.html) that 185,000 people attended the event in 2007. Besides the IndyCar and NASCAR circuits, there are the Champ Car Series, the Formula One Grand Prix series, the National Hot Rod Association, and various smaller racing circuits. Of these races, NASCAR has by far the greatest overall attendance numbers, drawing 4.4 million spectators in 2004, according to John W. Schoen, in "Auto Racing Revs Up Revenues, Profits" (May 28, 2005, http://

TABLE 2.20

Adult attendance at sports events, by frequency, 2005

[In thousands (2,664 represents 2,664,000), except percent. Based on survey.]

Event	Attend one or more times a month		Attend less than once a month	
	Number	Percent	Number	Percent
Auto racing—NASCAR	2,664	1.2	8,518	4.0
Auto racing—other	2,440	1.1	6,083	2.8
Baseball	8,502	3.9	18,575	8.6
Basketball:				
College games	4,383	2.0	7,485	3.5
Professional games	3,202	1.5	9,168	4.3
Bowling	1,749	0.8	3,533	1.6
Boxing	1,175	0.5	3,240	1.5
Equestrian events	574	0.3	3,534	1.6
Figure skating	696	0.3	3,330	1.5
Fishing tournaments	716	0.3	3,132	1.5
Football:				
College games	6,308	2.9	9,513	4.4
Monday night professional games	1,958	0.9	4,493	2.1
Weekend professional games	3,809	1.8	9,591	4.4
Golf	1,587	0.7	4,636	2.2
High school sports	12,087	5.6	8,363	3.9
Horse racing:				
Flats, runners	1,281	0.6	3,842	1.8
Trotters and harness	745	0.4	2,747	1.3
Ice hockey	1,973	0.9	6,754	3.1
Motorcycle racing	980	0.5	3,554	1.7
Pro beach volleyball	254	0.1	2,731	1.3
Rodeo/bull riding	1,190	0.6	4,267	2.0
Soccer	3,389	1.6	4,429	2.1
Tennis	903	0.4	3,655	1.7
Truck and tractor pull/mud racing	655	0.3	3,638	1.7
Wrestling professional	1,243	0.6	3,604	1.7

SOURCE: "Table 1224. Adult Attendance at Sports Events by Frequency: 2005," in *Statistical Abstract of the United States: 2007*, U.S. Census Bureau, 2006, http://www.census.gov/compendia/statab/tables/07s1224.xls (accessed July 24, 2007). Data from Mediamark Research, Inc.

www.msnbc.msn.com/id/8007370). However, by late 2006 the industry was concerned about an apparent dip in attendance at auto racing events, as reported by Nate Ryan, in "NASCAR's Growth Slows after 15 Years in the Fast Lane" (*USA Today*, November 15, 2006) and by Terry Blount, in "NASCAR Not Hitting Panic Button over Ratings" (November 16, 2006, http://sports.espn.go.com/rpm/columns/story?seriesId=2&columnis=blount_terry&id=2661800), reflecting a possible end to the NASCAR boom.

OTHER SPORTS. It can be assumed that what draws these hundreds of thousands of spectators to auto races such as the Indy 500 each year is the speed—the experience of watching people hurtle around a track at well over two hundred miles per hour. However, people also jam Boston's streets each year to watch a race in which the fastest entrant averages a mere twelve miles per hour. That race is the Boston Marathon, the most famous marathon in the world. Each year, according to the Boston Athletic Association (2007, http://www.bostonmarathon.org/BostonMarathon/RaceFacts.asp), 500,000 spectators line the streets along the marathon's 26.2-mile route. Few other sports in the world are witnessed live by as many people as is the Boston Marathon.

Table 2.20 presents information on 2005 attendance at various sporting events by adults. Table 2.21 puts attendance patterns for a handful of sports into historical perspective, using data dating back to 1990.

TABLE 2.21

Attendance at selected spectator sports, selected years 1990–2005

[55,512 represents 55,512,000]

Sport	Unit	1990	1995	2000	2001	2002	2003	2004	2005
Baseball, major leagues:									
Attendance	1,000	55,512	51,288	74,339	73,881	69,428	69,501	74,822	76,286
Regular season	1,000	54,824	50,469	72,748	72,267	67,859	67,568	73,023	74,926
National League	1,000	24,492	25,110	39,851	39,558	36,949	36,661	40,221	41,644
American League	1,000	30,332	25,359	32,898	32,709	30,910	30,908	32,802	33,282
Playoffs[a]	1,000	479	533	1,314	1,247	1,262	1,568	1,625	1,191
World Series	1,000	209	286	277	366	306	365	174	168
Players' salaries:									
Average	$1,000	598	1,111	1,896	2,139	2,296	2,372	2,313	2,476
Basketball:[b, c]									
NCAA Men's college:									
Teams	Number	767	868	932	937	936	967	981	983
Attendance	1,000	28,741	28,548	29,025	28,949	29,395	30,124	30,761	30,569
NCAA Women's college:									
Teams	Number	782	864	956	958	975	1,009	1,008	1,036
Attendance	1,000	2,777	4,962	8,698	8,825	9,533	10,164	10,016	9,940
National Hockey League:[d]									
Regular season attendance	1,000	12,580	9,234	18,800	20,373	20,615	20,409	22,065	e
Playoffs attendance	1,000	1,356	1,329	1,525	1,584	1,691	1,636	1,709	e
Professional rodeo:									
Rodeos	Number	754	739	688	668	666	657	671	662
Performances	Number	2,159	2,217	2,081	2,015	2,207	1,949	1,982	1,940
Members	Number	5,693	6,894	6,255	5,913	6,209	6,158	6,247	6,127
Permit holders (rookies)	Number	3,290	3,835	3,249	2,544	2,543	3,121	2,990	2,701
Total prize money	Million dollars	18.2	24.5	32.3	33.1	33.3	34.3	35.5	36.6

[a]Beginning 1997, two rounds of playoffs were played. Prior years had one round.
[b]Season ending in year shown.
[c]For women's attendance total, excludes double-headers with men's teams.
[d]For season ending in year shown.
[e]In September 2004, franchise owners locked out their players upon the expiration of the collective bargaining agreement. The entire season was cancelled in February 2005.

SOURCE: "Table 1230. Selected Spectator Sports: 1990 to 2005," in *Statistical Abstract of the United States: 2007*, U.S. Census Bureau, 2006, http://www .census.gov/compendia/statab/tables/07s1230.xls (accessed July 24, 2007). Data compiled from Major League Baseball, American League of Professional Baseball Clubs, National Collegiate Athletic Association, National Hockey League, Montreal, Quebec, Professional Rodeo Cowboys Association, and Official Professional Rodeo Media Guide.

CHAPTER 3
SPORTS AND THE MEDIA

Sports and the media are so thoroughly intertwined in the United States that it is difficult to think of them as two distinct industries. The financial relationship is complex and reciprocal. Media enterprises, mostly broadcast and cable television stations but also Web based, pay the sports leagues millions of dollars for the rights to broadcast their games. Leagues distribute this money to their member teams—the distribution formula varies from sport to sport—which then transfer most of this money to their players in the form of salaries. The media outlets try to recoup their huge expenditures by selling advertising time during sports broadcasts to companies that believe their products will appeal to the kinds of people who like to watch sports on television. These consumer product companies also pay large sums to individual athletes to endorse their products, or in some cases to teams to display their company logos on their uniforms or, in the case of auto racing, on their cars. Consumers then purchase these products, providing the money the companies use to buy advertising and pay for celebrity endorsements. The more people who watch a sport, the more the station can charge for advertising. The more the station can charge for advertising, the more it can offer the league for broadcast rights. The more the league gets for broadcast rights, the more the teams can pay their players.

THE HISTORY OF SPORTS ON TELEVISION

In "Sports and Television" (2004, http://www.museum.tv/archives/etv/S/htmlS/sportsandte/sportsandte.htm), Harry Coyle, a pioneering television sports director, states that "television got off the ground because of sports. Today, maybe, sports need television to survive, but it was just the opposite when it first started. When we [NBC] put on the World Series in 1947, heavyweight fights, the Army-Navy football game, the sales of television sets just spurted."

Even though it may be an exaggeration to credit the explosive growth of television in its early days solely to sports, sports certainly played a significant role. The first-ever televised sporting event was a baseball game between Columbia and Princeton universities in 1939. It was covered by one camera that was positioned along the third base line. The first network-wide sports broadcast came five years later with the premier of the National Broadcasting Corporation's (NBC) *Gillette Cavalcade of Sports*, the first installment of which featured a featherweight championship boxing match between Willie Pep (1922–2006) and Chalky Wright (1912–1957). Sports quickly became a staple of primetime network fare, accounting for up to one-third of primetime programming, but other genres began to catch up during the 1950s, perhaps spurred on by an increase in female viewers. The *Gillette Cavalcade of Sports* remained on the air for twenty years, before giving way to a new model in which sports programs were sponsored by multiple buyers of advertising spots rather than by a single corporation, as the cost of sponsorship became prohibitively expensive in the mid-1960s. The number of hours of sports programming on the networks continued to increase dramatically well into the 1980s, when advertising dollars generated by sports began to decline, making them less profitable for the networks to carry.

The amount of money involved in televising sports was growing fast by the 1970s. The Museum of Broadcast Communications notes that in 1970 the networks paid $50 million for the right to broadcast National Football League (NFL) games, $18 million for Major League Baseball (MLB), and $2 million for National Basketball Association (NBA) broadcast rights. By 1985 these numbers reached $450 million for football, $160 million for baseball, and $45 million for basketball. This explosive growth was fueled by a combination of increasing public interest, better—and therefore more expensive—coverage of events by the networks, and an effort on the part of the networks to lock in their position of dominance in sports programming in the face of challenges from emerging cable television networks. These skyrocketing fees did not cause much of a problem during the 1970s, as the networks were able to pass the high cost of producing sports programs along to their advertisers. However, things began to change during the early 1980s. According to the Museum of Broadcast Communications, between 1980 and 1984 professional football lost 7% of its viewing audience, and baseball lost 26% of its viewers. Meanwhile, advertisers became hesitant to pay increasing prices for commercials that would be seen by fewer people. The networks responded by airing more hours of sports. By 1985 the three major networks broadcast a total of fifteen hundred hours of sports, about twice as many hours as in 1960. However, by the mid-1980s the market for sports programming appeared saturated, and the presence of more shows made it harder for the networks to sell ads at top prices.

The first half of the 1980s marked the rise of sports coverage on cable. According to the Museum of Broadcast Communications, the all-sports station Entertainment and Sports Programming Network (ESPN), first launched in 1979, was reaching four million households by the middle of 1980. National stations such as WTBS and WGN, as well as the premium channel Home Box Office (HBO), were also airing a substantial number of sporting events. By 1986 thirty-seven million households were subscribing to ESPN.

Between the early 1990s and the early 2000s broadcast television ratings for the four major professional sports generally trended downward. There is no real consensus as to why this happened. Jere Longman, in "Pro Leagues' Ratings Drop; Nobody Is Quite Sure Why" (Scott R. Rosner and Kenneth L. Shropshire, eds., *The Business of Sports*, 2004), points to "a growing dislocation between fans and traditional sports, as players, coaches and teams move frequently, as athletes misbehave publicly, as salaries skyrocket, and as ticket prices become prohibitively expensive" as possible contributing factors in the decline of ratings during that period.

The key challenge for all the major sports leagues—beyond the obvious challenge of attracting as many viewers and listeners as possible—is to balance exposure and distribution of their product against consumer demand. In other words, in an era witnessing the emergence of new media such as the Internet, satellite radio, and even live feeds to cell phones, at what point does the coverage of a sport available for consumption outstrip the public's interest in that sport, thereby becoming a losing financial proposition?

BASEBALL AND TELEVISION: THE CONVERGENCE OF OUR TWO NATIONAL PASTIMES

By 1939 baseball was already known as "America's national pastime." Television was still a novelty at the time. The only option for those who could not attend a baseball game in person was to listen to a live broadcast on the radio. The first televised professional baseball game, between the Brooklyn Dodgers and the Cincinnati Reds, took place on August 26 of that year. The broadcast used two cameras: one positioned high above home plate and a second one along the third base line. Such a broadcast would appear primitive by twenty-first-century standards. To cover a typical World Series game in the modern era, broadcasters use perhaps a couple dozen cameras, some of them operated electronically, and at least one mounted on an airborne blimp. In addition, early broadcasts offered none of the additional features contemporary viewers take for granted, including color, instant replays, and statistics superimposed on the screen.

NBC was the network that first brought televised baseball to the American public. Because NBC used home-team announcers to call the World Series, and because the New York Yankees were in the World Series nearly every year, the Yankees announcer Mel Allen (1913–1996) became the first coast-to-coast voice of baseball. The Hall of Fame pitcher Dizzy Dean (1911–1974) became the first nationwide television baseball announcer when the network premiered the *Game of the Week* in 1953, thus initiating the long line of former ball players who have transformed themselves into commentators when their playing careers have ended.

By the 1960s baseball had lost a large share of its audience to other sports, particularly football. Baseball nevertheless remains a solid ratings draw, especially when teams with well-known stars located in large markets square off in the postseason. However, the overall ratings for World Series broadcasts have been declining for years. ESPN notes in "The Cardinals Won? Series Averages Record-Low Ratings" (October 29, 2006, http://sports .espn.go.com/mlb/playoffs2006/news/story?id=2642964) that the numbers rebounded somewhat in 2004, when the World Series received a 15.8 rating (meaning 15.8% of all households were tuned in) and a 25 share (meaning 25% of those watching something were watching the World Series). However, the 2006 World Series set a new record low for viewership, capturing only an average rating of 10.1 and a 17 share over the five games. The article "Fox Attributes Low Ratings to Labor Strife" (*Sports Illustrated*, October 29, 2002) states that this was a far cry from 1980, when the World Series had a 32.8% rating and a 56 share during the entire series.

MLB is currently operating under a round of television deals signed in 2005 and 2006. The *SportsBusiness Journal* states in *Sports Business Resource Guide & Fact Book* (2007, http://www.sportsbusinessjournal.com/images/random/resource2006_E-116,117.pdf) that ESPN agreed to pay $2.3 billion to start a series of Monday night baseball broadcasts as part of an eight-year contract, which runs through 2013. Under the terms of the deal, ESPN may televise up to eighty regular-season games per season. The agreement also affords ESPN substantial flexibility to move some of the games to Sunday nights. MLB also has a deal with Fox for the broadcast rights to the All-Star Game and the World Series through 2013. MLB's other major television partner is TBS, which is slated to air all regular-season tiebreaker games, Division Series games, and a Sunday afternoon regular-season package through 2013. Professional baseball has increased its media income substantially in recent years, according to the Associated Press, in "ESPN and Baseball Agree to Eight-Year Deal" (September 14, 2005, http://sports.espn.go.com/espn/print?id=2161569&type=story). The 2005 season marked the first year of a six-year contract with ESPN radio worth an average of $11 million per year; a six-year Internet deal with ESPN for an annual average of $30 million; and a $60 million-per-year deal with XM satellite radio to transmit baseball games for eleven years.

In "Is MLB Extending Its Reach or Overreaching?" in the *SportsBusiness Journal* (March 28, 2005, http://www.sportsbusinessjournal.com/index.cfm?fuseaction=page.feature&featureId=1561), Russell Adams observes that the 2005 MLB season marked "a critical juncture for MLB officials, who are charged with managing a perfect storm of peaking demand for content, the emergence of new technologies for delivering it, and the growing number of media outlets demanding a larger piece of both." Adams describes a situation in which baseball clubs' local television partners are clamoring for more content from a sport that has more games to offer than any other. Opportunities abound, many of them in new media, for a sport that has long been criticized for "underutilizing its product"; that is, not showing enough games in sophisticated enough ways, and for neglecting the younger portion of its potential audience. This neglect and underutilization no longer seem to be the case. According to Adams, the Internet division of MLB, known as MLB Advanced Media, has built a thriving subscription business by streaming live video of more than twenty-three hundred regular-season games and live audio of all games, and by packaging and selling video on an on-demand basis once the game has ended. Television contracts do not apply to these sales, because broadcast rights revert to the league once the game has taken place.

FOOTBALL: BIGGEST ATHLETES, BIGGEST AUDIENCE

Professional Football

It is not an exaggeration to say that television put football where it is today. Before the era of televised sports, baseball was much more popular than football. Stirring television moments such as the 1958 NFL Championship, a thrilling overtime victory by the Baltimore Colts over the New York Giants, helped establish professional football as a big-time spectator sport. A few years later, when *Time* put the Green Bay Packers coach Vince Lombardi (1913–1970) on its cover in 1962—accompanied by the pronouncement that football was "The Sport of the '60s"—it was clear that the sport had come of age as a media phenomenon.

In April 2005 the NFL signed a deal for $1.1 billion per year to move *Monday Night Football* from its long-standing home with the American Broadcasting Company (ABC)—which was paying about half that sum under its expiring contract—to ESPN from 2006 through the 2013 season. (See Table 1.4 in Chapter 1.) Under the terms of the deal, ESPN would continue to make its NFL games available on regular broadcast television in the markets of the participating teams each week. However, unlike basketball, which experienced a loss of casual viewers when games were moved to cable in 2002, regular network television would continue to play a large role in bringing football to the viewing public.

The same day it shook hands with ESPN, the league reached an agreement with NBC, which had not broadcast NFL games since 1997. The NBC contract provides $600 million per year for the rights to carry seventeen Sunday night games each season through 2011. (See Table 1.4.) Meanwhile, the NFL had agreed in November 2004 to extend its existing relationships with Columbia Broadcasting System (CBS) and Fox to carry regular-season American Football Conference and National Football Conference games, respectively. The new CBS agreement included two Super Bowls and guaranteed $622.5 million per year through 2011; the new Fox contract called for five years at $712.5 million per year, with two Super Bowls included in the deal. The league received another $700 million from DirectTV in a five-year agreement covering satellite transmission rights.

What do the networks get for all this money? They get plenty because advertisers know how firmly football is entrenched in U.S. households and sports bars. Football is by far the most popular sport to watch on television in the United States. In a December 2006 poll by the Gallup Organization, 43% of Americans named football as their top choice among sports on television. (See Figure 3.1 and Table 3.1.) This is nothing new; football has topped polls consistently since the early 1970s, when it overtook baseball as the public's favorite sport to watch. In the

FIGURE 3.1

Poll respondents' rating of their favorite sports to watch, December 11–14, 2006

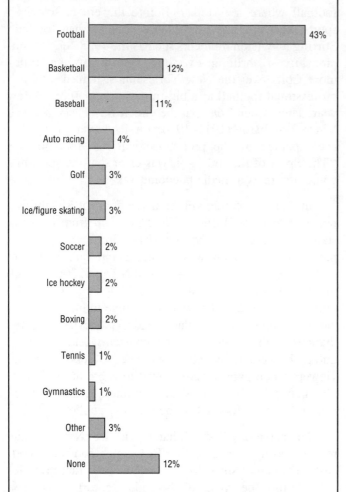

SOURCE: "Americans' Favorite Sport to Watch," in *Football Reaches Historic Popularity Levels in Gallup Poll*, The Gallup Organization, January 19, 2007, http://www.galluppoll.com/content/?ci=26188&pg=1 (accessed July 24, 2007). Copyright © 2007 by The Gallup Organization. Reproduced by permission of The Gallup Organization.

TABLE 3.1

Poll respondents' rating of the sports they like to watch most, 2003–06

WHAT IS YOUR FAVORITE SPORT TO WATCH?

	2006 Dec	2005 Dec	2004 Dec	2003 Dec
	%	%	%	%
Football	43	34	37	37
Basketball	12	12	13	14
Baseball	11	12	10	10
Auto racing	4	5	5	5
Golf	3	2	2	3
Ice/figure skating	3	3	4	6
Soccer	2	3	2	2
Ice hockey	2	4	3	5
Boxing	2	1	1	2
Tennis	1	3	2	1
Gymnastics	1	*	1	1
Rodeo	*	1	1	*
Volleyball	*	1	—	*
Motocross	*	*	1	*
Wrestling	*	1	1	1
Bowling	*	*	*	*
Fishing	*	1	*	*
Swimming	*	*	*	*
Other	3	4	4	4
None	12	13	12	9
No opinion	*	*	1	*

* = Less than .5%.
— = Zero respondents.

SOURCE: "What is your favorite sport to watch?" in *Sports*, The Gallup Organization, July 2, 2007, http://www.galluppoll.com/content/?ci=4735&pg=1 (accessed July 23, 2007). Copyright © 2007 by The Gallup Organization. Reproduced by permission of The Gallup Organization.

College Football

Televised college sports have nearly as much appeal as professional sports for American audiences, and since the 1980s they have become the subject of large media contracts as well. In the early days of televised sports, the National Collegiate Athletic Association (NCAA) determined which college teams could play on television. Officially, the NCAA's goal in making these decisions was to protect the schools from the loss of ticket-buying fans who were lured by the glowing screen in a warm home. The NCAA's dominance over the right to broadcast football games went virtually unquestioned for years. According to Welch Suggs, in "Football, Television, and the Supreme Court" (*Chronicle of Higher Education*, vol. 50, no. 44, July 9, 2004), the only case of a college losing its membership in the NCAA came in 1951, when the University of Pennsylvania was dismissed for attempting to schedule its own broadcasts in defiance of the NCAA. The school quickly repented, and its membership was restored.

The networks, however, aware of the potential audience for games between large universities with esteemed football programs, kept courting college athletic departments. By the 1970s several universities with top football programs had become frustrated with the limits the

2006 survey basketball was a distant second at 12%, and baseball was third at 11%. The preference for watching baseball has been on the decline since its peak in 1948, when 39% said it was their favorite sport to watch. (See Table 3.2.)

According to Nielsen Media Research, five of the ten top-rated U.S. television shows of all time have been sports programs, and of those five, four were Super Bowls. According to the NFL, in "Colts-Bears Draws No. 3 Audience of All-Time" (August 7, 2007, http://www.nfl.com/news/story?id=09000d5d800226d0&template=with-video&confirm=true), 93.2 million viewers watched Super Bowl XLI in February 2007, giving it the third-largest television audience of all time, behind only the 1996 Super Bowl and the final episode of the long-running comedy series *M*A*S*H* in 1983.

TABLE 3.2

Poll respondents' rating of the sports they like to watch most, long-term trend, selected years, 1937–2006

	Football	Baseball	Basketball	Auto racing	Ice/figure skating	Ice hockey
	%	%	%	%	%	%
2006 Dec 11–14	43	11	12	4	2	3
2005 Dec 5–8	34	12	12	5	3	4
2004 Dec 5–8	37	10	13	5	4	3
2003 Dec 11–14	37	10	14	5	6	5
2002 Dec 5–8	37	12	13	5	4	3
2001 Mar 26–28	28	12	16	6	4	3
2000 Mar 30–Apr 2	33	13	15	5	4	5
1998 Nov 20–22	36	16	12	3	2	3
1997 Apr 18–20	30	14	17	7	2	3
1995 Apr 17–19	32	16	15	2	2	3
1994 Sep 16–20	37	16	13	2	3	1
1994 Aug 8–9	35	21	11	2	3	3
1992 Sept	38	16	12	2	2	4
1990 Feb	35	16	15	1	2	3
1981 Jan	38	16	9	1	2	2
1972 Oct	32	24	9	2	1	4
1960 Dec	21	34	9	*	1	3
1948 Apr 9–14	17	39	10	1	*	3
1937 Mar 24–29						

SOURCE: "Long Term Trend," in *Sports*, The Gallup Organization, July 2, 2007, http://www.galluppoll.com/content/?ci=4735&pg=1 (accessed July 23, 2007). Copyright © 2007 by The Gallup Organization. Reproduced by permission of The Gallup Organization.

NCAA was placing on their television exposure. In 1977 five major conferences, along with a handful of high-profile independents, formed their own group, the College Football Association (CFA), to fight for their interests within the NCAA. A few years later the CFA signed its own television agreement with NBC, the second-largest sports television contract ever signed up to that time. Naturally, the NCAA was unhappy about this development and moved to ban the teams involved from all championship events. The University of Georgia and Oklahoma University sued the NCAA, and the case was eventually decided by the U.S. Supreme Court in *NCAA v. Board of Regents of the University of Oklahoma et al.* (468 U.S. 85, 1984). In the end, the NCAA was found to be in violation of antitrust laws. Thus, the NCAA's stranglehold on television broadcast of college football was broken.

In the wake of the Supreme Court decision, the CFA took on the role of coordinating the television coverage of most of the nation's leading football conferences. Still, some teams found the arrangement too restrictive. Following the defection of a handful of teams and conferences, the CFA folded in 1994, and the conferences were on their own to negotiate television contracts with the networks. The dollars began to flow in an ever-greater volume during this period. Suggs notes that the Southeastern Conference (SEC) signed a contract in 1990 that brought in $16 million to be divided among its members; in 2004 SEC teams, including the University of Alabama, the University of Arkansas, the University of Georgia, and Louisiana State University, split nearly seven times that amount.

With about a thousand universities participating in over one hundred fifty thousand sporting events each year by 2007, competition for the right to put these events on television is fierce. In 2003 a new station devoted strictly to collegiate athletics was launched under the name College Sports Television (CSTV). According to CSTV (2007, http://www.cstv.com/online/), in 2007 CSTV was available in more than twenty-one million homes via cable and satellite. CSTV also operates a network of 215 official athletic Web sites for top colleges, and streams audio and/or video for thousands of events per year on high-speed Internet to online subscribers. CSTV was purchased by CBS in January 2006. As often happens in the media world, success has bred competition. In March 2005 ESPN launched ESPNU, its own version of a college-only sports station.

BASKETBALL

NBA regular-season games have never drawn the kind of television audiences that NFL games routinely attract, simply because there are so many of them—the NBA season lasts eighty-two games, whereas the NFL's lasts just sixteen. In basketball, viewership increases significantly during the playoffs and is greatly influenced by the specific teams or personalities involved in a game. The NBA's television ratings have generally been sliding since Michael Jordan's (1963–) second retirement in 1999. Bob Wolfley notes in "NBA's Network Ratings Still Falling" (*Milwaukee Journal Sentinel*, April 13, 2006) that NBA regular-season broadcasts scored an average rating of 2.2 in 2006. A decade earlier, during the peak of the Jordan era, it had a 5.0 rating, according to Kevin Downey, in "'Monday Night Football' Takes a Hit" (*Media Life*, October 9, 2001). In "Fox's NASCAR Rainout Coverage Drove Ratings" (March 21, 2006, http://www.mediaweek.com/mw/news/cabletv/article_display.jsp?vnu_content_id =1002200021), John Consoli notes that a low point came in 2006, when a game between the Cleveland Cavaliers and the Los Angeles Lakers—pitting two of the sport's brightest stars in LeBron James (1984–) and Kobe Bryant (1978–) against each other—recorded lower ratings than a rained-out National Association for Stock Car Auto Racing (NASCAR) race being broadcast simultaneously on another network. In "Ratings for 2007 Finals down 27 Percent from Last Year" (June 15, 2007, http://sports.espn.go.com/nba/playoffs2007/news/story?id=2905923), ESPN reports that the 2007 NBA Finals, also featuring the emerging superstar James, scored record low ratings on ABC, capturing just a 6.2 rating and 11.0 share.

According to Erik Spanberg, in "NBA: Why Aren't You Watching?" (*Christian Science Monitor*, June 23, 2005), basketball's television ratings have been plummeting for a variety of reasons. Spanberg quotes the industry analyst David Carter of the Sports Business Group, who places the blame on a charisma gap: "The NBA is lacking chemistry and the style and personalities that drove it during the 1980s and 1990s." According to Carter, the slower pace of the game, which has been dominated by stifling defenses in recent years, also has a negative effect on ratings. Spanberg also raises the issue of the widening gulf between players and fans. Peter Roby, the director of the Center for the Study of Sport in Society at Northeastern University, notes, "There is a lack of connection between players and fans because the players make so much money now.... Players in the 1960s and 1970s used to live in the same neighborhoods as the fans. Now there is a wedge between fans and players, so there is no empathy."

Table 3.3 shows the history of the NBA's television contracts since 1953. The rate at which the money involved has increased is striking. The set of deals the league signed in 1990 with TNT and NBC were worth well under $1 billion for four years. The most recent contracts, signed in 2002 with TNT and ABC/ESPN, cover six years (from the 2002–03 season through the 2007–08 season) and have a total value of $4.6 billion. Under these contracts AOL/Time Warner (now Time Warner) agreed to pay nearly $2.2 billion to show fifty-two regular-season telecasts and up to forty-five postseason games on TNT. ESPN signed on to broadcast seventy-five regular-season games for $2.4 billion. The 2002 deal represented a key shift that saw most games moved from network television to cable. The terms of the latest contract call for ABC to air fifteen regular-season games per year, less than half of what NBC was airing under the previous contract. Rudy Martzke reports in

TABLE 3.3

NBA television contracts, by cable channel or broadcast network, 1953–2008

Seasons	Station	Contracts amount
1979–80 to 1981–82	USA	$1.5 million/3 years
1982–83 to 1983–84	USA/ESPN	$11 million/2 years
1984–85 to 1985–86	TBS	$20 million/2 years
1986–87 to 1987–88	TBS	$25 million/2 years
1988–89 to 1989–90	TBS/TNT	$50 million/2 years
1990–91 to 1993–94	TNT	$275 million/4 years
1994–95 to 1997–98	TNT/TBS	$397 million/4 years
1998–99 to 2001–02	TNT/TBS	$840 million/4 years
2002–03 to 2007–08	TNT	$2.2 billion/6 years
1953–54	DUMONT	$39,000/13 games
1954–55 to 1961–62	NBC	N/A
1962–63 to 1972–73	ABC	N/A
1973–74 to 1975–76	CBS	$27 million/3 years
1976–77 to 1977–78	CBS	$21 million/2 years
1978–79 to 1981–82	CBS	$74 million/4 years
1982–83 to 1985–86	CBS	$91.9 million/4 years
1986–87 to 1989–90	CBS	$173 million/4 years
1990–91 to 1993–94	NBC	$601 million/4 years
1994–95 to 1997–98	NBC	$892 million/4 years
1998–99 to 2001–02	NBC	$1.616 billion/4 years
2002–03 to 2007–08	ABC/ESPN	$2.4 billion/6 years

N/A=Not available

SOURCE: "NBA Cable Television Contracts" and "NBA Network Television Contracts," in *NBA TV Contracts*, InsideHoops.com, 2007, http://www.insidehoops.com/nba-tv-contracts.shtml (accessed August 20, 2007)

"NBA Finalizes TV Deals: Goodbye NBC" (*USA Today*, January 22, 2002) that during this contract period, which lasted from 1998–99 through 2001–02, the league's television ratings had fallen more than 35%. As a result, NBC was not inclined to make a particularly generous offer to extend its NBA contract; its bid of $325 million per year came in well below the $400 million offered by ESPN. Another factor in the shift from network to cable is the availability to cable stations of revenue from subscription fees. This additional source of income gives cable stations a negotiating advantage over traditional networks, which depend solely on advertising fees for their income.

In 2003 Time Warner Cable, Cox Communications, and Cablevision Systems teamed up on a multiyear agreement with the NBA for distribution of NBA-TV, the league's own twenty-four-hour network, which as of 2005 was available in about sixty-seven million U.S. homes, according to the NBA, in "NBA TV to Televise 25 D-League Games" (October 24, 2005, http://www.nba.com/dleague/nbdl/NBA_TV_to_Televise_25_DLeague-155010-95.html).

HOCKEY

The National Hockey League (NHL) has experienced a downturn in television viewership over the past decade. So apathetic was the viewing public in 2004 that the conference finals of the Stanley Cup Playoffs did not even draw a large enough share of the potential viewing audience to crack the top-fifteen program list for the week of May 17 through May 23. In June 2007 the final game of the Stanley Cup series between the Anaheim Ducks and Ottawa Senators pulled in the lowest audience for the championship in more than a decade, losing 28% of its 2006 audience with only two million households tuned in (http://www.sportingnews.com/yourturn/viewtopic.php?t=219101).

Given its declining performance as a television draw, it is not surprising that the NHL has the least lucrative national television deals among the major sports. NBC currently pays no fee for broadcast rights, and the NHL does not receive any money until NBC recoups all of its costs. Once this happens, the two entities share advertising revenues equally. In March 2007 NBC and the NHL agreed to extend the deal through the 2007–08 season, with an option to add another season afterward. This deal was set to expire at the end of 2008; NBC retains the option to renew the agreement for two additional years. ESPN, which had paid $60 million for broadcast rights through 2004–05, declined to extend its contract after that season was canceled because of a labor dispute between owners and players. Instead, the NHL signed a new agreement with the Comcast-owned Outdoor Life Network, in which the league is guaranteed $65 million for the first year and $70 million for the second. In "Look Who's Talking: ESPN, NHL" (July 30, 2007, http://www.sportsbusinessjournal.com/index.cfm?fuseaction=article.main&articleId=55770), John Ourand and Tripp Mickle report that ESPN and the NHL were conducting negotiations in 2007 to bring professional hockey back to ESPN2 beginning in 2008–09. As of September 2007 no contract had been signed, and the future of ice hockey as a first-tier major sport seemed doubtful, with many hometown newspapers discontinuing their coverage of teams during road trips to away games.

AUTO RACING

In "NASCAR TV Deals Done" (December 7, 2005, http://www.multichannel.com/article/CA6289818.html), Mike Reynolds reports that in 2005 NASCAR signed a set of eight-year television rights contracts with ESPN/ABC Sports ($270 million per year) and Turner Broadcasting's TNT network ($80 million per year). Soon after these lucrative deals were signed, NASCAR's television ratings began to sag. According to Nate Ryan, in "NASCAR's Growth Slows after 15 Years in the Fast Lane" (*USA Today*, November 15, 2006), in thirty of the first thirty-four races of 2006, ratings were lower than they were the previous year.

EXTREME SPORTS

Even though television ratings for extreme sports still have a long way to go before they are in the same league as professional football and basketball, the audience is growing. More important, at least from the perspective of advertisers, the audience watching extreme sports is youthful and predominantly male, with a lot of buying power. Not many sports can take credit for completely altering the public image of a soft drink, but extreme sports have done just that for Mountain Dew. Once perceived as a "hillbilly" drink, Mountain Dew is now almost universally associated with youth culture as personified by practitioners of extreme sports. In "Going to Extremes" (*American Demographics*, June 1, 2002), Joan Raymond states that the transformation started in 1992 with the appearance of the "Do the Dew" advertising campaign. The campaign, which featured attractive young people engaging in a variety of extreme activities, helped make Mountain Dew the fastest-growing soft drink during the 1990s.

Raymond notes that by the turn of the millennium, while *Monday Night Football*'s ratings were declining—viewership dropped from an average of 12.7% of the nation's households in 2000 to 11.5% in 2001—ratings for the two premier extreme sports events, the X Games and the Gravity Games, were increasing quickly. About two million households tuned in to the 2001 Gravity Games, up from 1.6 million the previous year. However, Chris Isidore states in "X-treme Marks the Spot" (August 6, 2004, http://money.cnn.com/2004/08/06/commentary/column_sportsbiz/sportsbiz/index.htm) that while the best ratings for the 2003 Summer X Games on ABC showed 2.2% of the nation's households watching, that number was still barely half the rating ABC achieved for the final game of NHL's Stanley Cup finals, which were themselves considered a ratings disappointment. In "Moto X Racing Added for Summer X Games 13" (March 22, 2007, http://sports.espn.go.com/espn/print?id=2808468&type=story), ESPN states that the 2006 X Games averaged a mere 0.9 rating on ESPN.

Broadcasters and advertisers are nevertheless optimistic about the future of extreme sports programming. According to Isidore, the sports' median (half are higher and half are lower) viewership age is twenty-seven, compared to a median age of forty-two for ESPN's NFL football broadcasts. The ages for some other sports are even higher: baseball's median is forty-eight and golf's is fifty-five. Media companies are scrambling to ride this youthful wave. Fox has launched a new digital cable channel called FuelTV, which is devoted to extreme sports and other programming that targets the under-forty demographic. Moreover, this young audience is also more comfortable with new media than their parents are, as reflected by the 1.4 million visits to EXPN.com, the official X Games Web site, on August 5, 2006, during the peak of the summer games. ESPN planned to expand its use of live streaming video and other newer technology in 2007.

ADVERTISING

The *SportsBusiness Journal* (2007, http://www. sports businessjournal.com/index.cfm?fuseaction=page.feature &featureId=43) estimates that sports in the United States are a $213 billion industry, making it twice as large as the U.S. auto industry. Of this $213 billion, $27.4 billion (or 14.1%) falls into the advertising category. Surprisingly, television does not account for the largest share of this total. The biggest share, $16.4 billion, is spent on billboards and signage at arenas and stadiums. National network television is the second largest expenditure, at $4.7 billion, followed by radio at $2.3 billion. Another $1.8 billion is spent on advertising on national cable television, and sports magazines account for $1.5 billion of the sports advertising total. The rest is spent on regional television, both network and cable, and national syndicated television. The *SportsBusiness Journal* classifies the $239 million that was spent on Internet advertising in a separate category. These totals do not include the $407 million spent on Internet advertising at sports-related Web sites—as estimated by Research and Markets in "Sports Site Marketing: A Whole New Ball Game" (July 2007, http://www .researchandmarkets.com/reports/c63687) for 2006.

A significant portion of sports advertising spending is on commercials aired during noteworthy games. The most expensive television advertisements of any kind are those placed during the NFL's Super Bowl. The article "Advertising History: 40 Years of Prices and Audience" (2007, http://adage.com/SuperBowlBuyers/superbowlhis tory07.html) indicates that a thirty-second spot during the 2007 Super Bowl cost advertisers $2.6 million, whereas in 1967 it cost only $40,000 (or about $245,350 in 2007 dollars). Given the cost, advertisers want maximum impact, and they create innovative and sometimes controversial ads just for the occasion. Table 3.4 shows a variety of facts about Super Bowl advertising, including the top advertisers and top product categories from 2002 through 2006.

Super Bowl commercials have in fact become something of a genre in themselves. Since 2004, however, advertisers appeared to have toned down the shock factor in the wake of that year's infamous halftime incident in which Janet Jackson's breast was exposed during the live broadcast. Advertising during baseball's World Series is a bargain in comparison, but it still yields large sums of money for the broadcaster. In *Sports, Inc.* (2004), Phil Schaaf explains that Fox charged $325,000 for a thirty-second spot during the 2002 World Series and took in nearly $20 million per game over the course of the series. This means that in just five games, Fox was able to recoup about a quarter of its yearly $400 million investment in MLB. It is worth noting that advertising spots during the first five games were sold out even before it was known which two teams would be participating.

TABLE 3.4

Super Bowl advertising, 2002–06

Top advertiser (seconds of exposure)

2006–Anheuser-Busch (270)
2005–Anheuser-Busch (300)
2004–Anheuser-Busch (330)
2003–Anheuser-Busch (330)
2002–Anheuser-Busch (300)

Average 30-second cost

2006–$2.5 million
2005–$2.4 million
2004–$2.3 million
2003–$2.15 million
2002–$2.2 million

2006 top categories (seconds of exposure)

1. Beer-270 seconds
   Motion pictures-270 seconds
2. Autos & trucks-240 seconds
3. Wireless telephone services-150 seconds

2006 top advertisers (seconds of exposure)

1. Anheuser-Busch-270 seconds
2. Pepsi-Cola-120 seconds
3. Gillette-90 seconds
   Mobile ESPN-90 seconds
   Walt Disney World-90 seconds
   Warner Brothers Entertainment-90 seconds

SOURCE: "Advertising Information," in *The Nielsen Company's Guide to the Super Bowl*, The Nielsen Company, January 31, 2007, http://www.nielsen .com/media/pr_070131_download.pdf (accessed August 1, 2007)

According to the Center for Media Research, at $2.5 million, the advertising rates for thirty-second commercials during the Super Bowl far exceeded rates for other sports championships in 2006 (http://www.centerforme diaresearch.com/cfmr_brief.cfm?fnl=070319). Network television advertising rates for other top-rated sports events in 2006 included $1.1 million for a thirty-second spot during the championship game of the NCAA Men's Basketball Tournament, $900–$956 million for a thirty-second ad during the AFC and NFC championship games leading up to the Super Bowl, $400,000 for an ad during the MLB World Series, $359 million for advertising time during the NBA Championship Series, and $268 million to $530 million for a thirty-second ad during a college football bowl game.

Advertising rates for nonchampionship sporting events, however, are usually negotiated in packages rather than for individual time slots. When broken down into thirty-second spots for comparison purposes, other estimated advertising rates that Schaaf mentions include ESPN's *SportsCenter*, $11,000; baseball divisional championship series, $90,000; U.S. Open tennis finals, $175,000; and *Monday Night Football*, $325,000.

Sports Advertising and Alcohol

Sports advertising is dominated by products that appeal to young adult males. However, one product in particular, beer, is the undisputed king of the sports

TABLE 3.5

Alcohol advertising on sports TV, 2001–03

	2001		2002		2003	
	Dollars	**Ads**	**Dollars**	**Ads**	**Dollars**	**Ads**
Alcohol						
Total sports	$491,695,626	59,461	$597,337,222	80,548	$540,841,358	90,817
Total all programs	$811,166,404	208,909	$990,225,497	289,381	$879,143,274	298,054
Sports as % of all programs	60.6%	28.5%	60.3%	27.8%	61.5%	30.5%
All categories						
Total sports	$7,435,202,670	2,166,842	$9,074,508,240	2,675,648	$8,212,413,180	2,777,224
Total all programs	$44,840,147,250	55,756,506	$49,384,436,500	66,399,304	$50,729,026,920	69,063,279
Sports as % of all programs	16.6%	3.9%	18.4%	4.0%	16.2%	4.0%

SOURCE: "Table 2. Alcohol Sports TV Advertising Relative to All Sports TV Advertising: 2001 to 2003," in *Alcohol Advertising on Sports Television 2001 to 2003*, The Center on Alcohol Marketing and Youth, October 2004, http://camy.org/factsheets/pdf/AlcoholAdvertisingSportsTelevision2001-2003.pdf (accessed August 20, 2007). Data from TNS Media Intelligence/CMR 2001–2003.

advertising jungle. According to the article "A-B Paces Ad Spending, Olympic Sponsors Climb List" (*SportsBusiness Journal*, March 21, 2005), the top sports advertiser for the last several years has been Anheuser-Busch Companies, which spends about $300 million—83% of its total advertising budget—on sports advertising each year.

The Center on Alcohol Marketing and Youth (CAMY) studies the relationship between sports programming and alcohol advertising. In the fact sheet *Alcohol Advertising on Sports Television, 2001 to 2003* (October 2004, http://camy.org/factsheets/pdf/AlcoholAdvertisingSportsTelevision2001-2003.pdf), CAMY finds that while sports programming accounted for only 16% to 18% of overall television advertising spending and only about 4% of all ads in those years, over 60% of the alcohol industry's advertising spending and around 30% of its ads were on sports programs. Overall, the alcohol industry spent $541 million to place 90,817 ads on television sports programming in 2003. (See Table 3.5.) CAMY notes that the percentage of commercials on sports shows that are for alcohol products is triple the percentage of ads on all programming that are for alcohol products. Even though beer advertisements have long been omnipresent on sports television, in recent years ads for hard liquor have been appearing with greater frequency. Sports television advertising for distilled spirits increased 350% between 2001 and 2003. CAMY also finds that alcohol advertising increased for the Super Bowl, *Monday Night Football*, and other top-rated games.

CAMY states that soccer outranked all other sports in terms of the percentage of its advertising that is for alcohol products; 8.3% of the commercials on televised soccer games were for alcohol. Hockey was second at 7.2%, followed by professional basketball at 6.8%. Overall, 3.2% of all ads shown during televised sporting events in 2003 were for alcohol products. Among professional sports, hockey games had the highest number of alcohol ads per broadcast. A typical televised hockey game featured 5.3 alcohol ads in 2003. (See Table 3.6.) Boxing matches averaged 4.5 alcohol ads, followed closely by professional basketball with 4.4.

According to CAMY, advertising on college sports presentations is at least as alcohol-oriented as on

TABLE 3.6

Average number of alcohol ads per game, by sport, 2001–03

	2001	2002	2003
Non-professional football—game	3.0	6.5	5.5
Hockey—game	5.0	4.9	5.3
Boxing	2.2	4.9	4.5
Professional basketball—game	4.2	3.7	4.4
Professional baseball—game	4.3	4.2	4.3
Non-professional basketball—game	2.9	4.7	4.2
Golf	2.0	2.4	3.4
Bowling	1.5	1.7	3.2
College baseball—game	3.1	2.8	3.1
Olympics	6.5	1.9	3.0
Auto racing	2.1	2.3	3.0
Other specific event—game	2.5	2.5	2.9
Soccer	2.1	2.4	2.8
College basketball—game	2.4	2.0	2.6
College football—game	2.9	2.2	2.5
Professional football—game	2.3	2.3	2.5
Non-professional basketball—game	5.0	2.2	2.5
Tennis	1.7	2.1	2.3
Horse racing	2.3	2.1	2.1
College baseball—pre-game	NA	2.0	1.7
College football—pre-game	2.6	1.9	1.6
Professional football—pre-game	1.4	1.2	1.5
Professional football—post-game	1.2	1.1	1.3
Professional basketball—pre-game	1.1	1.1	1.2
Professional baseball—post-game	NA	1.0	1.2
Professional basketball—post-game	1.5	1.1	1.1
Professional baseball—pre-game	1.1	1.0	1.1
College baseball—post-game	1.1	1.2	1.1
College basketball—pre-game	2.7	1.0	1.0
College football—post-game	1.0	NA	1.0
Non-professional basketball—pre-game	NA	NA	1.0

Note: NA=Not available

SOURCE: "Table 8. Average Number of Alcohol Ads per Sports Game: 2001 to 2003," in *Alcohol Advertising on Sports Television, 2001 to 2003*, Center on Alcohol Marketing and Youth, October 2004, http://camy.org/factsheets/pdf/AlcoholAdvertisingSportsTelevision2001-2003.pdf (accessed July 25, 2007). Data from TNS Media Intelligencer/CMR 2001–2003.

TABLE 3.7

Alcohol advertising on college sports TV, 2001–03

Sports program type	Alcohol			All categories			Alcohol as percent of all		
	2001 dollars	2002 dollars	2003 dollars	2001 dollars	2002 dollars	2003 dollars	2001 dollars	2002 dollars	2003 dollars
College baseball—game	$48,923	$108,159	$80,132	$2,115,000	$3,071,800	$2,976,840	2.3%	3.5%	2.7%
College baseball—pre-game	$0	$1,358	$11,243	$37,000	$124,000	$331,050	0.0%	1.1%	3.4%
College basketball—game	$32,440,775	$34,097,498	$28,260,794	$537,041,660	$569,391,450	$586,241,120	6.0%	6.0%	4.8%
College basketball—post-game	$191,370	$1,554,636	$1,179,731	$6,489,800	$13,363,200	$18,633,630	2.9%	11.6%	6.3%
College basketball—pre-game	$142,178	$34,247	$14,173	$5,086,000	$1,921,700	$3,381,930	2.8%	1.8%	0.4%
College football—game	$19,859,427	$21,947,490	$22,484,038	$447,809,650	$509,732,040	$531,923,940	4.4%	4.3%	4.2%
College football—post-game	$19,000	$0	$17,857	$1,849,400	$1,073,000	$1,485,350	1.0%	0.0%	1.2%
College football—pre-game	$258,128	$365,892	$180,387	$10,143,930	$6,200,370	$6,015,040	2.5%	5.9%	3.0%
College sports total	**$52,959,801**	**$58,109,280**	**$52,228,355**	**$1,010,572,440**	**$1,104,877,560**	**$1,150,988,900**	**5.2%**	**5.3%**	**4.5%**

SOURCE: "Table 9. Alcohol Advertising on College Sports TV: 2001 to 2003," in *Alcohol Advertising on Sports Television 2001 to 2003*, The Center on Alcohol Marketing and Youth, October 2004, http://camy.org/factsheets/pdf/AlcoholAdvertisingSportsTelevision2001-2003.pdf (accessed August 20,2007). Data from TNS Media Intelligence/CMR 2001–2003.

professional sports programming. In 2003 alcohol companies spent $52.2 million to place 4,747 ads on college sports programs. (See Table 3.7.) College basketball, at $28.2 million, accounted for more than half of this spending.

SPORTS VIEWING AND GENDER

In "Women Have Turned Chilly to TV Sports" (April 20, 2004, http://www.medialifemagazine.com/news2004/apr04/apr19/2_tues/news4tuesday.html), Toni Fitzgerald suggests that women and men watch sports for different reasons. Women, Fitzgerald proposes, watch sports for the story lines, meaning their primary interest is in the drama and personalities. By contrast, men are interested in the skills and statistics. Fitzgerald points to a report from the media research firm Magna Global USA, which finds that sports viewership by women had declined significantly between 1998 and 2003, as measured both by ratings and by total weekly hours spent watching sports. According to the Magna Global data, average broadcast (i.e., noncable) television ratings among women decreased by 18% during this period. The ratings drop was even more precipitous (44%) for women watching basic cable television sports. The total number of hours women spent watching sports on television—either broadcast or basic cable—dropped by 17%, from 1.5 hours per week in 1998 (with Olympic coverage excluded from the total) to 1.2 hours in 2003. Meanwhile, broadcast ratings for men decreased only 9% during this span, whereas cable ratings fell 36%. Men's viewing hours dropped only 6%, from 2.8 hours per week to 2.6. Fitzgerald argues that these numbers are the result of what is happening in the sports world. When the sports that women like to watch, such as figure skating and tennis, have relatively few appealing story lines in motion, women turn the television off. Therefore, injuries to Serena Williams (1981–) and Venus Williams (1980–)

in tennis and Michelle Kwan's (1980–) gradual decline in figure skating were seen to have a measurable effect on viewership among women.

GAMING

Not long ago there were only two options for sports enthusiasts: playing a sport yourself or watching others play it live or onscreen. In recent years, a third way has emerged in the form of sports gaming.

Sports-oriented video games have been around for years, but until the mid-1980s the graphics were mediocre and the action unexciting for a true sports buff. A big change took place during the late 1980s when Electronic Arts (EA), at the time a relatively new company making interactive entertainment software, introduced the first-ever football video game to offer realistic eleven-on-eleven action. To make the game as realistic as possible, the company consulted extensively with the former NFL coach and current football commentator John Madden (1936–). They eventually named the game after Madden, and in 1989 the first version of *John Madden Football* was released for Apple II computers. The game was an instant sensation. A version for the Sega Genesis home entertainment system was introduced the following year. Over the next few years the gaming industry grew exponentially, split about evenly between computer games and television-based systems. By the release of the 1995 version of the game, *Madden NFL '95*, EA had hashed out licensing deals with the NFL and the NFL Players Association, allowing it to use likenesses of real players and the official league and team logos and uniforms. *Madden NFL* was eventually made available for every major gaming system. According to Matthew Kirdahy, in "The Best-Selling Games of 2006" (December 15, 2006, http://www.forbes.com/technology/2006/12/15/video-games-bestsellers-tech-cx_mk_games06_1215sales.html), by 2006 *Madden NFL* had sold fifty-one million units worldwide since its 1989 launch; it was the best-selling video game of any kind, not just sports, in 2006, selling 2.3 million copies for various platforms.

However, *Madden NFL* is just one of a number of highly successful sports games. In "Video Gaming Is on a Roll, as NBA, NFL Lend Reality to Look" (*Sacramento Bee*, April 2, 2005), Clint Swett notes that sports game sales in the United States totaled $1.2 billion in 2004, representing nearly one-fifth of the entire $6.2 billion video game market. The latest development in sports gaming is the appearance of exclusive licensing contracts between sports leagues and individual game manufacturers. Swett reports that in December 2004 EA—which besides the *Madden NFL* series also makes *NBA Live*—signed a $400 million deal with the NFL, giving it exclusive rights to the likenesses of NFL players, uniforms, and stadiums for five years, effectively freezing out competitors such as Take-Two Interactive Software, which had eroded sales of *Madden NFL* by offering its *ESPN NFL* at sharply reduced prices. Take-Two's consolation prize was a seven-year, $250 million contract with MLB. EA was also one of five game companies to agree to pay a combined $400 million to the NBA for use of its imagery. In yet another licensing deal, EA is paying ESPN $850 million for fifteen years of use of ESPN features, including announcers and scoreboards.

CURRENT ISSUES IN SPORTS AND MEDIA
The Influence of Advertising on Young Sports Fans

The prevalence of alcohol in sports advertising noted earlier, and the potential harm it can cause to young viewers, is just one of many key issues in how sports are delivered to the American public via the media. In August 1999 the national, nonpartisan advocacy group Children Now published *Boys to Men: Sports Media* (http://www.la84foundation.org/9arr/ResearchReports/boys tomen.pdf), a report analyzing the content of sports programming during the late 1990s, and combines this information with data from polling and focus groups of young people. Children Now's intent was to connect the messages youths receive when watching sports programming—and the commercials placed therein—with their attitudes and behaviors. It finds that in 1999, 98% of U.S. boys between the ages of eight and seventeen consumed some form of sports-related media; 90% of them watched sports on television. Children Now notes that aggression and violence are often depicted in a positive light, and war metaphors are regularly employed. Furthermore, it highlights issues related to race and gender in sports. According to *Boys to Men*, more than three-quarters of sports announcers are white males. White females and African-American males each account for only 10% of sports commentators on U.S. broadcasts. Even though Children Now does not find significant evidence of overt racist content, sports pro-

grams sometimes reinforce racial stereotypes, such as by lauding African-American players for their "natural athleticism" or by remarking on the intelligence of white athletes. Women on sports programs, it suggests, are often treated as no more than props with sex appeal.

Native American Mascots

For the last fifty years Native American advocacy groups have expressed opposition to the use of Native American names and mascots by sports teams. Organizations such as the National Coalition on Racism in Sports and Media have embarked on a campaign to convince teams to discard cartoonish Native American mascots and to encourage teams with names such as the Braves, Chiefs, and Redskins to rename themselves. This movement has met with some success. In the 1970s activists convinced Stanford and Dartmouth universities to change their names from Indians to race-neutral names: the Cardinals and the Big Green, respectively. In 1994 Marquette University shed its Warriors nickname and became the Golden Eagles. The St. Johns University Redmen became the Red Storm the same year, and in 2007, after a long debate, the University of Illinois finally retired Chief Illiniwek, a school mascot since 1926. However, many more teams have resisted calls to retire their traditional mascots, so the debate continues.

Violence and Athlete Role-Models

Violence in sports is often a focus of media scrutiny and academic research because the behavior of high-profile athletes can have an impact on fan behavior, according to social scientists. In "Violence in Sports Reflects Society, Says IU Professor" (July 3, 2002, http://newsinfo.iu.edu/news/page/normal/449.html), Lynn Jamieson of Indiana University explains that "sport tends to reflect society, and we live in a violent era. We have a violent society where people use violence to solve problems instead of using other means.... The violence issue is not limited to professional sports. It filters down to the high schools and even to recreational activities.... This is because if it occurs at the professional level, it is likely to be imitated at the lower levels like Little League and city recreational programs."

Some sports include a measure of violence that is held in check by the rules of fair play and by officials who can enforce penalties or regulate the players' behavior to some extent. However, the violence below the surface can often erupt, and violent events involving professional athletes—either on or off the playing field—become major news stories covered by news and entertainment organizations in addition to the sports media. The 2004–05 NBA season was marred by a huge brawl during a game between the Detroit Pistons and the Indiana Pacers; the fracas spilled into the stands, resulting in the involvement of both spectators and players. Several players received long suspensions, and the entire season took place under the cloud of the melee. Another large basketball brawl, resulting in the ejection of ten players, took place during a December 2006 NBA game between the Denver Nuggets and the New York Knicks.

However, basketball is not alone in contending with image problems stemming from extended media coverage of the actions of its players. In October 2005 several members of the NFL's Minnesota Vikings were allegedly involved in a party aboard a chartered boat that erupted into a drunken sex orgy. In August 2007 Michael Vick (1980–) of the Atlanta Falcons was suspended indefinitely by the NFL after he pleaded guilty to felony charges stemming from his involvement in an illegal dog-fighting ring. According to author Michael MacCambridge in the *New York Times* (September 16, 2007, http://www.nytimes.com/2007/09/16/sports/football/16goodell.html), such incidents result from the unique position athletes are afforded within U.S. society. In MacCambridge's view, "There is a tremendous amount of money, free time and scrutiny in the lives of most pro football players, and the combination is more pronounced and more combustible than it was a generation ago." Vick's suspension indicated a no-nonsense response from Roger Goodell (1959–), who in his first year as commissioner of the NFL instituted a strict code of conduct for players and coaches.

CHAPTER 4
PROFESSIONAL TEAM SPORTS

For decades baseball, football, basketball, and hockey have been considered the four major professional team sports in the United States. Even though other sports, such as auto racing and soccer, are gaining ground in terms of popularity and hockey is struggling to maintain its status, it most likely will be some time before major league sports in the United States means anything other than the four core sports.

Besides being popular spectator events, professional league sports are also major industries that generate huge amounts of money—for team owners and managers, companies that sponsor teams, equipment and athletic gear manufacturers, and the athletes themselves.

MAJOR LEAGUE BASEBALL

Major League Baseball (MLB) is no longer as popular as professional football and is losing ground to other sports (particularly auto racing), yet it remains firmly ingrained in the American imagination, retaining the title of "national pastime." In 2004, 2005, and 2007 two teams with long histories of futility, the Boston Red Sox and the Chicago White Sox, saw World Series victories. Their success evoked an emotional response in fans across the United States and seemed to spark renewed interest in a sport that has had more than its share of bad publicity since the 1990s, mostly because of steroid scandals. Baseball's steroid problem was magnified in 2007, as Barry Bonds (1964–), the player most closely associated with the scandal, approached the all-time home-run record held by Hank Aaron (1934–) since 1974. Bonds broke Aaron's record on August 7, 2007, eliciting an ambivalent response from fans and the national media. It remains to be seen if the renewed interest in baseball will translate into long-term gains in attendance and television viewership in the face of stiff competition from other sports, old and new.

MLB Structure and Administration

As of 2007 MLB consisted of thirty teams. (See Table 4.1.) These teams are divided into two leagues: sixteen in the National League and fourteen in the American League. Each of these leagues is further split into three divisions—East, Central, and West—that are loosely based on geography. The MLB season normally runs from early April through late September and consists of 162 games. This season length was established in 1961, before which teams played a 154-game schedule. Most games are played against teams within each league, though not necessarily within each own division.

Following the regular season, the champions of each division (three teams in each league) plus a wild-card team—the team with the best record among those not winning their division—from each league compete in the playoffs. The playoffs consist of three rounds: two best-of-five Division Series in each league; a best-of-seven Championship Series in each league; and finally the World Series, a best-of-seven game series between the champions of each league to determine the major league champion team.

According to Plunkett Research, in "Sports Industry Overview" (2007, http://www.plunkettresearch.com/Industries/ Sports/SportsStatistics/tabid/273/Default.aspx), MLB took in $5.2 billion in revenue in 2006. The average player salary was $2.7 million. Table 4.2 shows the latest team values and revenue figures for each MLB team. The *SportsBusiness Journal* (2007, http://www.sportsbusiness journal.com/index.cfm?fuseaction=page.feature&feature Id=43) estimates that of the $10.5 billion worth of officially licensed sports merchandise sold annually, from banners to bobbleheads, $2.3 billion is spent on goods licensed by MLB and its member teams, second only to the NFL among the major sport leagues. Technically speaking, "Major League Baseball" refers to the entity that operates the National and American Leagues,

TABLE 4.1

Major League Baseball teams and divisions

American League	National League
East Division	**East Division**
Baltimore Orioles	Atlanta Braves
Boston Red Sox	Florida Marlins
New York Yankees	New York Mets
Tampa Bay Devil Rays	Philadelphia Phillies
Toronto Blue Jays	Washington Nationals
Central Division	**Central Division**
Chicago White Sox	Chicago Cubs
Cleveland Indians	Cincinnati Reds
Detroit Tigers	Houston Astros
Kansas City Royals	Milwaukee Brewers
Minnesota Twins	Pittsburgh Pirates
West Division	St. Louis Cardinals
Los Angeles Angels of Anaheim	**West Division**
Oakland Athletics	Arizona Diamondbacks
Seattle Mariners	Colorado Rockies
Texas Rangers	Los Angeles Dodgers
	San Diego Padres
	San Francisco Giants

SOURCE: Created by Robert Jacobson for The Gale Group, 2007. Data from Major League Baseball, http://www.mlb.com.

TABLE 4.2

Baseball team values and revenue, 2006

[In million dollars]

Rank	Team	Current value[a]	Revenues	Operating income[b]
1	New York Yankees	1,200	302	−25.2
2	New York Mets	736	217	24.4
3	Boston Red Sox	724	234	19.5
4	Los Angeles Dodgers	632	211	27.5
5	Chicago Cubs	592	197	22.2
6	St Louis Cardinals	460	184	14
7	San Francisco Giants	459	184	18.5
8	Atlanta Braves	458	183	14.8
9	Philadelphia Phillies	457	183	11.3
10	Washington Nationals	447	144	19.5
11	Houston Astros	442	184	18.4
12	Seattle Mariners	436	182	21.5
13	Los Angeles Angels of Anaheim	431	187	11.5
14	Baltimore Orioles	395	158	17.1
15	Chicago White Sox	381	173	19.5
16	San Diego Padres	367	160	5.2
17	Texas Rangers	365	155	11.2
18	Cleveland Indians	364	158	24.9
19	Detroit Tigers	357	170	8.7
20	Toronto Blue Jays	344	157	11
21	Arizona Diamondbacks	339	154	6.4
22	Colorado Rockies	317	151	23.9
23	Cincinnati Reds	307	146	22.4
24	Oakland Athletics	292	146	14.5
25	Minnesota Twins	288	131	14.8
26	Milwaukee Brewers	287	144	20.8
27	Kansas City Royals	282	123	8.4
28	Pittsburgh Pirates	274	137	25.3
29	Tampa Bay Devil Rays	267	134	20.2
30	Florida Marlins	244	122	43.3

Note: Revenues and operating income are for 2006 season.
[a]Value of team based on current stadium deal (unless new stadium is pending) without deduction for debt (other than stadium debt).
[b]Earnings before interest, taxes, depreciation and amortization.
NA: Not applicable.

SOURCE: Adapted from Kurt Badenhausen, Michael K. Ozanian, and Christina Settimi, "Special Report: The Business of Baseball," in *Forbes*, April 19, 2007, http://www.forbes.com/lists/2007/33/07mlb_The-Business-Of-Baseball_Rank.html (accessed July 25, 2007). Reprinted by permission of Forbes Magazine © 2007 Forbes LLC.

the two top professional baseball leagues in North America. MLB operates these two leagues under a joint organizational structure that was established in 1920 with the creation of the Major League Constitution. This constitution has been overhauled many times since then. MLB team owners appoint a commissioner, under whose direction MLB hires and maintains umpiring crews, negotiates marketing and television deals, and establishes labor agreements with the MLB Players Association.

MLB maintains a level of control over baseball that is somewhat unique among the major sports. This comes as a result of a 1922 U.S. Supreme Court decision in which baseball was deemed not to be "interstate commerce" and therefore not subject to federal antitrust law. Consequently, MLB is allowed to operate in monopolistic ways that would not be legal in most other industries. This privileged status allowed baseball to stave off player free agency (a professional athlete who is free to sign a contract with any team), and the high salaries that accompanied it, until the mid-1970s.

MLB History

The first professional baseball team was the Cincinnati Red Stockings, founded in 1869. That year the team—which still exists as the Cincinnati Reds—embarked on a fifty-seven-game national tour and went undefeated against local amateur teams. Their success led in 1871 to the creation of the first professional baseball league, the nine-team, eight-city National Association of Professional Baseball Players. Various other competing leagues were formed over the next decade, including a

precursor to the modern National League. The American League was founded in 1901. The champions of the American and National Leagues faced off in what became the first World Series in 1903. The popularity of professional baseball continued to grow over the next several years. A crisis unfolded in 1919, when several members of the Chicago White Sox were paid by gamblers to throw the World Series, in the so-called Black Sox scandal. In the wake of the scandal, club owners hired baseball's first commissioner, Kenesaw Landis (1866–1944), to clean up the game. As of 2007 the commissioner was Allan H. Selig (1934–), a founder of the Milwaukee Brewers. Selig, the ninth commissioner in MLB history, was appointed to the post by the team owners in 1998.

Baseball's golden era took place between the two world wars, marked by the rise of such all-time greats as Babe Ruth (1895–1948), Ty Cobb (1886–1961), and

Lou Gehrig (1903–1941). The major leagues survived the Great Depression (1929–1939) by introducing night games, which soon became the norm for games played during the week; weekend games were still played during the day. From its beginnings through World War II (1939–1945), MLB was racially segregated. That changed in 1947, when the African-American player Jackie Robinson (1919–1972) joined the Brooklyn Dodgers. Such legends as Willie Mays (1931–) and Hank Aaron followed over the next decade, and by the middle of the 1950s black players were fairly common on major league rosters. More recently, the number of African-American players in baseball has plummeted, as young African-American athletes have flocked to other sports. The 2005 World Series roster of the Houston Astros did not include a single black player; it was the first team to compete for the MLB championship without an African-American player in half a century.

After fifty years of stability, the 1950s brought changes to MLB in response to demographic shifts in the United States. The Boston Braves moved to Milwaukee in 1953. Two New York teams moved to the West Coast in 1957: the Brooklyn Dodgers departing for Los Angeles and the New York Giants to San Francisco.

Baseball started losing fans, especially younger ones, in big numbers during the 1960s and 1970s as labor conflicts and other challenges plagued the sport. In 1966 the MLB Players Association was formed. The association's main goal was to end the reserve clause, a contractual provision that essentially gave teams ownership of players, meaning they were bound to a particular team until they were traded or released. The reserve clause was finally overturned in 1975, ushering in the era of free agency in baseball, wherein players were free to negotiate with any team they wanted once their existing contract had expired. Labor squabbles continued over the next twenty years, and parts of several seasons were lost to work stoppages. The worst of these took place in 1994, when the final third of the season, including the World Series, was canceled.

The sport survived in spite of these distractions, however, thanks partly to a handful of individual accomplishments. These included Cal Ripken Jr.'s (1960–) destruction of Gehrig's long-standing record for consecutive games played, and Mark McGwire's (1963–) and Sammy Sosa's (1968–) 1998 competition to break the record for home runs in a season—a record that was broken again by Bonds just three years later. Unfortunately, enthusiasm over these feats has since been muted by ongoing scandals involving performance-enhancing drugs, which call into question the validity of the exploits of Bonds, McGwire, Sosa, and others who just a few years earlier had been credited with reviving public interest in the sport.

The Labor History of MLB: Players versus Owners

MLB's first major strike took place in 1981, as owners sought to blunt the impact of free agency. Team owners wanted to receive compensation when one of their players was signed by another team. The players went on strike in protest, and more than seven hundred games were canceled before the two sides agreed on a limited form of compensation for free-agent signings.

In 1990 owners proposed a sort of salary cap and the elimination of the arbitration system in place for resolving salary disputes. A thirty-two-day lockout ensued, resulting in the cancellation of spring training that year. The owners finally dropped their demands, and the full regular season took place, though its start was postponed by one week.

In "The Baseball Strike of 1994–95" (*Monthly Labor Review*, March 1997), Paul D. Staudohar reports that in June 1994 the owners proposed a salary cap that would have limited the players to 50% of total industry revenues. This represented a pay cut of about 15% for the players; not surprisingly, they declined the offer and went on strike in August. This strike resulted in the cancellation of the 1994 postseason, including the World Series. A ruling by the federal judge Sonia Sotomayor (1954–) ended the strike in March 1995. The 1995 and 1996 seasons were played under the terms of the expired contract.

In 2002 MLB appeared to be on the brink of another strike, the causes of which were mainly rooted in imbalances between teams in large and small markets that resulted in some financial disparities. The team owners lobbied for salary caps, but the players were understandably opposed to this. Instead, the owners came up with the idea of a luxury tax, which would be imposed on any team that spent more than a predetermined amount on player salaries. A strike was thus averted. The impact of the luxury tax, however, has been questionable. The New York Yankees, for example, have continued to spend vast sums to lure top players; in 2005 the Yankees became the first team in the history of sports to spend more than $200 million on salaries in a season. According to Barry M. Bloom, in "Yanks, Red Sox Hit with Luxury Tax Bills" (December 21, 2005, http://mlb.mlb.com/content/printer_friendly/mlb/y2005/m12/d21/c1286225.jsp), this was about $80 million over the luxury tax threshold, triggering a $34 million tax bill for team owner George Steinbrenner. The article "Yankees Hit with $26 Million Luxury Tax" (December 22, 2006, http://www.sportingnews.com/yourturn/viewtopic.php?p=1477875) indicates that the Yankees were billed another $26 million in December 2006. By contrast, only one other team, the Boston Red Sox, had to pay the luxury tax in 2006, so the tax is generally believed to work as a deterrent to reckless spending for most teams. However, the fines do not seem to have deterred big spending on the part of the

Yankees organization. Among the highest paid MLB players in 2007, only three were paid more than $20 million per year, and all three—Jason Giambi (1971–), Alex Rodriguez (1975–), and Derek Jeter (1974–)—played for the Yankees (*USA Today Salaries Databases*, 2007, http://asp.usatoday.com/sports/baseball/salaries/top25.aspx ?year=2007).

The other part of the 2002 deal was increased revenue sharing, meaning a greater share of each team's revenue was put into a pot to be divided among the entire major leagues. The biggest difference between baseball's revenue sharing system and football's is that baseball teams earn significant revenue from local television broadcasts, whereas almost all football coverage is national. MLB's 2002 contract brought a sharp increase in the amount of local revenue that teams must share. The 2002 collective bargaining agreement ran through the 2006 season; a new agreement, signed in the fall of 2006 and running through the 2011 season, preserved the luxury tax and revenue sharing systems with only minor alterations.

Current Issues in Baseball

One of the most critical issues facing baseball is how to respond to recent revelations of the rampant use of performance-enhancing drugs among top players (see Chapter 9 for more detailed information). As news has come to light about the use of steroids and other substances by some of the players credited with reviving the sport during the 1990s, professional baseball's credibility has come under fire. Important questions inevitably arise, such as how to account for records broken by players who were probably using banned substances. Bonds's eclipse in 2007 of one of the sport's most venerable records has brought this question to the fore. The ability of the league to handle such questions in a way that satisfies disgruntled fans will have a huge impact on the future of professional baseball in the United States.

NATIONAL FOOTBALL LEAGUE

The National Football League (NFL) is the premier U.S. professional football league. The United States is the only place where the term *football* refers to the game played by NFL teams; in most other parts of the world, this term refers to soccer. In "Sports Industry Overview," Plunkett Research estimates that the NFL's total league-wide revenue was $5.9 billion in 2006, and the average player earned a salary of $1.4 million. According to *SportsBusiness Journal*, sales of merchandise licensed by the NFL or its teams total $2.5 billion per year, the highest among the major sports. Table 4.3 shows current team values and revenue.

Figure 4.1 shows the gradual growth between 1998 and 2005 in the percentage of Americans who identify themselves as fans of professional football. The NFL's

TABLE 4.3

Football team values and revenue, 2005

Rank	Team	Current value ($mil)	Revenue ($mil)	Operating income ($mil)
1	Washington Redskins	1,423	303	108.4
2	New England Patriots	1,176	250	43.6
3	Dallas Cowboys	1,173	235	37.1
4	Houston Texans	1,043	222	57.6
5	Philadelphia Eagles	1,024	218	54.2
6	Denver Broncos	975	207	26.9
7	Cleveland Browns	970	206	47.1
8	Tampa Bay Buccaneers	955	203	56.9
9	Baltimore Ravens	946	201	27.8
10	Chicago Bears	945	201	51.5
11	Carolina Panthers	936	199	20.7
12	Miami Dolphins	912	194	33.4
13	Green Bay Packers	911	194	22.3
14	Kansas City Chiefs	894	186	28.2
15	New York Giants	890	182	26.9
16	Seattle Seahawks	888	189	5
17	Tennessee Titans	886	189	48.3
18	Pittsburgh Steelers	880	187	25.5
19	New York Jets	876	179	33.1
20	St Louis Rams	841	179	33.2
21	Detroit Lions	839	178	16.1
22	Indianapolis Colts	837	167	25
23	Cincinnati Bengals	825	175	20.9
24	Arizona Cardinals	789	158	16.6
25	Buffalo Bills	756	176	31.2
26	Jacksonville Jaguars	744	173	22.5
27	New Orleans Saints	738	160	−4.1
28	Oakland Raiders	736	171	9.1
29	San Francisco 49ers	734	171	11.8
30	San Diego Chargers	731	170	24.8
31	Atlanta Falcons	730	170	6.6
32	Minnesota Vikings	720	167	16.3

SOURCE: Adapted from Kurt Badenhausen, Michael K. Ozanian, and Maya Roney, "NFL Team Valuations," in "Special Report: The Business of Football," *Forbes*, August 31, 2006, http://www.forbes.com/lists/2006/30/06nfl_NFL-Team-Valuations_Rank.html (accessed July 25, 2007). Reprinted by permission of Forbes Magazine © 2007 Forbes LLC.

success can be credited in part to breakthroughs in the 1960s and 1970s in packaging the sport for television. No other sport has managed to capture the kind of spectacle that NFL broadcasts generate. The league has also benefited from labor relations that have been relatively stable, compared to those of the other major sports (a state some commentators attribute to the fact that the NFL Players Association is weak and ineffectual when compared to the unions in other sports). The NFL's revenue-sharing system is also generally considered the best among the major sports in terms of keeping small-market teams competitive.

NFL Structure and Administration

As of 2007 there were thirty-two teams in the NFL, sixteen each in the National and American Football Conferences. (See Table 4.4.) Each conference is divided into four divisions: East, North, South, and West, and each division has four teams. NFL teams play a sixteen-game regular season, which begins the weekend of Labor Day. Each team also has a bye weekend (no games are played)

FIGURE 4.1

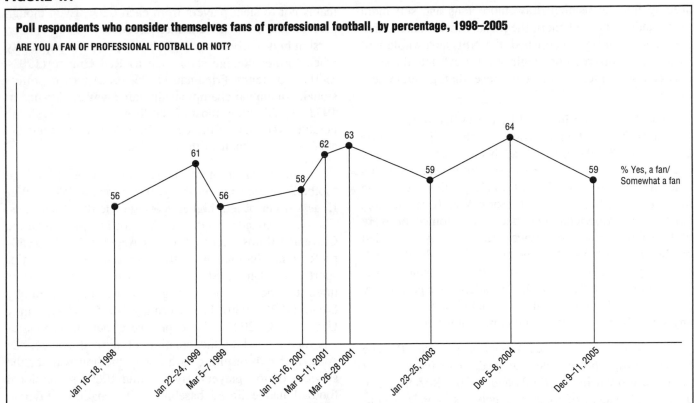

Poll respondents who consider themselves fans of professional football, by percentage, 1998–2005

ARE YOU A FAN OF PROFESSIONAL FOOTBALL OR NOT?

% Yes, a fan/
Somewhat a fan

Jan 16–18, 1998	Jan 22–24, 1999	Mar 5–7 1999	Jan 15–16, 2001	Mar 9–11, 2001	Mar 26–28 2001	Jan 23–25, 2003	Dec 5–8, 2004	Dec 9–11, 2005
56	61	56	58	62	63	59	64	59

SOURCE: "Are You a Fan of Professional Football or Not?" in *Football*, The Gallup Organization, July 2, 2007, http://www.galluppoll.com/content/?ci= 1705&pg=1 (accessed July 25, 2007). Copyright © 2007 by The Gallup Organization. Reproduced by permission of The Gallup Organization.

TABLE 4.4

National Football League teams and divisions

American Football Conference (AFC)	National Football Conference (NFC)
East Division	**East Division**
Buffalo Bills	Dallas Cowboys
Miami Dolphins	New York Giants
New England Patriots	Philadelphia Eagles
New York Jets	Washington Redskins
North Division	**North Division**
Baltimore Ravens	Chicago Bears
Cincinnati Bengals	Detroit Lions
Cleveland Browns	Green Bay Packers
Pittsburgh Steelers	Minnesota Vikings
South Division	**South Division**
Houston Texans	Atlanta Falcons
Indianapolis Colts	Carolina Panthers
Jacksonville Jaguars	New Orleans Saints
Tennessee Titans	Tampa Bay Buccaneers
West Division	**West Division**
Denver Broncos	Arizona Cardinals
Kansas City Chiefs	St. Louis Rams
Oakland Raiders	San Francisco 49ers
San Diego Chargers	Seattle Seahawks

SOURCE: Created by Robert Jacobson for The Gale Group, 2007. Data from the National Football League, http://www.nfl.com.

during the season; therefore, the full regular season lasts seventeen weeks. Sunday afternoons have long been the traditional time for professional football games. The exceptions have been one game per week on Sunday night and one on Monday night, although in recent years the league has begun scheduling occasional games on Thursday nights as well.

At the end of the regular season, six teams from each conference qualify for the playoffs: the four division champions and two wild-card teams (those with the best record that did not win their division). The champions of the two conferences square off in the Super Bowl. For much of its history, the Super Bowl has taken place in January; however, since 2002 it has been played in early February.

In the NFL revenue from television contracts and product licensing is shared equally among the teams. The idea behind this approach is to create parity, in contrast to MLB, where teams located in larger markets generally have a lot more money to spend than their rivals in smaller markets. Football teams also split money from ticket sales. Generally, the home team gets 60% of the money from the gate and the visiting team gets 40%. The exception is luxury boxes; the home team gets to keep all the money from selling its luxury box seating to corporations and other wealthy customers. This is one of the main reasons so many teams have been campaigning for new stadiums containing fewer regular seats and more premium boxes. Owners of teams that generate more money find the NFL's revenue-sharing system unfair, arguing that teams that draw more fans and sell more merchandise should benefit the most. Others contend that if revenue sharing is abolished, the NFL as a whole will suffer as team records begin to reflect the disparity between wealthier teams and those that generate less money.

The NFL is administered by the Office of the Commissioner. The first commissioner of the NFL was Elmer Layden (1903–1973), who had been a star player and later a coach at the University of Notre Dame. Layden held the post from 1941 until 1946, guiding the league through the difficult years of World War II, when most able-bodied American men had either joined or were drafted into the armed services. Layden was succeeded by Bert Bell (1895–1959), the cofounder of the Philadelphia Eagles. Under Bell, whose term as commissioner lasted until his death in 1959, NFL attendance grew every year. Bell is famous for his oft-quoted statement, "On any given Sunday, any team can beat any other team."

However, it was Bell's successor, Pete Rozelle (1926–1996), who led the league through its period of dramatic growth in the 1960s and 1970s. Rozelle introduced the concept of long-term network broadcast contracts and applied sophisticated marketing techniques to sell the NFL brand to the American public. Rozelle oversaw the merger between the American Football League (AFL) and the NFL and guided the league to what is generally considered a victory over the players' union during the 1987 labor strike. Rozelle retired in 1989 and was replaced by Paul Tagliabue (1940–). Under Tagliabue the NFL was marked by a great deal of team movement between cities, as owners sought to maximize the revenue they could generate from the sale of stadium naming rights and luxury skybox seating. Under Tagliabue the NFL largely avoided the labor disputes that have plagued the other major sports. Tagliabue retired after the 2005 season and was replaced by Roger Goodell (1959–). One of the key issues the commissioner must deal with before 2010 is the future of the NFL's revenue-sharing system, a debate that may pit owners of big-market teams against owners of teams who play in less populous cities.

NFL History

The NFL came to life in 1920 as the American Professional Football Association (APFA). The league adopted its current name two years later, but professional football actually dates back to 1892, when a Pittsburgh club paid Pudge Heffelfinger (1867–1954) $500 to play in a game.

The APFA—which was based in a Canton, Ohio, automobile dealership—consisted of eleven teams, all but one of them located in the Midwest. In its original form, the APFA was not really a league in the modern sense; it was essentially an agreement among member teams not to steal players from each other. Even though professional football remained secondary to the college version in its early years, it gradually gained in popularity when former college stars such as Red Grange (1903–1991) and Benny Friedman (1906–1982) turned professional. An annual championship game was established in 1933. By this time, most of the league's teams, with the notable exception of the Green Bay Packers, had left the small towns of their birth for bigger cities.

Professional football began to challenge college football's dominance in the years following World War II, as a faster-paced, higher-scoring style drew new fans. The NFL expanded to the West Coast in 1945, when the Cleveland Rams relocated to Los Angeles. By the 1950s professional football was firmly entrenched as a major sport in the United States, as television effectively captured the heroics of such glamorous stars as Bobby Layne (1926–1986), Paul Hornung (1935–), and Johnny Unitas (1933–2002). The explosive growth of professional football led to the creation of a rival league, the AFL, in 1960, resulting in a costly bidding war for the services of top players. By the mid-1960s professional football had eclipsed baseball as the nation's favorite sport. In 1970 the two football leagues merged. The AFL's ten teams plus three NFL teams became the American Football Conference; the remaining thirteen NFL teams became the National Football Conference. The champions of the two conferences would meet in the newly created Super Bowl to determine the world champion of professional football.

The NFL was the biggest spectator sport in the United States during the 1970s and 1980s. In most years the Super Bowl was the most watched television show of any kind, and *Monday Night Football* set a new standard for sports broadcasting with its innovative mixture of sports and entertainment. Since the 1990s the popularity of football has spread internationally. In 1993 the NFL launched the World League of American Football, whose name was changed to NFL Europe in 1997. NFL Europe, with teams in Germany and the Netherlands, served as a sort of development league in which a player's skills can be honed to reach NFL standards. In June 2007 the NFL abruptly announced that it was shutting down NFL Europe, but interest in the sport continues to grow in Europe.

Labor Disputes in the NFL

The NFL Players Union was formed in 1956, when players on the Green Bay Packers and Cleveland Browns utilized a collective approach to demand minimum salaries, team-paid uniforms and equipment, and other benefits from owners. The owners refused to respond to any of these demands. The union threatened to sue, a threat strengthened by *Radovich v. National Football League* (352 U.S. 445, 1957), in which the Supreme Court ruled that the NFL did not enjoy the same special status as MLB did with regard to antitrust laws. The owners eventually gave in to most of the players' demands but did not formally recognize the union for collective bargaining purposes. The NFL Players Association (NFLPA), as it was by then named, did not become the official bargaining agent for players until 1968, following a brief lockout and strike.

After the merger of the NFL and AFL, the NFLPA focused on antitrust litigation that challenged the so-called Rozelle Rule, which required a team signing a free agent to compensate the team losing the player, thereby severely limiting players' ability to benefit from free agency. The union succeeded in getting the Rozelle Rule eliminated in 1977.

When the NFLPA went on strike for a month in 1987, the owners responded by carrying on with the schedule using replacement players and a handful of veterans who chose to cross the picket line. With support weakening, the union ended its strike in October 1987. Free agency finally came to the NFL in 1992, and this was balanced by the introduction of salary caps during the mid-1990s. The NFL has experienced relatively smooth labor relations since then. The current collective bargaining agreement, which was renewed in March 2006, is active through the 2011 season.

Unlike MLB and the National Basketball Association (NBA), the NFL has a hard salary cap, meaning teams cannot spend more than a specified amount on salaries under any circumstances. For players and their union, free agency is considered an acceptable trade-off for the introduction of salary caps. With each new contract, the size of the salary cap is a subject of intense negotiation, but to date there have not been any work stoppages over it. Salary caps are considered an important way to ensure competition across the league: they stop the large-market teams from buying their way to the Super Bowl, and they give smaller-market teams such as Kansas City, Cincinnati, and Green Bay the ability to afford high-performing players.

Studies in sports economics show a strong correlation between total team salary and winning percentage. In "Buying Success: Relationships between Team Performance and Wage Bills in the U.S. and European Sports Leagues" (Rodney Fort and John Fizel, eds., *International Sports Economics Comparisons*, 2004), Robert Simmons and David Forrest analyze salary and percentages of wins of seven professional sports leagues in the 1980s and 1990s—three European soccer leagues, MLB, the National Hockey League (NHL), NBA, and the NFL. The results showed that, in general, a higher overall team salary was associated with a greater likelihood of higher point scoring (in the European leagues) and of entering playoffs (in the North American leagues). Salary caps were invented precisely to mitigate this effect, and by and large they have been effective at balancing the wealth within leagues. The NFL's cap is the "hardest" (it has the fewest loopholes), and as such has had the biggest balancing effect. Of course, wealth parity does not always translate into winning percentage parity, because there are so many other variables involved, such as whether management makes good decisions about how to distribute its limited payroll.

In recent years greater attention has been on the well-being of former players suffering from physical problems resulting from the pounding their bodies took during their active playing careers. Many players with disabilities severe enough to prevent them from working have faced financial hardships besides physical pain. One story that received a great deal of media attention is the case of Mike Webster (1952–2002), a Hall of Fame–caliber player for the Pittsburgh Steelers. Webster died homeless and destitute at the age of fifty after years of drug addiction and dementia that he believed was caused by the many concussions he suffered during his seventeen-year career. The NFL denied that Webster's injuries were football-related and withheld assistance. A court later ordered the league to pay Webster's estate more than $1 million.

In June 2007 congressional hearings revealed an NFL disability compensation system that had performed poorly, providing assistance to a shockingly low number of former players who had suffered debilitating injuries, ranging from multiple concussions to severe arthritis necessitating joint replacement. In 2007, in response to this problem, a number of former players—led by Jerry Kramer (1936–) and Mike Ditka (1939–)—formed the Gridiron Greats Assistance Fund (http://gridirongreats .org/), a nonprofit foundation that provides financial assistance to indigent former players who need help with medical or domestic issues.

NATIONAL BASKETBALL ASSOCIATION

Professional basketball has changed drastically since its early days; in fact, its evolution has perhaps been more pronounced than that of any other major sport—in dress, style of play, and, most noticeably, the racial composition of teams. Once a sport that featured white men in close-fitting uniforms hoisting up set shots from chest level, by the late twentieth century basketball was largely an African-American phenomenon, featuring loose-fitting fashions, a hip-hop sensibility, and an emphasis on the shortest-range shot of all: the slam dunk. Even though a sport such as hockey, for example, has always been dominated by white fans and players, basketball's racial shift has

TABLE 4.5

TABLE 4.6

National Basketball Association teams and divisions

Eastern Conference	Western Conference
Atlantic Division	**Southwest Division**
Boston Celtics	Dallas Mavericks
New Jersey Nets	Houston Rockets
New York Knicks	Memphis Grizzlies
Philadelphia 76ers	New Orleans Hornets
Toronto Raptors	San Antonio Spurs
Central Division	**Northwest Division**
Chicago Bulls	Denver Nuggets
Cleveland Cavaliers	Minnesota Timberwolves
Detroit Pistons	Portland Trail Blazers
Indiana Pacers	Seattle SuperSonics
Milwaukee Bucks	Utah Jazz
Southeast Division	**Pacific Division**
Atlanta Hawks	Golden State Warriors
Charlotte Bobcats	Los Angeles Clippers
Miami Heat	Los Angeles Lakers
Orlando Magic	Phoenix Suns
Washington Wizards	Sacramento Kings

SOURCE: Created by Robert Jacobson for The Gale Group, 2007. Data from the National Basketball Association, http://www.nba.com.

Basketball team values and revenue, 2005–06 season

[In million dollars]

Rank	Team	Current value[a]	Revenue[b]	Operating income[c]
1	New York Knicks	592	185	−39
2	Los Angeles Lakers	568	167	33.3
3	Dallas Mavericks	463	140	−24.4
4	Chicago Bulls	461	149	48.5
5	Houston Rockets	439	142	21.4
6	Detroit Pistons	429	138	21.8
7	Phoenix Suns	410	132	34.5
8	Miami Heat	409	132	20.5
9	San Antonio Spurs	390	122	11.7
10	Cleveland Cavaliers	380	115	23.9
11	Sacramento Kings	379	126	16.4
12	Philadelphia 76ers	375	110	−6.2
13	Boston Celtics	367	111	15.7
14	Indiana Pacers	340	110	−12.5
15	Washington Wizards	334	108	14.8
16	New Jersey Nets	325	93	−8
17	Toronto Raptors	315	105	8.4
18	Memphis Grizzlies	313	101	−18.5
19	Denver Nuggets	309	100	9.4
20	Minnesota Timberwolves	308	103	4.6
21	Utah Jazz	297	96	1.4
22	Los Angeles Clippers	285	95	15.7
23	Orlando Magic	283	89	−20.4
24	Charlotte Bobcats	277	89	11.9
25	Atlanta Hawks	275	92	12.9
26	Seattle SuperSonics	268	81	3.6
27	Golden State Warriors	267	89	6.3
28	Milwaukee Bucks	260	87	1.5
29	New Orleans Hornets	248	83	12.9
30	Portland Trail Blazers	230	77	−15.2

Note: Revenues and operating income are for 05–06 season and are net of revenue sharing.
[a]Value of team based on current arena deal (unless new arena is pending) without deduction for debt (other than arena debt).
[b]Net of arena revenues used for debt payments.
[c]Earnings before interest, taxes, depreciation and amortization.
NA: Not applicable.

SOURCE: Adapted from Kurt Badenhausen, Michael K. Ozanian, and Christina Settimi, "NBA Team Valuations," in "Special Report: The Business of Basketball," *Forbes*, January 25, 2007, http://www.forbes.com/lists/2006/32/biz_06nba_NBA-Team-Valuations_Rank.html (accessed July 25, 2007). Reprinted by permission of Forbes Magazine © 2007 Forbes LLC.

led to an identity crisis of sorts, with the issue of race becoming a major feature of discussion about the game.

NBA Structure and Administration

The thirty-team NBA is divided into two conferences: the Eastern Conference, which consists of the Atlantic, Central, and Southeast Divisions; and the Western Conference, which consists of the Northwest, Pacific, and Southwest Divisions. (See Table 4.5.) Each division contains five teams.

The NBA regular season begins in early November. A season consists of eighty-two games for each team, divided evenly between home and away games. Teams play each of the other teams in their own division four times per season; they play teams in the other divisions of their own conference three or four times, and they play teams in the other conference twice each. The NBA is currently the only one of the major sports leagues in which all teams play each other over the course of the regular season.

The NBA Playoffs begin in late April. Eight teams from each conference qualify: the winners of each of the three divisions plus the five teams with the next best records. Each round of the playoffs is a best-of-seven series. The third round of the playoffs is for the Conference Championship, and the winners of these two series compete against each other in the NBA Finals, the winner receiving the Larry O'Brien Trophy.

Plunkett Research reports in "Sports Industry Overview" that the NBA generated a total of $3.1 billion in revenue during the 2006–07 season. *SportsBusiness Journal* estimates that sales of NBA-licensed merchandise brings in approximately $1 billion per year. With such revenue teams can afford to pay high salaries. The average player salary was $5.2 million during the 2006–07 season, the highest among the major sports in the United States. In addition, as of 2006, twenty-one NBA players, the most in any professional sport, earned salaries greater than $15 million per year, according to the *USA Today Salaries Databases* (http://asp.usatoday.com/sports/football/nfl/salaries/top25.aspx?year=2006). Table 4.6 shows the current values of NBA teams and their most recent revenue figures.

NBA History

Basketball was invented in 1891 by James Naismith (1861–1939), a Canadian physical education instructor and physician. Working at a Young Men's Christian

Association (YMCA) in Springfield, Massachusetts, Naismith was directed by the head of the physical education department to create an indoor athletic game that would keep a class of young men occupied during the winter months. In two weeks Naismith had developed the game, including the original thirteen rules of basketball. Among them: "A player cannot run with the ball" and "The referee shall be judge of the ball and shall decide when the ball is in play, in bounds, to which side it belongs, and shall keep the time." Even though he never sought recognition for his invention, Naismith was present at the 1936 Olympic Games in Berlin, Germany, basketball's first appearance as an Olympic event.

Basketball was first played professionally in 1896, when members of a YMCA team in Trenton, New Jersey, left to form a squad that would play for money. Two years later a group of New Jersey sports journalists founded the National Basketball League (NBL), which consisted of six teams based in Pennsylvania and New Jersey. The NBL petered out after several years, but in the mid-1930s a new league with the same name was founded. A second professional league, the Basketball Association of America (BAA), was formed by a group of New York entrepreneurs. The BAA, which was in direct competition against the NBL, had teams in New York, Boston, Philadelphia, Chicago, and Detroit. Right before the start of the 1948–49 season, four NBL teams—Minneapolis, Rochester, Fort Wayne, and Indianapolis—joined the BAA, and the following year the NBL's six surviving teams followed suit. The BAA was then divided into three divisions and renamed the National Basketball Association. One division was eliminated the following year, leaving the two that became the forerunners of the modern Eastern and Western Conferences of the NBA.

The NBA had no competition for the next two decades. That changed in 1967 with the formation of the American Basketball Association (ABA). The ABA lured fans, and quite a few players, away from the NBA with a flashier style of play that featured a red, white, and blue ball. The ABA disbanded in 1976, and several of its teams became part of the NBA. However, by the late 1970s professional basketball's popularity was sagging. Revenue and television ratings were down, and the game had become dull. The league received a huge boost with the emergence of two new stars: Magic Johnson (1959–) of the Los Angeles Lakers and Larry Bird (1956–) of the Boston Celtics, who together are credited with ushering in a new era of popularity and prosperity to the NBA. Behind Johnson and Bird, the Lakers and Celtics completely dominated the NBA through the 1980s. During the 1990s the game was dominated by Michael Jordan (1963–) and the Chicago Bulls. With the charismatic Jordan leading the way, the NBA continued to thrive through most of the decade.

After the 1997–98 season, tensions between players and owners began to heighten, as the salary cap and other issues came to a head. The owners instituted a player lockout, and the two sides did not reach an agreement until January 1999, by which time more than a third of the regular season had been canceled.

At the turn of the twenty-first century there was a dramatic increase in the number of foreign-born players in the NBA. The U.S. Olympic basketball team's mediocre performance in 2004 demonstrated that the rest of the world was starting to catch up with the United States in terms of basketball talent. Players from Europe appeared to have a better grounding in basketball fundamentals such as passing and long-range shooting. In "Solving USA Basketball's Long List of Problems" (September 6, 2002, http://espn.go.com/nba/columns/aldridge_david/1427992.html), David Aldridge notes that the top NBA coaches George Karl (1951–) and Larry Brown (1940–) (who coached the U.S. team to a bronze medal in the 2002 World Championships) have complained for years that there is less emphasis on skill development and fundamentals on U.S. teams than on teams in other countries. Bringing foreign-born players into the NBA is believed to be one possible solution to the problem. Tim Receveur notes in "Foreign Players Help San Antonio Win Basketball Championship" (June 19, 2007, http://usinfo.state.gov/xarchives/display.html?p=washfile-english&y=2007&m=June&x=20070619155528btrueveceR0.3644831&t=livefeeds/wf-latest.html) that in 2007 NBA rosters included eighty-five foreign-born players (about 20% of all league players) from thirty-seven different countries and territories. Some of them, including German-born Dirk Nowitzki (1978–) of the Dallas Mavericks, French-born Tony Parker (1982–) of the San Antonio Spurs, and Chinese-born Yao Ming (1980–) of the Houston Rockets, are among the best players in the league. In fact, the league's Most Valuable Player award was won by an individual born outside the United States for three straight years from 2005 to 2007—one by Nowitzki and two by the Canadian Steve Nash (1974–) of the Phoenix Suns.

Current Issues in the NBA

SALARY CAPS. Basketball has a soft salary cap, meaning the amount a team can spend on salaries is limited, but there are loopholes and complications. As a result, there are still great disparities in how much the teams spend. For example, the article "NBA Salary Report" (*Sports Illustrated*, December 14, 2006) reports that the New York Knicks started the 2006–07 season with a payroll totaling $117 million, whereas the Charlotte Bobcats paid their players a total of $38 million. Table 4.7 shows the history of the NBA salary cap since 1984.

TABLE 4.7

NBA salary cap history, 1984–2008

NBA season	NBA salary cap
1984–85	$3.6 million
1985–86	$4.233 million
1986–87	$4.945 million
1987–88	$6.164 million
1988–89	$7.232 million
1989–90	$9.802 million
1990–91	$11.871 million
1991–92	$12.5 million
1992–93	$14.0 million
1993–94	$15.175 million
1994–95	$15.964 million
1995–96	$23.0 million
1996–97	$24.363 million
1997–98	$26.9 million
1998–99	$30.0 million
1999–2000	$34.0 million
2000–01	$35.5 million
2001–02	$42.5 million
2002–03	$40.271 million
2003–04	$43.84 million
2004–05	$43.87 million
2005–06	$49.5 million
2006–07	$53.135 million
2007–08	$55.630 million

SOURCE: "NBA Salary Caps History," in *NBA Salary Cap*, InsideHoops.com, July 10, 2007, http://www.insidehoops.com/nba-salary-cap.shtml (accessed July 25, 2007)

Beginning in the late 1980s it became increasingly common for top college players to leave school before graduating and enter the NBA draft. By the mid-1990s the best high school players were foregoing college altogether and moving straight into the professional ranks. The NBA has long sought to discourage players from making the jump from high school to the pros. Toward that end, in 1995 the league enacted a salary limit for rookies, in the hopes of making the move less enticing.

In June 2005, as another labor dispute seemed possible, the league and the players union reached a new collective bargaining agreement. In "The NBA's New Labor Deal: What It Means, Who It Impacts" (*Sports-Business Journal*, June 27, 2005), Liz Mullen and John Lombardo explain that the agreement's key provisions included a new rule preventing players from entering the NBA straight out of high school, increased drug testing, a 3% increase in the salary cap, and a reduction in the maximum length of free-agent contracts from seven to six years. This agreement remains in effect through the 2010–11 season.

MINIMUM AGE. Among the issues addressed in the NBA's contract, the minimum age requirement generated the most public attention. This provision requires that a player be at least nineteen years old and be out of high school for at least one year. Proponents of age restrictions argue that allowing teens in the NBA does them a disservice and that they are much better off playing college basketball—even if it is just for a year—or playing in the

NBA Developmental League than they are sitting on the end of an NBA team's bench rarely seeing significant playing time. They also say the NBA's skill level can become diluted with players who have not yet mastered the fundamentals of the game. According to the article "David Stern Media Conference" (April 12, 2004, http://www.insidehoops.com/stern-interview-041104.shtml), the NBA commissioner David Stern (1942–) has been the most vocal advocate of age limits, arguing that the presence of NBA recruiters in high school gyms has an overall negative influence on young players, that teens lack the maturity to handle the rigors of NBA life without getting into trouble, and that too many young urban Americans are unrealistically looking to basketball as a pathway out of poverty.

Opponents of the minimum age requirement point out that practicing every day against the best players in the world is not such a bad way to learn the game and wonder what young men can gain from waiting just one extra year before entering the professional league. In "Hunter Still Opposed to Raising NBA Age Limit" (*USA Today*, May 12, 2005), Chris Sheridan notes that Billy Hunter (1943–), the director of the NBA players' union, also questions the possible racial motivations behind the move toward age limits: "I'm still strongly philosophically opposed to it, and I can't understand why people think one is needed except for the fact that the NBA is viewed as a predominantly black sport. You don't see that outcry in other sports, and the arguments that have been in support of an age limit have been defeated."

RACE AND THE NBA. The debate over teens in the NBA and its possible relation to race is related to the broader issue of public image. Because it is dominated by young African-American males, the NBA struggles with the image the league projects to a predominantly white American public. Some basketball executives, particularly Stern, express concern about the message sent by the appearance and behavior of certain players. The arrests of high-profile players on sexual assault, drugs, and weapons charges have not helped matters. According to Jeff Benedict, in *Out of Bounds: Inside the NBA's Culture of Rape, Violence, and Crime* (2004), a startling 40% of NBA players have police records, although, not surprisingly, the NBA disputes this claim. Interestingly, it is not the younger players who are getting in trouble the most. In "Illegal Defense: The Irrational Economics of Banning High School Players from the NBA Draft" (*Virginia Sports and Entertainment Law Journal*, vol. 3, 2004), Michael A. McCann of the Mississippi College School of Law analyzes arrests of NBA players from 1995 to 2004 and finds that 57.1% of the NBA players arrested actually went to college for four years. Another 17.9% of the arrested players went to college for three years. Only 4.8% of those arrested did not go to college at all.

Nonetheless, the question of public image persists. As one way of addressing the image problem, Stern announced in October 2005 a new dress code that would apply to all players when they are participating in NBA-related activities, including arriving at and leaving games, participating in interviews, and making promotional appearances. The new rules banned sleeveless shirts, shorts, T-shirts, chains or medallions worn over the clothes, sunglasses while indoors, and headphones (except on a team bus or plane or in the locker room). The code also required players to wear a sport coat when on the bench but not in uniform. Reactions to the code among players were at best mixed. Some players applauded the league's effort to clean up the game's image. Others were outraged. According to the article "Spurs Superstar Tim Duncan Is Known to Be Understated and Shy, But Not about the NBA's New Dress Code" (FoxSports.com, October 20, 2005), Tim Duncan (1976–) of the San Antonio Spurs, a player often touted by the league as a model citizen, described the dress code as "basically retarded." The article "Pacers' Jackson: Dress Code Is 'Racist': Forward Wears Jewelry to Protest Rules, Which He Says Attacks Culture" (October 20, 2005, http://www.msnbc.msn.com/id/9730334/) reports that Stephen Jackson (1978–) of the Indiana Pacers openly accused the league of targeting black players. Jackson was particularly critical of the ban on wearing chains, noting that chains are associated with hip-hop culture and are a common fashion choice among young black men.

A new image problem for the NBA emerged in July 2007, when it was revealed that the veteran referee Tim Donaghy (1967–) was under investigation for allegedly betting on the outcome of NBA games, including games in which he had officiated. The following month he pleaded guilty to two felony charges, admitting that he personally bet on NBA games and that he provided inside information to associates about likely game outcomes.

WOMEN'S NATIONAL BASKETBALL ASSOCIATION

The Women's National Basketball Association (WNBA) started play in June 1997 following the celebrated gold medal run of the U.S. women's basketball team in the 1996 Olympics. There had been other professional women's basketball leagues before, but the WNBA was launched with the full support of the NBA, making it much more viable than other upstart leagues. At its inception, the WNBA already had television deals in place with the National Broadcasting Corporation, the Entertainment and Sports Programming Network (ESPN), and Lifetime network.

TABLE 4.8

WNBA teams and divisions

Eastern conference

Chicago Sky
Connecticut Sun
Detroit Shock
Indiana Fever
New York Liberty
Washington Mystics

Western conference

Houston Comets
Los Angeles Sparks
Minnesota Lynx
Phoenix Mercury
Sacramento Monarchs
San Antonio Silver Stars
Seattle Storm

SOURCE: Created by Robert Jacobson for The Gale Group, 2007

In its first season, the WNBA had eight teams. By 1999 four more teams had joined the league. That year, players and the league signed the first collective bargaining agreement in the history of women's professional sports. Four more teams were added in 2000. Following the 2002 season, the league's ownership structure was changed. Before that, the NBA owned all the teams in the WNBA. In 2002, however, the NBA sold the women's teams either to their NBA counterparts in the same city or to outside parties. As a result of this restructuring, two teams moved to other cities and two teams folded. Another team dropped out after the 2003 season.

As of 2007, there were thirteen teams in the WNBA: six in the Eastern Conference and seven in the Western Conference. (See Table 4.8.) Each team plays a thirty-four-game regular-season schedule, with the top four teams in each conference competing in the playoffs. The first and second rounds of the playoffs are best-of-three series. The WNBA Finals are best of five. The WNBA season starts in the summer, when the NBA season ends.

Even though the WNBA has gained in popularity, it has not been a big financial success. Through 2006, the league had not yet turned a profit in any year, although league officials expressed optimism that 2007 would be the season in which the league finished in the black. Average attendance at WNBA games is only about half that of NBA games. Player salaries are much lower as well. In "Free Agency 101" (September 27, 2007, http://www.wnba.com/shock/news/freeagency101.html), the WNBA indicates that the maximum salary for a WNBA player was $93,000 in 2007; this figure was less than one-fourth the minimum salary for an NBA rookie.

NATIONAL HOCKEY LEAGUE

Even though professional hockey has a long and storied history in the United States, it is currently at a

TABLE 4.9

Hockey team values and revenue, 2005–06 season

[In million dollars]

Rank	Team	Current value[a]	Revenue[b]	Operating income[c]
1	Toronto Maple Leafs	332	119	41.5
2	New York Rangers	306	109	17.7
3	Detroit Red Wings	258	89	5.8
4	Dallas Stars	248	89	10
5	Philadelphia Flyers	246	88	0.9
6	Boston Bruins	235	86	4.8
7	Montreal Canadiens	230	90	17.5
8	Colorado Avalanche	219	81	5.9
9	Los Angeles Kings	205	82	7.1
10	Vancouver Canucks	192	80	1.1
11	Tampa Bay Lightning	172	82	5
12	Chicago Blackhawks	168	67	3.1
13	Minnesota Wild	163	71	4.7
14	Ottawa Senators	159	76	4.2
15	Anaheim Ducks	157	75	−0.2
16	St Louis Blues	150	66	1
17	Buffalo Sabres	149	70	4.6
18	New Jersey Devils	148	62	−6.7
19	Edmonton Oilers	146	75	10.7
20	San Jose Sharks	145	69	1.8
21	Carolina Hurricanes	144	72	0.5
22	Phoenix Coyotes	143	63	−6
23	Florida Panthers	142	65	−1.9
24	New York Islanders	140	56	−9.2
25	Columbus Blue Jackets	139	66	−4
26	Calgary Flames	135	68	2.3
27	Nashville Predators	134	61	−1.1
28	Pittsburgh Penguins	133	63	4.8
29	Atlanta Thrashers	128	64	−5.4
30	Washington Capitals	127	63	4.6

Note: Revenues and operating income are for 2005–06 season and are net of revenue sharing.
[a]Value of team based on current arena deal (unless new arena is pending) without deduction for debt (other than arena debt).
[b]Net of stadium revenues used for debt payments.
[c]Earnings before interest, taxes, depreciation and amortization.
NA: Not applicable.

SOURCE: Adapted from Michael K. Ozanian and Kurt Badenhausen, eds., "NHL Team Valuations," in "Special Report: The Business of Hockey," *Forbes*, November 9, 2006, http://www.forbes.com/lists/2006/31/biz_06nhl _NHL-Team-Valuations_Rank.html (accessed July 25, 2007). Reprinted by permission of Forbes Magazine © 2007 Forbes LLC.

crossroads. Its popularity in the United States is declining, whereas other sports such as soccer and auto racing are eagerly courting disenchanted hockey fans. The cancellation of the 2004–05 NHL season because of a bitter labor dispute certainly did not help matters. Regardless, hockey is still big business. Plunkett Research notes in "Sports Industry Overview" that league-wide revenue in the NHL was about $2.2 billion during the 2006–07 season, less than half that of the NFL or MLB, and nearly a billion dollars less than the NBA, which has the same number of teams and games in a season. NHL players earn an average annual salary of $1.5 million. The *SportsBusiness Journal* estimates that sales of merchandise licensed by the NHL and member teams generate about $900 million annually, the lowest among the major sports. The values and recent revenue figures for NHL teams are shown in Table 4.9.

TABLE 4.10

National Hockey League teams and divisions

Eastern Conference	Western Conference
Atlantic Division	**Central Division**
New Jersey Devils	Chicago Blackhawks
New York Islanders	Columbus Blue Jackets
New York Rangers	Detroit Red Wings
Philadelphia Flyers	Nashville Predators
Pittsburgh Penguins	St. Louis Blues
Northeast Division	**Northwest Division**
Boston Bruins	Calgary Flames
Buffalo Sabres	Colorado Avalanche
Montreal Canadiens	Edmonton Oilers
Ottawa Senators	Minnesota Wild
Toronto Maple Leafs	Vancouver Canucks
Southeast Division	**Pacific Division**
Atlanta Thrashers	Anaheim Ducks
Carolina Hurricanes	Dallas Stars
Florida Panthers	Los Angeles Kings
Tampa Bay Lightning	Phoenix Coyotes
Washington Capitals	San Jose Sharks

SOURCE: Created by Robert Jacobson for The Gale Group, 2007. Data from the National Hockey League, http://www.nhl.com.

NHL Structure and Administration

The NHL is divided into the Eastern and Western Conferences. (See Table 4.10.) Each conference consists of three divisions, and each division has five teams. The Eastern Conference is split into the Northeast, Atlantic, and Southeast Divisions. The divisions that make up the Western Conference are the Northwest, Central, and Pacific. NHL teams play an eighty-two-game regular season, split evenly between home and away games. Before the 2004–05 lockout each team played all the others at least once during the season, but this is no longer the case. Teams now play ten games against opponents outside of their own conference, and forty games against teams in a different division within their own conference.

At the conclusion of the regular season, the champion of each division plus the five teams in each conference with the next best records compete in the Stanley Cup Playoffs. The structure is similar to that of the NBA: a single-elimination tournament consisting of four rounds of best-of-seven series, culminating in the Stanley Cup Finals, usually played in the late spring.

NHL History

Even though hockey in North America started in Canada, the first professional version of the game was launched in the United States. In 1904 the International Pro Hockey League was founded in the iron mining areas of Michigan's Upper Peninsula. That league lasted only a few years, but in 1910 a new league, the National Hockey Association (NHA), arose. The Pacific Coast League (PCL) was founded soon after the NHA. It was arranged that the champions of the two leagues would play a championship series, the winner gaining possession of the coveted Stanley Cup, a trophy named for Frederick A. Stanley (1841–1908), a former British governor-general of Canada.

World War I (1914–1918) put a temporary halt to the fledgling sport, but when the war ended professional hockey reorganized itself as the National Hockey League. At first the NHL was strictly a Canadian affair. The league initially consisted of five teams: Montreal Canadiens, Montreal Wanderers, Ottawa Senators, Quebec Bulldogs, and Toronto Arenas (later renamed the Maple Leafs). The first game took place in December 1917. The NHL expanded into the United States in the 1920s, adding the Boston Bruins in 1924; the New York Americans and Pittsburgh Pirates in 1925; and the New York Rangers, Chicago Blackhawks, and Detroit Cougars (which later became the Red Wings) in 1926. By the end of the 1930–31 season, there were ten teams in the NHL. The Depression and World War II took their toll on the league, however, and by its twenty-fifth birthday the NHL was reduced to six teams. Those six teams—the Canadiens, Maple Leafs, Red Wings, Bruins, Rangers, and Blackhawks—are commonly referred to, though not very accurately, as the "Original Six" of the NHL.

The NHL did not expand again until 1967, when six new teams were added, forming their own division. Two other franchises came on board three years later. In 1972 a new rival league, the World Hockey Association (WHA), was formed. In response, the NHL accelerated its own plans for expansion, adding four new teams over the next three years. This double-barreled expansion of professional hockey in North America diluted the pool of available players, however, and the quality of play suffered as a result. The WHA folded in 1979, and four of its teams joined the NHL. The league continued to expand over the next two decades, as league officials sought to follow demographic trends in the United States. The NHL reached its current total of thirty teams in 2000. Unfortunately, the league's southward and westward expansion has not been entirely successful, as interest is weak in warm-weather regions. Even though many Canadian towns have lost their teams to U.S. cities, and suffered economically as a result, a large percentage of Canadians remain diehard hockey fans. In "'Hockey Night' Features Flicks Instead of Sticks" (November 1, 2004, http://sports.espn.go.com/nhl/columns/story?id=1913770), Damien Cox notes that the television show *Hockey Night in Canada* is consistently the highest-rated Canadian-produced television program on Canadian television. In the United States, though, hockey is in danger of losing its major sport status.

Labor Issues in the NHL: A Season on Ice

In its long history the NHL has been interrupted only three times by labor strife. The first, a 1992 strike by the NHL Players Association (NHLPA), lasted only ten days, short enough for all missed games to be made up. A lockout at the start of the 1994–95 season was more disruptive. It lasted three months and resulted in the cancellation of thirty-six games, nearly half of the regular season.

With the 1995 deal moving toward its 2004 expiration date, negotiations between players and owners turned bitter. Unlike the 1994 lockout, which came at a time when the NHL was enjoying strong fan support and rising popularity, interest in the league had been waning for several years by 2004. As in other major sports, one of the biggest points of contention was proposed limits on the amount teams could spend on player salaries. The league proposed what it called cost certainty, which the players' union argued was just a fancy term for a salary cap. The union rejected the idea and instead proposed a luxury tax. Not surprisingly, the owners were opposed. The two sides failed to reach an agreement, and the entire 2004–05 season, from preseason training through the Stanley Cup Finals, was canceled—the first time a major sport had lost a whole season to labor unrest.

In July 2005 the NHLPA and the league finally agreed to the terms of a new collective bargaining agreement, which was published as the *Collective Bargaining Agreement, 2005* (http://www.nhlpa.com/CBA/2005CBA.asp). The deal, which runs through the 2010–11 season, gives players 54% to 57% of league-wide revenues, depending on the total. The agreement includes a salary cap that tops out at about $39 million and enhances revenue sharing to help the smaller market teams remain competitive. It does not include a luxury tax.

Naturally, hockey fans across North America were greatly disappointed by the loss of an entire season. In response, the NHL took measures to try to lure fans—both those who had wandered away from the sport before the lockout and those who lost interest directly because of it—back. These measures included a handful of rule changes designed to speed up the pace of the game and increase scoring.

A bigger challenge to the NHL remains: making hockey popular in parts of the United States that do not have long-standing hockey traditions. The expansion that the league undertook in the last two decades of the twentieth century was focused primarily in the southern and southwestern regions of the United States, the very parts of the country experiencing rapid population growth. Even though this expansion strategy made sense at the time, to date it has not produced the expected new generation of hockey fans in these regions.

MAJOR LEAGUE SOCCER

Major League Soccer (MLS), the premier professional soccer league in the United States, was launched in

TABLE 4.11

Major League Soccer teams and divisions

- **Eastern conference**
  - Chicago Fire
  - Columbus Crew
  - D.C. United
  - Kansas City Wizards
  - New England Revolution
  - Red Bull New York
  - Toronto FC
- **Western conference**
  - Chivas USA
  - Colorado Rapids
  - FC Dallas
  - Houston Dynamo
  - Los Angeles Galaxy
  - Real Salt Lake
  - San Jose Earthquakes (beginning 2008)

SOURCE: Created by Robert Jacobson for The Gale Group, 2007. Data from Major League Soccer, http://www.mlsnet.com.

April 1996. MLS has a unique ownership and operating structure that is unlike those of other major U.S. sports leagues. Even though the other leagues are confederations of independent franchise owners, MLS has a single-entity structure, which allows investors to own a share of the league as well as individual teams.

As of the 2007 season, MLS consisted of thirteen teams that were divided into two conferences: Eastern and Western. (See Table 4.11.) Teams compete through a season that runs from April through the MLS Cup championship in November. Each team plays thirty regular-season games, four games against each opponent within their division, and two against nonconference opponents. With the addition of the San Jose Earthquake in 2008, this structure will likely be adjusted. The MLS Cup Playoffs begin in mid-October and culminate in the crowning of a new MLS Cup champion.

Plans to start up MLS were first announced in December 1993. Twenty-two cities submitted bids to secure teams, of which ten were selected. A player draft was conducted in February 1996. The league's first game took place a few months later. According to MLS (2007, http://ww2.mlsnet.com/about/), a full stadium of 31,683 spectators and a national ESPN viewing audience watched the San Jose Clash defeat the D.C. United.

Two additional teams were added in 1998. The following year the Columbus Crew built the first major league stadium ever constructed specifically for soccer in the United States. The Crew ended up leading the league in attendance for the year. In 2002 the league was forced to cut two teams for financial reasons, returning MLS to its original ten-team size. Two new teams were added in 2005, bringing the league to twelve teams once again. The addition of Toronto FC before the 2007 season made the league thirteen strong.

MLS is far more ethnically diverse than any of the traditional four major sports in the United States. MLS rosters during the 2006 season included ninety-two players born outside the United States, representing forty-four different countries. MLS has also played a huge role in preparing American players for greater impact on the international soccer scene.

Attempts to establish a women's professional soccer league in the United States have not met with great success. The Women's United Soccer Association, the first women's professional outdoor league to be sanctioned by U.S. Soccer, was launched in 2001. It featured stars from the popular 2000 U.S. Olympic team, including Mia Hamm (1972–), Brandi Chastain (1968–), and Julie Foudy (1971–). Faced with financial struggles, the association suspended operations in September 2003. In 2004 a new nonprofit organization, the Women's Soccer Initiative, was established with the goal of reviving women's professional soccer in the United States. In September 2007, with seven confirmed teams already in place, the Women's Soccer Initiative (http://wsii.typepad.com/) announced plans to relaunch a professional women's league in 2009.

DIVERSITY IN THE MAJOR SPORTS

Diversity has long been an issue in major league sports in the United States. MLB was all white until Jackie Robinson crossed the color line in 1947. Over the next few decades the number of prominent black ballplayers grew, and baseball took on the appearance of an inclusive sport (at least on the field; managerial jobs for African-Americans have always been scarce). However, the trend has reversed itself. Once again, MLB teams have few African-Americans on their rosters, although the number of Hispanic players has increased dramatically. Enrique Rojas reports in "Robinson Opened Door for Black Hispanics" (April 14, 2007, http://sports.espn.go.com/mlb/jackie/columns/story?id=2836488) that 210 players born in Latin American countries were on the 2007 opening-day rosters of MLB teams, more than a quarter of the league's total number of players. The percentage of foreign-born players was only 19% on opening day in 1997, according to the Associated Press, in "More Foreigners in Majors for Sixth Straight Year" (April 2, 2003, http://espn.go.com/mlb/news/2003/0402/1532956.html).

Concerns about diversity in professional sports extend beyond the playing field. Coaching and management opportunities have traditionally been limited for minorities, though this trend may be shifting. The University of Central Florida's Institute for Diversity and Ethics in Sport issues annual racial and gender report cards that examine the front office, support staff, playing, and coaching opportunities for women and minorities in football, basketball, baseball, and soccer at the professional and college levels. The most recent report, *The 2006–07 Season Racial and Gender Report Card: National Basketball Association* (May 9, 2007, http://www.bus.ucf .edu/sport/public/downloads/2006_NBA_RGRC_PR.pdf), by Richard Lapchick, gives top marks for racial diversity to the NBA, noting that during the 2006–07 season the league had twelve African-American head coaches, people of color in 15% of team vice president positions, and the only African-American team majority owner in professional sports (Robert Johnson [1946–], owner of the Charlotte Bobcats). For gender diversity, Richard Lapchick reports in *The 2006 Racial and Gender Report Card: Women's National Basketball Association* (July 31, 2007, http://www.bus.ucf.edu/sport/public/downloads/ 2006_Racial_Gender_Report_Card_WNBA.pdf) that the WNBA outperformed all other sports, which is not surprising because it was the only professional sport analyzed that has female players.

THE STADIUM SCRAMBLE

Since the early 1990s there has been an unprecedented boom in the construction of new stadiums for U.S. sports teams. The main reason is that team owners believe that they can make more money selling skyboxes to wealthy corporate customers than they can by selling cheaper seats to the masses, and many older stadiums lack luxury accommodations. A skybox can sell for upward of $200,000 a season. Table 4.12 shows the typical cost of a luxury skybox at venues that host each of the major sports. An additional incentive is that the revenue from sales of these luxury skyboxes is exempt from the revenue-sharing formulas of both MLB and the NFL, meaning that teams get to keep all the money generated by skybox sales.

Owners have been further encouraged by the success of their peers in obtaining public funding for the construction of their new stadiums. A number of team owners have succeeded in securing public dollars for their new stadiums by threatening to move to a different city if the taxpayers did not foot the bill. Owners usually argue that a new stadium will generate additional tax revenue, as fans flock to the new facility and, so they claim, spend vast sums of money at nearby businesses. In "Stadium Subsidies Scalp the Public" (*Boston Globe*, March 27, 2000), Ralph Nader (1934–), a consumer advocate and former presidential candidate, claims that the economic benefits of taxpayer-subsidized stadium construction are

TABLE 4.12

Average prices for luxury suites within major sports leagues, 2007

Sport/league	Averages		
	Quantity	Low	High
Major League Baseball	76	$99,203	$190,764
National Football League	143	$62,338	$195,933
National Basketball Association	88	$135,900	$246,236
National Hockey League	94	$118,451	$230,133

SOURCE: "Luxury Suites," in *Free Venue Information*, Revenues from Sports Venues, 2007, http://www.sportsvenues.com/info.htm#Suites (accessed July 25, 2007)

negligible, citing research that indicates no positive economic impact over the course of thirty years from twenty-seven out of thirty existing taxpayer-funded stadiums. Nevertheless, team owners have met with great success in selling their proposed public-financed stadium plans to lawmakers.

Another source of revenue from stadiums comes from the sale of naming rights. Where in the past most stadiums had straightforward names such as Tiger Stadium or the Houston Astrodome, in the twenty-first century an increasing number of facilities bear the name of a corporate sponsor that has paid millions of dollars for the privilege. The following are only three out of several examples that Revenues from Sports Venues cites in *Free Venue Information* (August 27, 2007, http://www.sports venues.com/pdf/names.pdf):

- Comerica Park in Detroit, home of MLB's Detroit Tigers ($66 million for thirty years)

- San Francisco's 3Com Park, where the San Francisco Giants play baseball ($4 million for five years)

- American Airlines Center in Dallas, home of both basketball's Mavericks and hockey's Stars ($195 million for thirty years)

Sometimes these deals backfire. Darren Rovell reports in "Astros Stuck with Enron Name—For Now" (January 25, 2002, http://espn.go.com/sportsbusiness/s/ 2002/0124/1316712.html) that in 1999 Enron, a U.S. energy company, signed a thirty-year, $100 million deal with the Houston Astros. In 2001 Enron filed for bankruptcy following an accounting scandal. The collapse of the company forced the Astros to buy their way out of the deal to get Enron's name off their stadium.

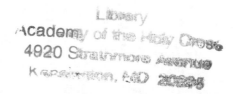

CHAPTER 5
OTHER PROFESSIONAL SPORTS

As important as professional team sports are in the United States, Americans' sports obsession extends well beyond them. Not every sports enthusiast is engrossed by the hoopla of *Monday Night Football* or the high-flying acrobatics of the National Basketball Association. Some fans prefer the quiet beauty of a perfect putt or the battle of wills that takes place across the Centre Court net at Wimbledon. Others are attracted to the blunt truth of boxing or the raw speed of the National Association for Stock Car Auto Racing (NASCAR). This chapter considers several sports that fall below the top tier of U.S. sports in terms of audience or revenue but are nevertheless important components of the nation's professional sports culture.

GOLF

Professional golf in the United States is coordinated by the Professional Golfers' Association (PGA) of America, a nonprofit organization that promotes the sport while enhancing golf's professional standards. The PGA of America (2007, http://www.pga.com/home/pgaofamerica/about-the-pga.cfm) states that in 2007 there were more than twenty-eight thousand PGA professionals in the United States, both men and women. However, most of these members were primarily golf instructors; only a small fraction compete in high-profile tournaments.

The PGA of America traces its roots to 1916, when a group of golf professionals and serious amateurs in the New York area got together at a luncheon sponsored by the department store magnate Rodman Wanamaker (1863–1928). The point of the meeting was to discuss forming a national organization to promote golf and elevate the occupation of golf professionals. The meeting led to the organization of the first PGA Championship tournament, which was played later that year. The PGA Championship has grown to become one of professional golf's four major championships, along with the British Open, the Masters, and the U.S. Open. Together, these four tournaments make up the unofficial Grand Slam of golf. (See Table 5.1.) Besides the PGA Championship, the PGA of America sponsors three other top golf events: the Senior PGA Championship; the Ryder Cup, which every two years pits a team of top American golfers against their European counterparts; and the PGA Grand Slam of Golf, an annual event in which the winners of the four major championships compete head to head. Besides these championships, the PGA of America also conducts about forty tournaments for PGA professionals.

However, while professional golfers in the United States are members of the PGA of America, most of the actual golf they play is under the auspices of other organizations. Worldwide, professional golf is organized into several regional tours, each of which usually holds a series of tournaments over the course of a season. There are approximately twenty of these tours around the world, each run by a national or regional PGA, or by an independent tour organization. Each tour has members who may compete in as many of its events as they want. Joining a tour usually requires that a golfer achieve some specified level of success, often by performing well in a qualifying tournament. A player can be a member of multiple tours.

The world's top tour by far, in terms of money and prestige, is the PGA Tour, which since 1968 has been a completely separate organizational entity from the PGA of America. In 2007 the PGA Tour (http://www.pgatour.com/r/schedule/) had forty-eight official events offering more than $280 million in total prize money. The PGA Tour organization also runs two other tours: the Champions Tour for golfers over age fifty; and the Nationwide Tour, a sort of minor league of professional golf.

The History of the PGA

According to the PGA Tour (2007, http://www.pgatour.com/company/pgatour_history.html), the first U.S.

TABLE 5.1

Golf Grand Slam events

Event	Location	Scheduled time
The Masters	Augusta, Georgia	April
U.S. Open	Location varies	June
British Open	Location varies	July
PGA Championship	Location varies	August

SOURCE: Created by Robert Jacobson for The Gale Group, 2007

Open took place in 1895 in Newport, Rhode Island. Ten professionals and one amateur competed in the event. The Western Open made its debut in Chicago, Illinois, four years later. Tournaments were initiated throughout the country at about this time, although there was no coordination or continuity among them. English players dominated the competition in U.S. tournaments. As interest in golf continued to grow, American players improved. Enthusiasm for the sport began to increase after John McDermott (1891–1971) became the first U.S.-born player to win the U.S. Open in 1911. By the 1920s professional golf had spread to the West Coast and southward to Florida, and the prize money was becoming substantial.

The PGA Tour was formally launched in late 1968, when the Tournament Players Division of the PGA broke away from the parent organization. The tour grew during the 1970s and 1980s, with its total annual revenue increasing from $3.9 million in 1974 to $229 million in 1993.

The Champions Tour

The Champions Tour, which is run by the PGA Tour organization, hosts thirty events each year in the United States and Canada for golfers at least fifty years old. The tour grew out of a highly successful 1978 event called the Legends of Golf, which featured two-member teams composed of some of the game's best-known former champions. Following on the success of the Legends event, the Senior PGA Tour was established in 1980, with two tournaments and $250,000 in prize money. The Senior Tour proved remarkably popular, as fans flocked to golf courses and tuned in on television to see legendary competitors such as Arnold Palmer (1929–) and Sam Snead (1912–2002) in action. Even though their playing skills may have diminished somewhat from the level of their prime playing years, the former champions proved popular with golf lovers across the country. At the start of the 2003 season the Senior Tour changed its name to the Champions Tour. The 2008 Champions Tour (2007, http://www.pgatour.com/2007/s/06/28/2008_schedule/index.html) offered total prize money of nearly $58 million over twenty-nine tournaments.

Most tournaments on the Champions Tour are played over three rounds (fifty-four holes) rather than the cus-

tomary four rounds (seventy-two holes) typical of PGA tournaments. The five majors of the senior circuit are exceptions, because they are played over four rounds. The major tournaments of the Champions Tour are the Senior PGA Championship, the Senior Players Championship, the Senior British Open, the U.S. Senior Open, and The Tradition.

The Nationwide Tour

The Nationwide Tour is the developmental tour for the PGA Tour. Its players are professionals who have missed the criteria to get into the main tour by failing to score well enough in the PGA Tour's qualifying tournament, known as Qualifying School, or who have made it into the main tour but failed to win enough money to stay there. The Nationwide Tour gets its name from the company that bought the naming rights in 2003, the Nationwide Mutual Insurance Company of Columbus, Ohio. It was called the Nike Tour and the Buy.com Tour before that. When the tour was first launched in its original form in 1990, it was known as the Ben Hogan Tour.

In 2007 the Nationwide Tour (http://www.pgatour.com/h/schedule/) consisted of thirty-two events. Three of them were in Australia, New Zealand, and Panama, and the rest were in the United Sates. The prize money for Nationwide Tour events is typically about one-tenth that of a PGA Tour tournament, ranging from about $450,000 to $750,000.

The Nationwide Tour has proven to be an excellent feeder system for the PGA Tour. The PGA Tour reports in "Wilson Gets Nationwide Tour's 200th PGA Tour Win" (March 5, 2007, http://www.pgatour.com/2007/h/03/04/200_tour/index.html?eref=sitesearch) that Nationwide Tour alumni have won two hundred PGA Tour titles, including eleven major championships, as of 2007. A number of top players, including Ernie Els (1969–), David Duval (1971–), Jim Furyk (1970–), David Toms (1967–), and Stuart Appleby (1971–), played the Nationwide circuit before achieving success on the PGA Tour.

Other Men's Tours

As noted earlier, the PGA Tour is merely the biggest and richest of the world's many professional golf tours. There are many others around the world, some of which—such as the Nationwide Tour—prepare players for entry into the PGA Tour. In 1996 the International Federation of PGA Tours was formed by golf's five chief governing bodies around the world. As of 2007 the International Federation (http://www.worldgolfchampionships.com/wgcinfo/international/index.html) had six members: the PGA Tour (United States), the Asian Tour (Singapore), the Japan Golf Tour, the PGA European Tour, the PGA Tour of Australasia, and the Sunshine Tour (South

Africa). Together, these tours sanction the Official World Golf Rankings.

The PGA European Tour, headquartered in England, is the premier professional golf tour in Europe and is second only to the PGA Tour in money and international prestige. The European tour was established by the British PGA, but in 1984 it became a separate entity, just as the PGA Tour became independent from the PGA of America in 1968. In 2006 the European Tour (2007, http://www.europeantour.com/) consisted of forty-nine tournaments in twenty-six countries, offering prize money totaling about $168 million (based on August 2007 exchange rates). Most of the top players on the European Tour, including Els, Retief Goosen (1969–), Sergio Garcia (1980–), and Padraig Harrington (1971–), are also members of the PGA Tour. Like the PGA Tour, the European Tour has a developmental tour, called the Challenge Tour, and a senior tour, called the European Seniors Tour.

The Japan Golf Tour is the third biggest professional men's tour (not counting senior tours) in terms of prize money available. However, prize money in the Japanese Tour has not kept pace with the growth of money in the PGA and European tours in recent years.

Performance in all the previously mentioned tours—the six International Federation members, plus the Nationwide and Challenge Tours—earns Official World Golf Ranking points. Other regional tours worth noting are the Tour de las Americas, which is seeking to be included in World Ranking calculations; the Indian Golf Tour; and the Hooters NGA Tour, which is the third-tier U.S.-based professional tour, below the Nationwide Tour in money and prestige.

Women's Tours

Women's professional golf, like men's golf, is organized into several regional tours. The top tour for female professional golfers is the Ladies Professional Golf Association (LPGA), which operates the LPGA Tour. Unlike the PGA Tour, the LPGA Tour and the LPGA are not distinct organizations. Both of these terms generally refer to the LPGA that is based in the United States. Internationally, there are other regional LPGAs and tours, including the LPGA of Japan, the LPGA of Korea, the Australian Ladies Professional Golf tour, and the Ladies European Tour.

Founded in 1950 by a group of thirteen golfers, the LPGA is the oldest continuing women's professional sports organization in the United States. It features the best female golfers from all over the world. The 2007 LPGA Tour (http://www.lpga.com/content_1.aspx?mid=0&pid=52) consisted of thirty-five events offering total prize money of over $54 million. Most LPGA Tour events take place in the United States. In 2007 there were also two events in Mexico and one each in Canada, Sweden, Japan, and Australia. Four LPGA tournaments are considered the tour's majors: the Kraft Nabisco Championship, McDonald's U.S. LPGA Championship Presented by Coca-Cola, the U.S. Women's Open, and the Ricoh Women's British Open (held jointly with the Ladies European Tour).

Besides the main tour, the LPGA also coordinates a developmental tour called the Duramed Futures Tour. The Futures Tour began in Florida in 1981 as the Tampa Bay Mini Tour but is now a national tour that functions as a feeder system for the LPGA, filling the same role as the Nationwide Tour does for the men. In 2007 the Duramed Futures Tour (http://www.duramedfuturestour .com/AboutUs.asp) featured a nineteen-tournament national schedule and a total purse of about $1.6 million.

In 2001 the LPGA created the Women's Senior Golf Tour for players over age forty-five. Its name was changed to the Legends Tour before the 2006 season. As of 2007 the Legends Tour had only six events.

TENNIS

The modern sport of tennis developed out of various games that involved hitting a ball with a racket or the hand dating back to ancient times. Lawn tennis was developed in 1873 in Wales by Walter C. Wingfield (1833–1912). It is based on the older sport of Real tennis (French for Royal tennis), which was itself based on earlier forms of racket sports. Tennis gained popularity across Great Britain, and the first world tennis championship was held just four years later at the All England Croquet Club at Wimbledon. This tournament evolved into the famous Wimbledon Championships, which remain the most prestigious tennis titles to this day. A women's championship was added at Wimbledon in 1884. Over the next several years, tennis spread across many parts of the British Empire, becoming especially popular in Australia.

Tennis arrived in the United States early on in this process. A tennis court was set up in Staten Island, New York, in about 1874. The first National Championship in the United States—for men only—was held in 1881 in Newport, Rhode Island. A women's championship was added six years later. The National Championship moved to Forest Hills, New York, in 1915, where it remained under various names for more than sixty years. Now known as the U.S. Open, the event has been held at the National Tennis Center in Flushing, New York, since 1978.

The Development of Professional Tennis

As tennis spread around the British empire early in the twentieth century, national federations were formed in countries where the sport caught on. These federations eventually joined forces to form the International Tennis

Federation (ITF), which was the worldwide sanctioning authority for tennis. International competitions between national teams soon arose, the most important being the Davis Cup tournament, founded in 1900, and the Wightman Cup, an annual competition between women's teams from England and the United States, founded in 1923.

Most sports turned professional during the first half of the twentieth century, but tennis remained primarily an amateur endeavor, largely a pastime for wealthy country club members. By the late 1920s it became economically feasible for a top player to make a decent living on the professional tour, but it meant giving up the sport's most prestigious, amateur-only events, such as those at Wimbledon and Forest Hills. The move toward professionalism accelerated after Will T. Tilden II (1893–1953), the best player of his time and a winner of seven U.S. singles championships and three Wimbledon titles as an amateur, turned professional in 1931. Over the next few decades more and more top players trickled into the professional ranks, but the professional tour was not glamorous and the money was mediocre. The ITF fought hard against the professionalization of tennis. In 1968 the All England Lawn Tennis and Croquet Club decided to open Wimbledon to professional players, thus ushering in the "open era" of tennis in which professional players are allowed to compete in the sport's biggest tournaments.

About this time women players became frustrated at the gender disparity in tennis prize money. Women winning a tournament often received a mere fraction of what the men's champion in the same tournament took home. In 1971 a women-only professional tour was formed to address these inequities. This new Virginia Slims Tour was an instant hit. It made Billie Jean King (1943–) the first woman athlete in any sport to earn more than $100,000 in a single year.

Men's Professional Tennis

Men's professional tennis is coordinated by the Association of Tennis Professionals (ATP), which organizes the ATP Tour (the principal worldwide tennis tour), and the ITF, which coordinates international play including the Davis Cup and the Grand Slam tournaments. (See Table 5.2.) The ATP was originally formed in 1972 as a sort of trade union to protect the interests of male professional tennis players. The organization assumed its role as the chief coordinating body of the professional tour in 1990. The most important professional tennis tournaments are those that comprise tennis's Grand Slam: the Australian Open, the French Open, the U.S. Open, and Wimbledon. Only two men have ever won the Grand Slam of tennis: Don Budge (1915–2000) in 1938 and Rod Laver (1938–) in both 1962 and 1969. Total prize money for Wimbledon in 2007 was approximately $23 million, with the men's and ladies' singles champions each receiving a prize of $1.4

TABLE 5.2

Tennis Grand Slam events

Event	Location	Scheduled time
Australian Open	Melbourne	Last fortnight of January
French Open	Paris	May/June
Wimbledon	Wimbledon, England	June/July
U.S. Open	Flushing Meadows, Queens, New York	August/September

SOURCE: Created by Robert Jacobson for The Gale Group, 2007

million (based on 2007 exchange rates; http://www.wimbledon.org/en_GB/about/guide/prizemoney.html). According to the U.S. Open (2007, http://www.usopen.org/en_US/about/history/prizemoney.html), the tournament offered a payout of $19.6 million, with possible bonuses bringing the total to about $22 million. The ATP also operates the Challenger Series, a second-tier professional circuit in which many top players have started their professional careers.

Women's Professional Tennis

Women's professional tennis is coordinated by the Women's Tennis Association (WTA, which is to the women's game what the ATP is to the men's game). The WTA runs the premier professional women's tour, which in 2005 became known as the Sony Ericsson WTA Tour. In 2007 the Sony Ericsson Tour (http://www.sonyericssonwtatour.com/3/thewtatour/) involved more than fourteen hundred players representing seventy-five nations and competing for $62 million in prize money at sixty-two events in thirty-five countries. Women also compete in the same four Grand Slam events, governed by the ITF, as do the men.

The WTA was born in 1973, initially, like the ATP, as a professional organization to protect the interests of the players. The tour itself, which started out as the Virginia Slims Tour, was originally formed out of protest at the disparity between the prize money for men and women. At the dawn of the open era (1968), when professionals were first allowed to compete in Grand Slam tournaments, the male singles winner sometimes received as much as ten times what the female champion was paid. By 1980 more than 250 women were playing professionally all over the world in a tour consisting of forty-seven global events, offering a total $7.2 million in prize money. The tour remained under the governance of the Women's Tennis Council, an umbrella agency run by representatives from the ITF, the tournament promoters, and the players, into the 1990s. The WTA Tour in its current form was created in 1995 through the merger of the WTA Players Association and the Women's Tennis Council. Several sponsors have funded the tour over the years, including Colgate, Avon, Toyota, Kraft General Foods, and Sony Ericsson.

AUTO RACING

There are several different top-level auto-racing circuits in the United States, in which different kinds of cars race. The two most popular types of racecars are stock cars and open-wheeled racers. From the outside, stock cars essentially look like the regular cars that populate U.S. highways, only covered with corporate logos. Stock car racing is dominated by the National Association for Stock Car Auto Racing (NASCAR). Open-wheel cars are single-seat vehicles with special aerodynamic features that allow them to travel at speeds well over two hundred miles per hour without flying off the track. Open-wheel racing is currently in a state of civil war between its two chief circuits, the Indy Racing League and the Champ Car Series. Another open-wheel circuit, Formula One Grand Prix, is dominant in Europe.

NASCAR

The largest sanctioning body of motor sports in the United States is NASCAR, which oversees a number of racing series, the largest among them being the NEXTEL Cup, the Busch Series, and the Craftsman Truck Series. In all, NASCAR (2007, http://www.nascar.com/races/cup/2007/data/schedule.html) sanctions more than fifteen races per year at more than one hundred different tracks in thirty-eight states, Mexico, and Canada. The article "NASCAR Evolution: Survival of the Fastest" (*Sports Illustrated*, February 19, 2007) notes that thirteen million NASCAR fans regularly fill twenty-two tracks in nineteen states and that licensed NASCAR products bring in $2.1 billion per year. Once merely a regional diversion in the South, NASCAR has exploded into a nationwide phenomenon, rivaling baseball for the number-two spot behind football for the hearts and viewing hours of American sports fans, though attendance and television viewership both slumped in 2006 after a decade of impressive growth.

Stock car racing evolved out of bootlegging in the rural South. Alcohol runners would modify their cars to make them faster and more maneuverable. It was natural for these drivers to start racing their souped-up autos against one another.

NASCAR was founded in 1948 by William France Sr. (1909–1992) and Ed Otto (1908–1986) as a way to organize, standardize, and promote racing of unmodified, or stock, cars for entertainment. The first NASCAR Strictly Stock race took place at North Carolina's Charlotte Speedway in June 1949. Over time, modifications were allowed into the sport, and by the mid-1960s only the bodies of the cars looked stock; the innards were specially built for speed.

NASCAR's rapid growth began in the 1970s, when R. J. Reynolds Tobacco Company began to sponsor racing as a way to promote its products after they had been banned from television advertising. The top series, formerly known as the Grand National Series, became the Winston Cup. At about this time, television networks began to occasionally cover stock car racing. Columbia Broadcasting System's broadcast of the 1979 Daytona 500 was the first time a stock car race had been aired nationwide from start to finish.

In 2004 Nextel assumed sponsorship of the series formerly known as the Winston Cup. The Nextel Cup remains the most prominent and lucrative NASCAR racing series. That year, NASCAR established a new ten-race playoff system called the Chase for the Cup, in which the top ten drivers (according to NASCAR's point system) after twenty-six races compete for the series championship. In 2008 the Nextel Cup becomes the Sprint Cup Series to reflect the merger of Nextel Communications with the phone company Sprint.

Open-Wheel Cars

The two major open-wheel series, the Indy Racing League (IRL) and the Champ Car Series, have been struggling since 2000, as millions of fans have flocked to stock car racing. The reasons for this are complex, but it is reasonable to attribute the situation in part to the acrimonious relationship between the IRL and the Champ Car. Neither has done well financially in recent years, although the success of the rookie Danica Patrick (1982–) breathed some life into IRL in 2005.

Indy Racing League

The IRL is the top circuit for single-seat, open-wheel racecars specially designed for high-speed racing on oval tracks. The IRL was formed in 1994 by a group of drivers breaking away from the Championship Auto Racing Teams (CART; now known as the Champ Car Series), which had coordinated Indy car racing since breaking away from the U.S. Auto Club (USAC) in 1979. The IRL consists of two series: the IndyCar Series, which is virtually synonymous with the IRL, and the Indy Pro Series, which functions as a developmental series for drivers aspiring to join the IndyCar circuit.

Before 1979 the term *IndyCar* was generically used to refer to cars racing in USAC events. By the 1980s IndyCar was a term commonly used to refer to CART, which by that time was the preeminent sanctioning body for open-wheel racing in the United States. The name "IndyCar" became the subject of fierce legal battles in the 1990s. The Indianapolis Motor Speedway, home of the Indianapolis 500, trademarked the name in 1992 and licensed it to CART, which in turn renamed its championship the IndyCar World Series. Two years later,

Tony George (1959–), the president of the speedway, started his own racing series called the Indy Racing League. In 1996 CART sued to protect its right to continue using the IndyCar name. The speedway countered with its own suit. The two groups eventually reached a settlement in which CART agreed to stop using the IndyCar name after the 1996 season, and the IRL could start using it after the 2002 season. The IRL's premier series has been called the IRL IndyCar Series since the beginning of the 2003 season. The 2007 IndyCar Series (http://www.indycar.com/schedule/) featured sixteen races from March to September.

Champ Car Series

The USAC was formed in 1956 to take over coordination of the national driving championship from the American Automobile Association, which had launched the championship in 1909. The USAC controlled the championship until 1979, when a group of car owners formed the Championship Auto Racing Teams that they hoped would give them power in negotiations with the USAC over media contracts, race purses, promotion, and other issues. The two entities immediately clashed, and CART soon separated from the USAC to establish its own racing series. Most of the top teams defected from the USAC, and CART quickly became the dominant open-wheel racing circuit. The USAC held its last National Championship in 1979, before reluctantly handing the reins over to CART.

The IRL's split from CART threw open-wheel racing into a tailspin from which it has not yet recovered entirely. The rivalry may have helped pave the way for NASCAR's rise, as both competing organizations struggle for control over the sport's available pot of money. In 2003 CART declared bankruptcy, and its assets were liquidated and put up for sale. A group of CART car owners bought the company and opened the 2004 season under the new name Champ Car Series. Since 2005 Champ Car ran both the Champ Car World Series and the Champ Car Atlantic Championship, which functions as a developmental circuit for drivers trying to get into Champ Car. The Champ Car series (2007, http://www.champcar worldseries.com/Event/EventSchedule.asp?Year=2007) included sixteen races in 2007, which took place between April and December.

BOXING

Boxing is unique among professional sports in that there is no nationwide commission that oversees it, no regular schedules, no seasons, and few universal rules. Every set of matches (called a card) is set up separately, usually by one of a handful of top-level boxing promoters. Each state has its own boxing commission with its own set of rules. Some state boxing commissions regulate the sport more rigorously than others, and the different governing organizations establish their own regulations. For example, variations exist regarding whether a boxer who has been knocked down can be "saved by the bell," whether a referee or a ringside physician has the authority to stop a match, and whether a match should automatically be stopped if a fighter is knocked down three times within one round.

Boxing matches in the United States consist of a maximum of twelve three-minute rounds with one minute of rest between rounds. Opponents in a fight must belong to the same weight class, with competitors being weighed before the fight to ensure that neither holds an unfair weight advantage. The three judges at ringside score the fight according to a ten-point must system; that is, each judge must award ten points to the winner of the round and fewer points to the loser of the round. Matches end in one of five ways:

- Knockout—one fighter is unable to return to his feet within ten seconds of a knockdown

- Technical knockout—a decision is made to stop the fight because one fighter is clearly losing

- Decision—the fight ends without a knockout or technical knockout and is won based on the scoring of the three judges at ringside

- Draw—the fight ends without a knockout or technical knockout, and the scorecards award each fighter the same number of points

- Disqualification—the fight is stopped because of a rule infraction on the part of one of the fighters

Unlike other professional sports, boxing does not use a playoff series or point system to name a champion. In fact, there is not necessarily even a consensus about who is the champion of any given weight class. Different champions are recognized by several competing boxing organizations. The most prominent boxing organizations are the World Boxing Association, the World Boxing Council, the World Boxing Organization, and the International Boxing Federation. A fighter may be recognized as champion in his weight class by more than one of these organizations at a time, or each may have a different champion at any given time. Some of the biggest boxing matches are unification bouts between champions recognized by two different sanctioning organizations, the winner walking away with both titles.

Because boxing competitions are often international in nature, it is difficult to gauge the size of the boxing industry in the United States. In "The Shame of Boxing" (*Nation*, November 12, 2001), Jack Newfield estimates professional boxing to be a $500-million-a-year business. Much of the money comes from cable television, where championship fights are usually broadcast on a pay-per-view basis.

Boxing has a long history of both glamour and corruption. It has inspired famous writers such as Norman Mailer (1923–2007), Albert Camus (1913–1960), Ernest Hemingway (1899–1961), and Joyce Carol Oates (1938–), and landmark films such as *The Champ* (1931), *Body and Soul* (1947), *On the Waterfront* (1954), *Requiem for a Heavyweight* (1962), *Raging Bull* (1980), *Million Dollar Baby* (2004), and the *Rocky* series (1976–2006). However, because the scoring system is complex and because the overall rankings often appear somewhat arbitrary, the sport has long been a tempting target for organized crime and others seeking illicit financial gain. Even in the twenty-first century bribery is thought to be rampant. Mysterious judging decisions and bizarre rankings are not at all rare. Boxing's reputation also suffers because of the sheer brutality of the sport. Fighters have sometimes died or suffered disabling brain trauma as a result of a particularly violent bout. Mike Tyson (1966–), a former heavyweight champ and convict, once bit off part of an opponent's ear in the ring. Newfield cites several cases of fixed fights, rigged rankings, cronyism, and instances of money being prioritized over safety.

World Boxing Association

The World Boxing Association (WBA; 2005, http://www.wbaonline.com/wba/History/wbahistory.asp) was the first sanctioning body of professional boxing. It was formed as the National Boxing Association (NBA) in 1921. The first NBA-sanctioned match was a heavyweight championship fight between Jack Dempsey (1895–1983) and Georges Carpentier (1894–1975). Brilliant and colorful champions such as Joe Louis (1914–1981) carried the WBA through the World War II (1939–1945) era. The dawn of television boosted the popularity of professional boxing in the 1950s. The sport's globalization during this period led the organization to change its name to the World Boxing Association in 1962.

World Boxing Council

The World Boxing Council (WBC; 2005, http://www.wbcboxing.com/WBCboxing/Portal/cfpages/contentmgr.cfm?docId=22&docTipo=1) was formed in 1963 by representatives of eleven countries (United States, Mexico, Venezuela, Panama, Peru, Brazil, Japan, Argentina, Spain, Great Britain, and the Philippines) and Puerto Rico. Its purpose, according to WBC founders, was to improve the standards of professional boxing, including the safety of fighters. Among the WBC's innovations was the 1983 shortening of world championship fights from fifteen to twelve rounds, a move that was eventually adopted by the other sanctioning organizations. In 2003 the WBC filed for bankruptcy in an attempt to avoid paying $30 million in damages from a lawsuit over questionable handling of title fight eligibility. The following year, the lawsuit was settled for a lesser amount, allowing the WBC to avoid having to disband and liquidate its assets.

International Boxing Federation

Herb Goldman, in "Boxing Bodies: A Brief Chronology and Rundown" (January 1998, http://www.ibroresearch.com/Boxing%20History/BOXING%20BODIES.htm), explains that the International Boxing Federation (IBF) was formed in 1983 by a group of WBA representatives upset with political machinations within that agency. Its creation was spearheaded by Robert W. Lee, the president of a smaller regional organization called the U.S. Boxing Association (USBA). The new group was originally called the IBF-USBA. In its first year of operation, the IBF remained fairly obscure. In 1984, however, the IBF decided to recognize as champions a number of high-profile fighters who were already established as other organizations' title holders, including Larry Holmes (1949–) and Marvin Hagler (1952–). When Holmes opted to relinquish his WBC title to accept the IBF's, it instantly gave the IBF the credibility it had previously lacked. The IBF's reputation took a major hit in 1999, when Lee was convicted on racketeering and other charges. It nevertheless remains one of professional boxing's major sanctioning bodies.

World Boxing Organization

The World Boxing Organization (WBO) was formed in 1988 by a group of Puerto Rican and Dominican businessmen disenchanted with what they perceived as illegitimate rules and rating systems within the WBA. The WBO's first championship fight was a junior welterweight championship match between Héctor Camacho (1962–) and Ray Mancini (1961–). The WBO achieved a level of legitimacy comparable to that of the WBA, the WBC, and the IBF, largely thanks to its recognition as champions of many of the sport's best-known competitors. The WBO has also tended at times to provide more opportunities for non-U.S.-based fighters than the other organizations. Even though the WBO was formed out of protest against allegedly corrupt practices, it has certainly exhibited its share of inexplicable decisions that raise questions about the organization's integrity. In "New WBO Division: Dead Weight" (February 20, 2001, http://espn.go.com/boxing/columns/graham/1097210.html), Tim Graham notes that a particularly embarrassing example took place in 2001, when the WBO twice moved Darrin Morris (1966–2000) up in its super-middleweight rankings, even though he had fought only once in the past three years, and, more important, was dead.

CHAPTER 6
COLLEGE AND HIGH SCHOOL SPORTS

College athletics function as a minor, or preparatory, league for some professional sports, particularly football and basketball, but there is nothing minor about Americans' passion for them or about the sums of money intercollegiate sports generate. Just as college sports serve as a feeder system for professional leagues, high schools fill the same role for colleges, and schools often compete for the services of elite teenage athletes. For the most part, high school and college athletes participate in sports for their own rewards. Most of them understand that the chances of striking it rich as a professional athlete are remote. For example, out of 156,096 boys who play on high school basketball teams during their senior year, only forty-four (0.03%) will become professional basketball players. (See Table 6.1.) Regardless, the money that flows through the sports industry—an industry of which intercollegiate sports are an integral part—is so abundant that its influence can be felt even in U.S. high schools.

COLLEGE SPORTS

In contrast to professional sports, where turning a profit is the motivating force behind most decisions, college sports must reconcile commercial interests, educational priorities, and a jumble of other influences ranging from alumni pride to institutional prestige. Even though it may make high-minded university officials uncomfortable to admit it, college sports have become big business in the United States.

The most important governing organization of college sports in the United States is the National Collegiate Athletic Association (NCAA), although there are other governing bodies as well.

National Collegiate Athletic Association

The NCAA is a voluntary association whose members comprised 1,282 institutions, conferences, organizations, and individuals in 2007; 1,027 of them were active member schools. (See Table 6.2.) The NCAA's main purpose, according to its constitution, is to "maintain intercollegiate athletics as an integral part of the educational program and the athlete as an integral part of the study body and, by so doing, retain a clear line of demarcation between intercollegiate athletics and professional sports." In other words, college sports are supposed to be strictly amateur and are supposed to fulfill an educational role.

Organizationally, the NCAA's structure consists of more than 125 committees, which, since a new governance structure was adopted in 1997, have enjoyed a fair amount of autonomy. Several of these committees are association-wide, including the Executive Committee and committees having to do with ethics, women's opportunities, and minority opportunities. The rest are specific to one of the NCAA's three divisions—Divisions I, II, and III—which classify the schools by the number of sports they sponsor and other factors. NCAA member schools and organizations vote on the rules they will have to follow. It is then up to the NCAA National Office staff of about three hundred to implement and enforce the rules and bylaws dictated by the members.

The NCAA's divisions are based on factors such as the number of sports sponsored, attendance at the school's sporting events, and financial support to athletes. Division I is further divided into Divisions I-A, I-AA, and I-AAA. Intercollegiate sports under the auspices of the NCAA are also divided into conferences, which function like the leagues and divisions in professional sports. The most prominent conferences, often referred to collectively as the Big Six, are shown in Table 6.3. The colleges in these conferences sponsor many sports, have big athletic budgets, and draw many fans. Table 6.4 shows that among both men and women, basketball is the sport sponsored by the greatest number of colleges and universities.

TABLE 6.1

Estimated probability of competing in athletics beyond high school

Student athletes	Men's basketball	Women's basketball	Football	Baseball	Men's ice hockey	Men's soccer
High school student athletes	546,335	452,929	1,071,775	470,671	36,263	358,935
High school senior student athletes	156,096	129,408	306,221	134,477	10,361	102,553
NCAA student athletes	16,571	15,096	61,252	28,767	3,973	19,793
NCAA freshman roster positions	4,735	4,313	17,501	8,219	1,135	5,655
NCAA senior student athletes	3,682	3,355	13,612	6,393	883	4,398
NCAA student athletes drafted	44	32	250	600	33	76
Percent high school to NCAA	3.00%	3.30%	5.70%	6.10%	11.00%	5.50%
Percent NCAA to professional	1.20%	1.00%	1.80%	9.40%	3.70%	1.70%
Percent high school to professional	0.03%	0.02%	0.08%	0.45%	0.32%	0.07%

Note: These percentages are based on estimated data and should be considered approximations of the actual percentages.

SOURCE: "Estimated Probability of Competing in Athletics Beyond the High School Interscholastic Level," National Collegiate Athletic Association, 2006, http://www.ncaa.org/research/prob_of_competing/ (accessed July 26, 2007)

TABLE 6.2

Composition of NCAA Membership

	Division I				Division II	Division III	Total
	I-FBS	I-FCS	I	Total			
Active	119	116	91	326	281	420	1,027
Provisional	0	0	1	1	15	21	37
Voting conference	11	10	10	31	22	43	96
Nonvoting conference	0	3	18	21	1	13	35
Corresponding							15
Affiliated							72
Total							**1,282**

Notes:
Prior to the 2006 season, the NCAA changed the nomenclature for its top two football divisions, though the labels I-A and I-AA are still used informally. FBS is Football Bowl Subdivision, formerly known as I-A. It includes teams in major divisions that compete for berths in bowl games. FBC, fomerly known as I-AA, is Football Championship Subdivision. Its national champion is determined through a playoff system.

Active member

An active member is a four-year college or university or a two-year upper-level collegiate institution accredited by the appropriate regional accrediting agency and duly elected to active membership under the provisions of the association bylaws. Active members have the right to compete in NCAA championships, to vote on legislation and other issues before the association, and to enjoy other privileges of membership designated in the constitution and bylaws of the association.

Provisional member

A provisional member is a four-year college or university or a two-year upper-level collegiate institution accredited by the appropriate regional accrediting agency and that has applied for active membership in the association. Provisional membership is a prerequisite for active membership in the association. The institution shall be elected to provisional membership under the bylaws of the association. Provisional members shall receive all publications and mailings received by active members in addition to other privileges designated in the constitution and bylaws of the association. Provisional membership is limited to a three-year period.

Member conference

A member conference is a group of colleges and/or universities that conducts competition among its members and determines a conference champion in one or more sports (in which the NCAA conducts championships or for which it is responsible for providing playing rules for intercollegiate competition), duly elected to conference membership under the provisions of the bylaws of the association. A member conference is entitled to all of the privileges of active members except the right to compete in NCAA championships. Only those conferences that meet specific criteria as competitive and legislative bodies and minimum standards related to size and division status are permitted to vote on legislation or other issues before the association.

Affiliated member

An affiliated member is a nonprofit group or association whose function and purpose are directly related to one or more sports in which the NCAA conducts championships, duly elected to affiliated membership under the provisions of the association bylaws. An affiliated member is entitled to be represented by one nonvoting delegate at any NCAA convention and enjoys other privileges as designated by the bylaws of the association.

Corresponding member

A corresponding member is an institution, a nonprofit organization or a conference that is not eligible for active, provisional, conference or affiliated membership and desires to receive membership publications and mailings. A corresponding member duly elected under the provision of the association bylaws receives all publications and mailings received by the general NCAA membership and is not otherwise entitled to any membership privileges.

SOURCE: "Composition," in *Composition & Sport Sponsorship of the NCAA*, NCAA, March 1, 2007, http://www1.ncaa.org/membership/membership_svcs/membership_breakdown.html (accessed July 31, 2007)

History of the NCAA

Up until the middle of the nineteenth century, there was no governing body that oversaw intercollegiate ath-letics. Typically, it was students rather than faculty or administrators who ran the programs. Even so, there was already a fair amount of commercialization and illicit

TABLE 6.3

NCAA "Big 6" conferences, 2007

Atlantic Coast conference (ACC)

Boston College
Clemson University
Duke University
Florida State University
George Tech
University of Maryland
University of Miami
University of North Carolina
North Carolina State University
University of Virginia
Virginia Tech
Wake Forest University

Big East conference

University of Cincinnati
University of Connecticut
DePaul University
Georgetown University
University of Louisville
Marquette University
University of Notre Dame
University of Pittsburgh
Providence College
Rutgers University
St. John's University
Seton Hall University
University of South Florida
Syracuse University
Villanova University
West Virginia University

Big Ten conference

University of Illinois
Indiana University
University of Iowa
University of Michigan
Michigan State University
University of Minnesota
Northwestern University
Ohio State University
Pennsylvania State University
Purdue University
University of Wisconsin

Big 12 conference

Baylor University
University of Colorado
Iowa State University
University of Kansas
Kansas State University
University of Missouri
University of Nebraska
University of Oklahoma
Oklahoma State University
University of Texas
Texas A&M University
Texas Tech

Pacific-10 conference (Pac-10)

University of Arizona
Arizona State University
University of California, Berkeley (Cal)
University of Oregon
Oregon State University
Stanford University
University of California, Los Angeles (UCLA)
University of Southern California
University of Washington
Washington State University

TABLE 6.3

NCAA "Big 6" conferences, 2007 [CONTINUED]

Southeastern conference (SEC)

University of Alabama
University of Arkansas
Auburn University
University of Florida
University of Georgia
University of Kentucky
Louisiana State University
University of Mississippi (Ole Miss)
Mississippi State University
University of South Carolina
University of Tennessee
Vanderbilt University

SOURCE: Created by Robert Jacobson for The Gale Group, 2007

suite of rooms in the dorm, free University Club meals, profits from the sale of programs, and a ten-day vacation to Cuba. However, what finally led administrators to the conclusion that formal oversight was necessary was the sheer brutality of college sports, particularly football. According to *The Business of Sports* (2004), edited by Scott R. Rosner and Kenneth L. Shropshire, there were at least eighteen deaths and more than one hundred major injuries in intercollegiate football in 1905 alone. In response to the growing violence of college football, President Theodore Roosevelt (1858–1919) convened a White House conference of representatives from Harvard, Princeton, and Yale universities to review the rules of the game. When the deaths and serious injuries continued, Henry M. Mac-Cracken (1840–1918), the chancellor of the University of the City of New York (now New York University), called for a national gathering of representatives from the major football schools. In early December 1905 representatives of thirteen schools, including West Point, Columbia, and the University of Kansas, met with MacCracken and formed a Rules Committee. This group held another meeting on December 28 that was attended by representatives of more than sixty college football programs, during which the Intercollegiate Athletic Association (IAA) was formed. The IAA was a national organization with sixty-two founding members, including schools in Minnesota, Nebraska, New Hampshire, New York, Ohio, Pennsylvania, and Texas. The IAA became the NCAA in 1910.

Initially, the NCAA did not really govern college sports. Its chief role was simply to make rules to keep the sports safe and fair. It also served as a forum for discussion of any other issues that happened to arise in the world of intercollegiate athletics, such as the formation of conferences and the transition of oversight responsibilities from students to faculty. In 1921 the NCAA organized its first national championship, the National Collegiate Track and Field Championships. More championships in other sports followed, as did an increasingly complex bureaucracy featuring additional rules committees.

professionalism in college sports. For example, James Hogan (1876–1910), the captain of the Yale football team in 1904, was compensated with, among other things, a

TABLE 6.4

NCAA sports sponsorship, by sport and division, 2007

	Men's				Women's				Mixed			
	I	II	III	Total	I	II	III	Total	I	II	III	Total
Baseball	284	246	367	897								
Basketball	326	293	403	1022	325	294	431	1050				
Bowling	1	1	1	3	28	17	6	51				
Cross country	297	246	358	901	322	275	378	975				
Fencing	20	3	12	35	26	4	14	44	1	0	0	1
Field hockey					78	26	155	259				
Football	234	157	234	625								
(I-FBS 118)												
(I-FCS 116)												
Golf	287	214	277	778	231	131	156	518				
Gymnastics	17	0	2	19	65	5	16	86				
Ice hockey	58	7	70	135	33	2	43	78				
Lacrosse	57	32	138	227	81	40	169	290				
Rifle	5	0	2	7	11	1	2	14	17	2	5	24
Rowing	30	4	30	64	86	15	43	144				
Skiing	13	8	17	38	14	9	19	42				
Soccer	196	174	393	763	301	227	415	943				
Softball					269	270	405	944				
Swimming	139	55	195	389	190	73	242	505				
Tennis	259	170	318	747	306	224	265	795				
Track, indoor	241	117	223	581	290	127	230	647				
Track, outdoor	262	164	254	680	302	173	259	734				
Volleyball	22	15	46	83	315	275	419	1009				
Water polo	21	5	15	41	31	10	20	61				
Wrestling	89	45	95	229								

Note: FBS = Football Bowl Subdivision; FCS = Football Championship Subdivision

SOURCE: "Sports Sponsorship," in *Composition & Sport Sponsorship of the NCAA*, National Collegiate Athletic Association, March 1, 2007, http://www1.ncaa.org/membership/membership_svcs/membership_breakdown.html#sponsorship (accessed July 26, 2007)

By the 1920s college athletics were firmly entrenched both as an integral part of college life and as a subject of intense public interest. Along with this interest came creeping commercialism. In 1929 the Carnegie Foundation for the Advancement of Education issued a major report on college sports, which stated that "a change of values is needed in a field that is sodden with the commercial and the material and the vested interests that these forces have created. Commercialism in college athletics must be diminished and college sport must rise to a point where it is esteemed primarily and sincerely for the opportunities it affords to mature youth."

In response to the Carnegie report, token attempts were made to reduce commercial influences on college sports, but the trend continued. A dramatic increase in access to higher education following World War II (1939–1945) further accelerated both interest in and commercialization of college athletics. A series of gambling scandals and questionable recruiting incidents finally moved the NCAA to act. In 1948 the NCAA adopted the Sanity Code, which established guidelines for recruiting and limited financial aid. In addition, the code set academic standards for players and defined the status of college athletes as amateurs—that is, those "to whom athletics is an avocation." The NCAA also created a Constitutional Compliance Committee to enforce the Sanity Code and investigate possible violations. The Sanity Code did not have much of an impact and was repealed in 1951. The Constitutional Compliance Committee was replaced by the Committee on Infractions, which was given broader authority to sanction institutions that broke the rules. The NCAA also hired its first full-time executive director, Walter Byers (1922–), that same year. A national headquarters was established in Kansas City, Missouri, the following year. The 1950s also brought the first lucrative television broadcast contracts, which provided the NCAA with the revenue it needed to become more active. Its capacity to enforce rules expanded throughout the 1950s and 1960s. Nevertheless, the influence of money on college sports continued to grow. In 1956 the NCAA moved to regulate athletic scholarships, but the eight schools of the Ivy League— Brown, Columbia, Cornell, Dartmouth, Harvard, Penn, Princeton, and Yale—refused to comply.

In 1973 the NCAA divided its membership into three divisions to group schools by their competitive firepower. Three years later, the NCAA acquired the authority to penalize colleges directly for violating rules, opening itself up to criticisms of unfair enforcement practices. In 1978, in response to the rapid growth in the number of football programs relative to other sports, Division I members voted to break the division solely for football purposes into two subdivisions, I-A and I-AA.

During the 1970s and 1980s major football colleges began to see that they could make more money from broadcast revenue by negotiating their own deals. A group of schools, led by the University of Georgia and Oklahoma University, began to challenge the NCAA's monopoly on negotiation of lucrative television contracts. In 1984 the U.S. Supreme Court ruled in *NCAA v. Board of Regents of the University of Oklahoma et al.* (468 U.S. 85) that the NCAA had violated antitrust laws. This ruling allowed colleges to start negotiating broadcast deals directly. Meanwhile, the relationship between sports and academics remained a matter of intense debate, as reports of student-athletes ignoring the first half of this role proliferated. In 1986 the NCAA implemented Proposition 48, later modified by Proposition 16 (1995), which set down minimum academic standards for athletes entering college. Among the requirements, student-athletes needed to maintain a 2.0 grade point average (GPA) in academic courses and have a Scholastic Assessment Test (SAT) score of 1010 or a combined American College Text (ACT) score of 86.

SCANDALS AND SANCTIONS IN NCAA SPORTS PROGRAMS. More than a century after Hogan's royal treatment at Yale, payments and other special perks for student-athletes remain prevalent in college sports, in spite of the NCAA's enforcement efforts. There have been several cases of institutions and their boosters making illicit payments to players. In the early 1980s Southern Methodist University (SMU) was a football powerhouse. Its ability to attract top football players was enhanced by a highly organized system of player payments in blatant violation of NCAA rules. According to Chris DuFresne, in "Life after Death" (*Newsday*, December 28, 2005), the payoff system, which had been in place for decades, began to unravel in November 1986, when SMU linebacker David Stanley admitted to reporters that he had accepted $25,000 from boosters. Within days another player, Albert Reese, told the *Dallas Morning News* that he had been living in a rent-free apartment provided by a booster. After an investigation that turned up widespread corruption and cover-ups that went as high as the Texas governor's office, the NCAA hit the university with what became known in college sports as the death penalty. The sanctions included cancellation of SMU's entire 1987 football season and restriction of the following season to eight games.

The NCAA has not wielded the death penalty again since then. Moreover, its threat has not halted these practices on the part of boosters elsewhere. A recent high-profile case involved the National Basketball Association star Chris Webber (1973–). On July 14, 2003, Webber pleaded guilty to criminal contempt related to charges that he had received tens of thousands of dollars from the booster Ed Martin while a member of the University of Michigan basketball team in 1994. Martin

pleaded guilty to money laundering in May 2002. Webber's sentence, a fine of $100,000, was announced in August 2005.

Special treatment of student-athletes does not always involve money. Sometimes it comes in the form of academic breaks. In 1998 Texas Tech was penalized by the NCAA for, among other things, allowing a star running back to play despite maintaining a 0.0 GPA. David Lagesse reports in "Troubleshooting" (*U.S. News & World Report*, March 18, 2002) that nine Texas Tech sports departments were sanctioned after the resulting investigation, and the football team's ban from postseason bowl games cost the school an estimated $1.7 million. In "Case Study: Minnesota's Basketball Cheating Scandal" (February 15, 2003, http://www.concernedjournalists.org/node/424), the Committee of Concerned Journalists reports that in 1999 a University of Minnesota employee told the *St. Paul Pioneer Press* that she had completed course work for at least twenty members of the school's basketball program. Four top sports officials at Minnesota lost their jobs in the resulting scandal.

One highly charged college sports scandal that developed in 2006 turned out to be manufactured. The Associated Press notes in "North Carolina State Bar Issue Formal Disbarment Order for Nifong" (July 12, 2007, http://sports.espn.go.com/ncaa/news/story?id=2933841) that in March 2006 a stripper accused three members of the Duke University men's lacrosse team of sexually assaulting her at a party. The three students were indicted, the remainder of the lacrosse team's 2006 season was canceled, and the team coach was forced to resign. However, all charges against the players were dropped in April 2007 after many inconsistencies in the alleged victim's story were revealed, and deoxyribonucleic acid (DNA) evidence came to light that did not support the allegations. It also became clear that the prosecutor in the case, Mike Nifong (1950–), had employed a number of illegal and unethical tactics in his handling of the case; he was disbarred in June 2007 for fraud, misrepresentation, and withholding exculpatory DNA evidence.

College Sports Participation

The *1981–82—2005–06 Sports Sponsorship and Participation Report* (May 2007, http://www.ncaa.org/library/research/participation_rates/1982-2006/1982_2006_participation_rates.pdf), by Nicole Bracken of the NCAA, contains detailed information on participation across the full range of college sports. As of 2005–06, there were 393,509 student-athletes participating in championship sports at NCAA schools. Even though women's teams outnumbered men's teams, there were more men— 57.2% of the total—than women actually playing on those teams. The average NCAA institution had about 375 student-athletes in 2005–06, 214 of them men and 161

TABLE 6.5

NCAA participation in women's sports, by division, 2005–06

	Division I			Division II			Division III			Overall		
	Teams	Athletes	Avg. Squad	Teams	Athletes	Avg. Squad	Teams	Athletes	Avg. Squad	Teams	Athletes	Avg. Squad
Championship Sports												
Basketball	325	4,867	15.0	286	4,040	14.1	428	6,189	14.5	1,039	15,096	14.5
Bowling	24	209	8.7	15	124	8.3	5	50	10.0	44	383	8.7
Cross Country	322	5,258	16.3	265	3,002	11.3	371	4,968	13.4	958	13,228	13.8
Fencing*	26	402	15.5	4	48	12.0	14	208	14.9	44	658	15.0
Field Hockey	77	1,693	22.0	27	604	22.4	154	3,171	20.6	258	5,468	21.2
Golf	231	2,020	8.7	130	936	7.2	143	1,025	7.2	504	3,981	7.9
Gymnastics	65	1,076	16.6	6	92	15.3	15	246	16.4	86	1,414	16.4
Ice Hockey	31	730	23.5	2	54	27.0	42	943	22.5	75	1,727	23.0
Lacrosse	80	2,079	26.0	38	806	21.2	153	3,114	20.4	271	5,999	22.1
Rifle*	27	167	6.2	3	15	5.0	7	35	5.0	37	217	5.9
Rowing	86	5,134	59.7	15	476	31.7	41	1,292	31.5	142	6,902	48.6
Skiing*	16	239	14.9	9	80	8.9	15	184	12.3	40	503	12.6
Soccer	301	7,630	25.3	220	5,025	22.8	409	9,054	22.1	930	21,709	23.3
Softball	267	5,082	19.0	266	4,763	17.9	399	6,764	17.0	932	16,609	17.8
Swimming/Diving	188	4,966	26.4	72	1,375	19.1	237	4,670	19.7	497	11,011	22.2
Tennis	310	2,860	9.2	218	1,881	8.6	360	3,793	10.5	888	8,534	9.6
Track, Indoor	289	10,371	35.9	117	3,114	26.6	224	5,605	25.0	630	19,090	30.3
Track, Outdoor	299	10,509	35.1	165	4,132	25.0	258	6,230	24.1	722	20,871	28.9
Volleyball	311	4,496	14.5	269	3,698	13.7	412	5,816	14.1	992	14,010	14.1
Water polo	31	649	20.9	10	204	20.4	20	320	16.0	61	1,173	19.2
Championship Sports subtotal	**3,306**	**70,437**		**2,137**	**34,469**		**3,707**	**63,677**		**9,150**	**168,583**	
Emerging Sports												
Archery	2	21	10.5	0	N/A	N/A	0	N/A	N/A	2	21	10.5
Badminton	0	N/A	N/A	0	N/A	N/A	3	30	10.0	3	30	10.0
Equestrian	15	663	44.2	6	148	24.7	24	475	19.8	45	1,286	28.6
Rugby	1	25	25.0	1	37	37.0	2	87	43.5	4	149	37.3
Squash	8	115	14.4	0	N/A	N/A	18	245	13.6	26	360	13.8
Synchronized swimming	4	51	12.8	1	11	11.0	3	35	11.7	8	97	12.1
Team handball	0	N/A	N/A	0	N/A	N/A	0	N/A	N/A	0	N/A	N/A
Emerging Sports subtotal	**30**	**875**		**8**	**196**		**50**	**872**		**88**	**1,943**	
Total	**3,336**	**71,312**		**2,145**	**34,665**		**3,757**	**64,549**		**9,238**	**107,526**	

Notes: 1. Participation totals are adjusted to reflect all institutions sponsoring each sport.
2. Provisional members are included in these numbers.
3. Coed sport teams from the sports sponsorship database were added to both the men's AND women's team data. The following sports had coed teams: a) equestrian, b) fencing, c) golf, d) rifle, e) swimming & diving, f) indoor track & field and g) outdoor track & field.
N/A=Not applicable.
*Coed championship sport.

SOURCE: Nicole Bracken, "2005–06 Participation Study—Women's Sports," in *1981–82—2005–06 NCAA Sports Sponsorship and Participation Rates Report*, National Collegiate Athletic Association, May 2007, http://www.ncaa.org/library/research/participation_rates/1982–2006/1982_2006_participation_rates.pdf (accessed July 26, 2007)

women. Even though the gender gap has widened some since 2004, it has actually been closing since the 1980s.

Table 6.5 shows participation in women's sports at NCAA schools in 2005–06. According to Bracken, 10,509 women participated on the NCAA's 299 Division I outdoor track and field teams that year, the highest total of any women's sport. Nearly as many participated during the indoor track season. (These are essentially the same group of athletes; a few schools offer only outdoor track and field.) The NCAA's 301 women's Division I soccer teams had 7,630 total participants in 2005–06. Including all sports, both championship and emerging, 71,312 women participated in Division I sports that year. Another 34,665 women played at the Division II level; Division III had 64,549 female athletes.

Table 6.6 shows participation in men's collegiate sports in 2005–06. Bracken indicates that 88,085 student-athletes participated on 2,907 Division I men's teams that year. The sport with the greatest number of Division I teams was basketball, with 326. However, basketball squads are relatively small, averaging 15.3 members per school in Division I. Therefore, several other sports actually have more participants. Over twenty-five thousand men played football at either the Division I-A or I-AA level in 2005–06. Baseball was second, with 10,011 participants, followed closely by outdoor track and field with 9,813. Division II sports included 50,624 men participants in 2005–06 and Division III had 89,397. Football had the most participants at both of these levels as well.

TABLE 6.6

NCAA participation in men's sports, by division, 2005–06

	Division I			Division II			Division III			Overall		
	Teams	Athletes	Avg. Squad	Teams	Athletes	Avg. Squad	Teams	Athletes	Avg. Squad	Teams	Athletes	Avg. Squad
Championship Sports												
Baseball	286	10,011	35.0	241	8,100	33.6	363	10,656	29.4	890	28,767	32.3
Basketball	326	4,996	15.3	289	4,594	15.9	398	6,981	17.5	1,013	16,571	16.4
Cross Country	299	4,337	14.5	234	2,819	12.0	346	4,737	13.7	879	11,893	13.5
Fencing*	20	378	18.9	3	28	9.3	12	226	18.8	35	632	18.1
Football	235	25,180	107.1	153	14,767	96.5	230	21,305	92.6	618	61,252	99.1
I-A	*119*	*13.912*	*116.9*	*N/A*	*N/A*	*N/A*	*N/A*	*N/A*	*N/A*	*N/A*	*N/A*	*N/A*
I-AA	*116*	*11.268*	*97.1*	*N/A*	*N/A*	*N/A*	*N/A*	*N/A*	*N/A*	*N/A*	*N/A*	*N/A*
Golf	287	3,029	10.6	214	2,289	10.7	276	2,932	10.6	*777*	8,250	10.6
Gymnastics	17	290	17.1	0	0	0.0	2	31	15.5	19	321	16.9
Ice Hockey	58	1,649	28.4	7	218	31.1	68	2,106	31.0	133	3,973	29.9
Lacrosse	56	2,445	43.7	34	1,077	31.7	132	4,349	32.9	222	7,871	35.5
Rifle*	26	140	5.4	2	11	5.5	8	56	7.0	36	207	5.8
Skiing*	14	245	17.5	8	90	11.3	14	190	13.6	36	525	14.6
Soccer	199	5,496	27.6	166	4,274	25.7	387	10,023	25.9	752	19,793	26.3
Swimming/Diving	139	3,547	25.5	52	966	18.6	190	3,258	17.1	381	7,771	20.4
Tennis	266	2,660	10.0	173	1,584	9.2	315	3,355	10.7	754	7,599	10.1
Track, Indoor	242	8,908	36.8	108	3,382	31.3	217	6,845	31.5	567	19,135	33.7
Track, Outdoor	265	9,813	37.0	155	4,628	29.9	250	7,634	30.5	670	22,075	32.9
Volleyball	22	402	18.3	15	241	16.1	45	567	12.6	82	1,210	14.8
Water Polo	21	511	24.3	9	161	17.9	15	270	18.0	45	942	20.9
Wrestling	87	2,563	29.5	44	1,234	28.0	97	2,342	24.1	228	6,139	26.9
Championship Sports subtotal	**2,865**	**86,600**		**1,907**	**50,463**		**3,365**	**87,863**		**8,137**	**224,926**	
Non-Championship Sports												
Archery	1	11	11.0	0	N/A	N/A	0	N/A	N/A	1	11	11.0
Badminton	0	N/A	N/A	0	N/A	N/A	0	N/A	N/A	0	N/A	N/A
Bowling	0	N/A	N/A	1	18	18.0	1	15	15.0	2	33	16.5
Equestrian	0	N/A	N/A	0	N/A	N/A	8	95	11.9	8	95	11.9
Rowing	26	1,243	47.8	4	135	33.8	30	761	25.4	60	2,139	35.7
Rugby	0	N/A	N/A	0	N/A	N/A	2	84	42.0	2	84	42.0
Sailing	7	95	13.6	1	8	8.0	16	314	19.6	24	417	17.4
Squash	8	136	17.0	0	N/A	N/A	17	259	15.2	25	395	15.8
Non-Championship Sports subtotal	**42**	**1,485**		**6**	**161**		**74**	**1,469**		**122**	**3,115**	
Total	**2,907**	**88,085**		**1,913**	**50,624**		**3,439**	**89,397**		**8,259**	**228,106**	

Notes:
1. Participation totals are adjusted to reflect all institutions sponsoring each sport,
2. Provisional members are included in these numbers.
3. Coed sport teams from the sports sponsorship database were added to both the men's AND women's team data. The following sports had coed teams: a) equestrian, b) fencing, c) golf, d) rifle, e) swimming & diving, f) indoor track & field and g) outdoor track & field.
N/A=Not applicable.
*Coed championship sport.

SOURCE: Nicole Bracken, "2005–06 Participation Study—Men's Sports," in *1981–82—2005–06 NCAA Sports Sponsorship and Participation Rates Report*, National Collegiate Athletic Association, May 2007, http://www.ncaa.org/library/research/participation_rates/1982–2006/1982_2006_participation_rates.pdf (accessed July 26, 2007)

Table 6.7 puts college sports participation in historical perspective. In 1981–82 there were 231,445 athletes competing in NCAA championship sports, all divisions; 167,055 of them were men. By 1994–95 the total number of athletes had grown to 294,212. About twice as much of this growth was on the women's side as on the men's. The total number of athletes had grown to 393,509 by 2005–06. However, it is important to note a change in the way the total is calculated: provisional NCAA members were included in the count beginning in 1995–96. In addition, the numbers for 1995–96 and 1996–97 were adjusted to comply with the Equity in Athletics Disclosure Act, making it difficult to compare current participation numbers with data from before 1995.

Table 6.8 shows the number of sports sponsored by NCAA member schools over the same period. There were 11,025 teams in NCAA championship sports in 1981–82. By 1994–95 there were 13,799. Much more of this growth was in women's sports than in men's. The number of women's teams surpassed the men's total in 1996–97 and has remained higher since then. The total number of teams was 17,287 in 2005–06, though the same caveat pertaining to comparisons of older and newer participation data apply.

Table 6.9 vividly illustrates the trend in the number of sports offered per school since the early 1980s. Even though the overall average number of teams per college,

TABLE 6.7

Overall NCAA championship sports participation, 1981–82 to 2005–06

Year	Men	Percent change men	Women	Percent change women	Total	Percent change total
1981–82	167,055	N/A	64,390	N/A	231,445	N/A
1982–83	176,822	5.85	78,027	21.18	254,849	10.11
1983–84	186,008	5.20	82,452	5.67	268,460	5.34
1984–85	197,446	6.15	89,072	8.03	286,518	6.73
1985–86	196,437	−0.51	92,192	3.50	288,629	0.74
1986–87	187,561	−4.52	89,640	−2.77	277,201	−3.96
1987–88	176,396	−5.95	88,266	−1.53	264,662	−4.52
1988–89	178,521	1.20	90,180	2.17	268,701	1.53
1989–90	175,539	−1.67	88,206	−2.19	263,745	−1.84
1990–91	182,836	4.16	92,473	4.84	275,309	4.38
1991–92	183,675	0.46	94,922	2.65	278,597	1.19
1992–93	184,732	0.58	97,978	3.22	282,710	1.48
1993–94	186,939	1.19	102,994	5.12	289,933	2.55
1994–95	186,607	−0.18	107,605	4.48	294,212	1.48
1995–96*	206,385	10.60	125,250	16.40	331,635	12.72
1996–97*	199,391	−3.39	129,289	3.22	328,680	−0.89
1997–98*	200,030	0.32	133,445	3.21	333,475	1.46
1998–99*	207,685	3.83	145,873	9.31	353,558	6.02
1999–00*	208,481	0.38	146,617	0.51	355,098	0.44
2000–01*	214,154	2.72	155,698	6.19	369,852	4.15
2001–02*	209,890	−1.99	153,601	−1.35	363,491	−1.72
2002–03*	214,464	2.18	158,469	3.17	372,933	2.60
2003–04*	214,854	0.18	160,997	1.60	375,851	0.78
2004–05*	219,744	2.28	164,998	2.49	384,742	2.37
2005–06*	224,926	2.36	168,583	2.17	393,509	2.28

*Provisional members are included in these numbers.
N/A=Not applicable.

SOURCE: Nicole Bracken, "NCAA Championship Sports Participation, Divisions I, II and III Overall 1981–82—2005–06," in *1981–82—2005–06 NCAA Sports Sponsorship and Participation Rates Report*, National Collegiate Athletic Association, May 2007, http://www.ncaa.org/library/research/participation_rates/1982–2006/1982_2006_participation_rates.pdf (accessed July 26, 2007)

across all divisions, has increased slightly during this period, the gender balance has shifted. For example, in 1981–82 the average number of Division I teams was 10.3 for men and 7.3 for women; by 2005–06 the average number of Division I men's teams declined to 8.9, whereas the women's teams increased to 10.2. (See Table 6.9.) This trend is apparent in the other two divisions as well. Per Table 6.10, the average number of Division I male student-athletes per college has also declined, from 273.5 in 1981–82 to 269.3 in 2005–06, whereas the average number of female student-athletes per college has risen from 114.8 in 1981–82 to 218.1 in 2005–06.

Women's Sports and Gender Equity

Figure 6.1 graphically illustrates what has happened to the gender gap since 1991 at the Division I level. In 1991–92 the average number of female and male athletes per institution were 112 and 250, respectively; by 2003–04 this average increased to 212 for women and 261 for men. Overall, the average number of women athletes per institution grew by one hundred between 1991 and 2004, whereas the average number of male athletes grew by only eleven. In terms of average expenses, however, the gender gap has not narrowed significantly in Division I. In 1995–96 the average athletic expense for men's sports was $3,398, whereas for women it was $1,525—a difference of $1,837. By 2003–04 this difference had

increased, rather than decreased, to $3,091, in that $7,286 was expended on men's sports and $4,195 on women's. (See Figure 6.2.) In spite of this, considerable progress has been made in equalizing scholarship spending. In 1991–92 an average of $373,000 in scholarships was awarded to women, whereas $849,000 was given to men. This average increased to $1.6 million for women and $1.9 million for men in 2003–04. (See Figure 6.3.)

In *Women in Intercollegiate Sport: A Longitudinal, National Study—Twenty Nine Year Update, 1977–2006* (2006, http://www.womenssportsfoundation.org/binary-data/WSF_ARTICLE/pdf_file/1107.pdf), Linda Jean Carpenter and R. Vivian Acosta of Brooklyn College examine the status of women's college athletics over a twenty-nine-year period, between 1977 and 2006. Carpenter and Acosta find that nationwide, college women have more athletic teams available to them than ever before. Since 1978 (the mandatory compliance date for Title IX) the number of women's athletic teams per school rose from 5.6 to 8.5 in 2006. There were a total of 8,702 varsity women's intercollegiate teams in the NCAA in 2006.

According to Carpenter and Acosta, the sport most frequently found in women's intercollegiate athletic programs was basketball, which was offered by 98.4% of NCAA schools in 2006. (See Table 6.11.) Basketball was

TABLE 6.8

Overall NCAA championship sports teams, 1981–82 to 2005–06

Year	Men	Women	Total
1981–82	6,746	4,279	11,025
1982–83	6,807	4,915	11,722
1983–84	6,807	5,053	11,860
1984–85	6,826	5,217	12,043
1985–86	6,787	5,504	12,291
1986–87	6,715	5,570	12,285
1987–88	6,721	5,635	12,356
1988–89	6,644	5,661	12,305
1989–90	6,628	5,708	12,336
1990–91	6,824	5,870	12,694
1991–92	6,940	6,032	12,972
1992–93	7,026	6,173	13,199
1993–94	7,127	6,430	13,557
1994–95	7,172	6,627	13,799
1995–96*	7,857	7,447	15,304
1996–97*	7,608	7,618	15,226
1997–98*	7,602	7,765	15,367
1998–99*	7,838	8,201	16,039
1999–00*	7,803	8,271	16,074
2000–01*	8,057	8,699	16,756
2001–02*	8,037	8,792	16,829
2002–03*	8,002	8,831	16,833
2003–04*	8,009	8,948	16,957
2004–05*	8,016	8,991	17,007
2005–06*	8,137	9,150	17,287

*Provisional members are included in these numbers.

SOURCE: Adapted from Nicole Bracken, "NCAA Championship Sports Sponsorship, Divisions I, II and III Overall 1981–82—2005–06," in *1981–82—2005–06 NCAA Sports Sponsorship and Participation Rates Report*, National Collegiate Athletic Association, May 2007, http://www.ncaa.org/library/research/participation_rates/1982–2006/1982_2006_participation_rates.pdf (accessed July 26, 2007)

the most popular sport throughout the period covered in the study. It ranked number one in 1977, when it was offered at 90.4% of colleges. The only other women's sport offered at more than 90% of colleges in 2006 was volleyball, which was available at 95.2% of NCAA schools. Like basketball, volleyball has maintained its ranking since 1977, when it was offered at 80.1% of schools.

Title IX

No piece of legislation has had a greater impact on gender equity in sports participation than Title IX of the Education Amendments of 1972 of the Civil Rights Act of 1964, usually referred to simply as Title IX. In 1971 the gender disparity in sports participation was overwhelming. According to the Women's Sports Foundation, in "Playing Fair: A Guide to Title IX in High School and College Sports" (October 8, 2001, http://www.womenssportsfoundation.org/cgi-bin/iowa/issues/geena/record.html?record=829), 294,015 girls were participating in interscholastic sports programs that year, compared to 3.5 million boys. Title IX was based on the notion that unequal federal funding between genders was an illegal form of discrimination. Title IX requires institutions receiving federal funding—including both

secondary schools and colleges—to provide resources equally to male and female students. In practice, this has meant that schools must attempt to maintain equal facilities, equal coaching staffs, and a gender ratio among athletes similar to the ratio among the student body as a whole. Critics of Title IX have been dismayed by the fact that compliance has sometimes meant cuts in men's sports programs, but the biggest impact has been an explosion in the prevalence and popularity of women's sports. In 2002 President George W. Bush (1946–) officially renamed Title IX the Patsy T. Mink Equal Opportunity in Education Act, after the legislation's author, a congresswoman from Hawaii. However, it is still generally referred to as Title IX.

The Women's Sports Foundation (2007, http://www.womenssportsfoundation.org/cgi-bin/iowa/issues/article.html?record=1017) notes that there is both good and bad news regarding gender equity in high school and college sports in the Title IX era. Female high school sports participation increased by 904% between 1972, when Title IX went into effect, and 2007, and female college sports participation increased by 456% during this same period. By contrast, women athletes in college received only 38% of sports operating dollars, 45% of athletic scholarship dollars, and 33% of recruitment spending in 2007. In high school, where girls represented 49% of all students, they received only 41% of the opportunities to participate in school athletics.

Women Coaches in College

One ironic consequence of the increase in the number of women's sports offered in college is a decrease in the percentage of teams that are coached by women. In 1972 women coached more than 90% of women's college sports teams. (See Table 6.12.) By 1978 the percentage had dropped to 58.2%. Acosta and Carpenter suggest that this drop was because of the rapid increase in the number of women's sports teams, which was not accompanied by a comparable growth in the number of qualified female coaches. However, the percentage has continued to fall since 1978, and in 2006 it stood at 42.4%, an all-time low. Acosta and Carpenter argue that this decline in women's representation in college coaching is due in part to discrimination and differences in the way male and female coaches are recruited. The percentage varies substantially from sport to sport. Table 6.13 shows that 60.8% of women's college basketball teams had female coaches in 2006 and 53.5% of volleyball coaches were female. However, men dominated the coaching ranks of women's cross country (19.5% women) and soccer (29.9%).

Acosta and Carpenter note that the percentage of female coaches is higher among schools at which the athletic director is also a woman. However, they also

TABLE 6.9

Average number of teams per college, 1981–82 to 2005–06

Year	Division I			Division II			Division III			Overall		
	Men's	Women's	Overall	Men's	Women's	Overall	Men's	Women's	Overall	Men's	Women's	Overall
1981–82	10.3	7.3	17.5	7.9	5.5	13.4	8.8	6.0	14.8	9.1	6.4	15.5
1982–83	10.2	6.9	17.1	7.4	5.7	13.1	8.3	6.2	14.6	8.8	6.3	15.1
1983–84	10.2	7.1	17.3	7.5	5.9	13.4	8.2	6.3	14.6	8.7	6.5	15.3
1984–85	10.2	7.3	17.4	7.5	6.1	13.6	8.2	6.6	14.8	8.7	6.7	15.5
1985–86	10.1	7.7	17.9	7.3	6.3	13.6	8.2	6.8	15.0	8.7	7.0	15.7
1986–87	9.7	7.8	17.5	7.1	6.2	13.3	8.4	7.0	15.4	8.6	7.1	15.7
1987–88	9.6	7.8	17.4	7.1	6.2	13.3	8.4	7.1	15.6	8.6	7.2	15.7
1988–89	9.4	7.7	17.2	6.9	6.1	13.0	8.3	7.2	15.4	8.4	7.1	15.5
1989–90	9.4	7.8	17.2	6.9	6.2	13.1	8.2	7.2	15.4	8.3	7.2	15.5
1990–91	9.5	7.8	17.3	6.8	6.0	12.8	8.3	7.2	15.4	8.3	7.1	15.4
1991–92	9.6	8.1	17.6	6.7	5.9	12.6	8.2	7.2	15.4	8.3	7.2	15.5
1992–93	9.5	8.2	17.7	6.7	5.9	12.6	8.1	7.3	15.3	8.2	7.2	15.4
1993–94	9.6	8.4	18.0	6.5	5.9	12.4	7.9	7.4	15.3	8.1	7.3	15.4
1994–95	9.5	8.5	18.0	6.1	5.6	11.7	7.3	7.0	14.3	7.7	7.1	14.8
1995–96*	9.6	9.0	18.6	6.5	6.1	12.5	7.8	7.7	15.5	8.0	7.6	15.6
1996–97*	9.4	9.1	18.5	6.3	6.1	12.4	7.6	7.8	15.5	7.8	7.7	15.5
1997–98*	9.3	9.3	18.7	6.4	6.4	12.8	7.7	8.0	15.7	7.8	8.0	15.8
1998–99*	9.4	9.6	19.0	6.3	6.5	12.8	7.6	8.1	15.7	7.8	8.1	15.9
1999–00*	9.1	9.7	18.8	6.1	6.4	12.4	7.5	8.2	15.7	7.8	8.1	15.7
2000–01*	9.2	10.0	19.2	6.4	6.8	13.2	7.9	8.5	16.4	7.9	8.5	16.3
2001–02*	9.2	10.1	19.2	6.5	7.0	13.4	7.9	8.6	16.5	7.9	8.6	16.5
2002–03*	9.0	10.1	19.1	6.4	7.1	13.5	7.9	8.7	16.6	7.9	8.7	16.5
2003–04*	8.9	10.1	19.1	6.5	7.2	13.7	7.8	8.6	16.4	7.8	8.7	16.5
2004–05*	8.9	10.2	19.0	6.4	7.1	13.6	7.8	8.6	16.4	7.8	8.7	16.5
2005–06*	8.9	10.2	19.1	6.5	7.2	13.7	7.8	8.5	16.3	7.8	8.7	16.4

*Provisional members are included in these numbers.

SOURCE: Nicole Bracken, "NCAA Sports Sponsorship, 1981–82—2005–06, Average Number of Teams per Institution," in *1981–82—2005–06 NCAA Sports Sponsorship and Participation Rates Report*, National Collegiate Athletic Association, May 2007, http://www.ncaa.org/library/research/participation_rates/1982–2006/1982_2006_participation_rates.pdf (accessed July 26, 2007)

note that only 18.6% of NCAA schools had female athletic directors in 2006.

College Sports and Ethnicity

According to Roberto Vicente of the NCAA, in *1999–00—2004–05 NCAA Student-Athlete Race and Ethnicity Report* (June 2006, http://www.ncaa.org/library/research/ethnicity_report/2004-05/2004-05_race_ethnicity_report.pdf), the percentage of African-American male student-athletes increased from 16.3% in 1999–2000 to 18% in 2004–05. During this same period the percentage of African-American female athletes increased from 9.4% to 10.9%.

Table 6.14 breaks down sports participation ethnic percentages (all divisions combined) by ethnicity and sport. Some sports, such as lacrosse at just over 90% for each gender, are overwhelmingly white. In contrast, a substantial portion of college basketball players—42.2% of men and 28.5% of women—are non-Hispanic black. The overall ethnic balance across all divisions has remained fairly stable over the last several years, among both male and female athletes. This stability is represented visually in Figure 6.4 and Figure 6.5, which trace the ethnicity percentages of student-athletes between 1999 and 2005. In these two graphs, the line representing

non-Hispanic white male athletes hovers at just over 70% across the entire time span; the line representing non-Hispanic white women similarly hovers at a little under 80%. Table 6.15, however, shows that there have indeed been small increases in participation, in both genders, among African-American, Hispanic, and nonresident alien athletes. The only nonwhite ethnic category that did not show a significant increase was Native American/Alaskan. Among both genders, about 0.3% of participants have been members of this ethnic group throughout the time period.

Spending on College Sports

In "Athletic Spending Grows as Academic Funds Dry Up" (February 18, 2004, http://www.usatoday.com/sports/college/2004-02-18-athletic-spending-cover_x.htm), Mary Jo Sylwester and Tom Witosky indicate that in 2004 spending on Division I sports increased at more than twice the rate of overall average university spending between 1995 and 2001. Spending on athletics, adjusted for inflation, grew an average of about 25% during this period, whereas university spending increased only 10% on average. According to Sylwester and Witosky, part of this disparity is due to increases in basic costs, such as scholarships and travel; however, a bigger factor is simply the desire by schools to have winning teams, which translates into higher

TABLE 6.10

Average number of student-athletes per college, 1981–82 to 2005–06

Year	Division I			Division II			Division III			Overall		
	Men's	Women's	Overall	Men's	Women's	Overall	Men's	Women's	Overall	Men's	Women's	Overall
1981–82	273.5	114.8	388.3	185.8	81.6	267.4	206.5	94.7	301.1	225.8	98.7	324.5
1982–83	293.3	120.3	413.6	180.2	78.1	258.3	202.8	100.3	303.1	228.7	101.6	330.3
1983–84	301.8	120.3	422.0	194.1	91.2	285.3	213.8	107.5	321.3	239.9	107.9	347.8
1984–85	318.2	127.2	445.4	203.6	97.8	301.4	227.1	116.6	343.7	254.2	115.9	370.1
1985–86	315.2	133.0	448.2	199.5	103.8	303.3	227.0	118.3	345.3	251.9	120.1	372.0
1986–87	290.8	128.7	419.5	186.7	95.3	282.0	224.2	114.0	338.2	239.9	115.0	354.9
1987–88	275.6	125.9	401.5	177.1	94.3	271.4	207.5	112.5	320.0	225.7	113.3	338.9
1988–89	277.9	127.8	405.7	172.2	92.7	264.9	208.2	114.7	322.9	225.2	114.3	339.4
1989–90	275.8	126.0	401.7	168.4	90.1	258.5	202.2	110.5	312.7	220.9	111.2	332.1
1990–91	277.7	128.3	405.9	171.2	87.3	258.6	206.3	113.2	319.4	222.9	112.1	335.0
1991–92	278.7	132.9	411.6	168.6	87.6	256.2	200.1	114.2	314.3	219.7	113.9	333.5
1992–93	277.5	137.8	415.3	164.5	86.2	250.7	197.2	115.4	312.7	216.5	115.6	332.1
1993–94	286.5	147.4	433.8	159.1	85.8	244.9	186.2	116.1	302.3	212.6	118.3	330.9
1994–95	278.8	153.1	431.8	146.6	81.3	227.9	173.7	112.4	286.0	199.7	116.7	316.4
1995–96*	284.9	169.4	454.3	157.3	90.7	248.0	189.5	129.2	318.7	209.4	130.3	339.7
1996–97*	276.8	172.3	449.1	154.3	90.6	244.9	185.0	129.7	314.7	204.4	131.5	335.9
1997–98*	277.7	180.4	458.1	157.4	96.6	254.0	186.6	132.4	319.0	206.8	137.2	344.0
1998–99*	274.1	194.1	468.3	160.0	103.0	263.0	185.6	136.7	322.3	205.0	144.4	349.4
1999–00*	267.3	195.6	463.0	152.5	99.4	251.9	188.9	136.8	325.7	202.7	144.3	346.9
2000–01*	272.3	203.2	473.6	159.4	107.6	266.4	195.5	143.6	338.5	209.0	151.8	359.8
2001–02*	263.9	203.2	467.2	156.6	104.6	261.2	192.4	140.6	333.1	204.8	150.1	354.9
2002–03*	266.1	210.0	476.1	163.4	108.9	272.2	197.9	144.5	342.4	210.0	155.5	365.6
2003–04*	265.5	213.4	478.9	165.5	112.5	278.0	194.9	142.5	337.4	209.2	156.6	365.8
2004–05*	268.5	216.8	485.2	166.8	114.4	281.2	202.0	146.1	348.1	213.2	159.5	372.8
2005–06*	269.3	218.1	487.4	171.0	117.1	288.1	202.7	146.4	349.1	214.4	160.3	374.6

*Provisional members are included in these numbers.

SOURCE: Nicole Bracken, "NCAA Sports Participation 1981–82—2005–06, Average Number of Student-Athletes per Institution," in *1981–82—2005–06 NCAA Sports Sponsorship and Participation Rates Report*, National Collegiate Athletic Association, May 2007, http://www.ncaa.org/library/research/participation_rates/1982–2006/1982_2006_participation_rates.pdf (accessed July 26, 2007)

attendance at sports events, better television ratings, and increased alumni support.

Revenue generated by university sports does not typically cover the costs of running the programs. Sylwester and Witosky state that only about forty schools had self-sustaining athletic departments in 2004. Therefore, most departments were reliant on the school for financial support. About 60% of Division I schools used student fees, usually ranging from $50 to $1,000 per year for full-time students, to help fund their athletic department.

The trend toward university-subsidized sports appears to be accelerating, leading to growing tensions between athletics and academics on the campuses of many top schools. The debate has gotten more fierce as substantial cuts in higher education funding by state governments has led many schools to eliminate jobs, downsize academic programs, increase class sizes, and raise tuition.

The NCAA actively rebuts the argument that college sports have become "big business." In "Is College Sports Big Business?" (*NCAA News Online*, August 29, 2005), Gary T. Brown asserts that the money that flows through college athletic programs pales in comparison to the dollars that professional sports and the corporate world overall generate. Brown notes that Myles

Brand (1942–), the president of the NCAA, places the blame on the media for creating the impression that college sports are all about money. For example, Brand argues that media coverage of college sports mentions the NCAA's $6.2 billion television contract, but rarely mentions the fact that the $6.2 billion is spread over eleven years. Brad Wolverton, in "College Presidents Call for Increased Disclosure of Athletics Spending" (*Chronicle of Higher Education*, November 10, 2006), quotes Brand as saying that the revenue generated by college sports is well spent in educationally valid ways, including the $1.2 billion spent by Division I schools on athletic scholarships in 2005–06 and $150 million on academic support programs for student-athletes.

In *2002–03 NCAA Revenues and Expenses of Divisions I and II Intercollegiate Athletics Programs Report* (February 2005, http://www.ncaa.org/library/research/i_ii_rev_exp/2003/2002-03_d1_d2_rev_exp.pdf), an analysis of revenue from and spending on athletic programs, Daniel L. Fulks of the NCAA states that in 1985 the average Division I-A athletic program had total revenues of $6.8 million ($6.7 million of it from men's sports) and expenses of $6.9 million ($6.2 million on the men's side). By 2003 the average sports revenue for Division I-A schools had more than quadrupled to $29.4 million, with $18.6 million of this total coming from men's

FIGURE 6.1

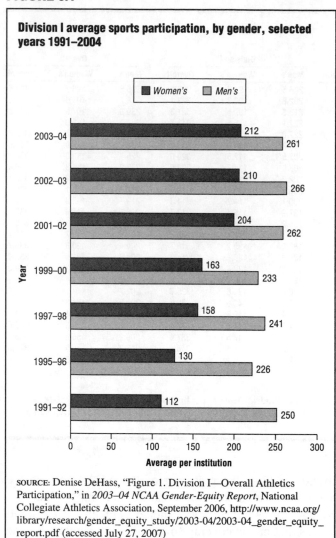

Division I average sports participation, by gender, selected years 1991–2004

SOURCE: Denise DeHass, "Figure 1. Division I—Overall Athletics Participation," in *2003–04 NCAA Gender-Equity Report*, National Collegiate Athletics Association, September 2006, http://www.ncaa.org/library/research/gender_equity_study/2003-04/2003-04_gender_equity_report.pdf (accessed July 27, 2007)

FIGURE 6.2

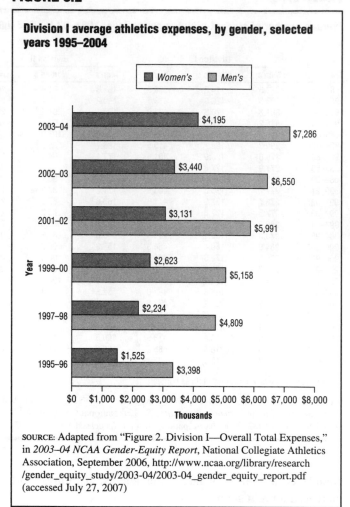

Division I average athletics expenses, by gender, selected years 1995–2004

SOURCE: Adapted from "Figure 2. Division I—Overall Total Expenses," in *2003–04 NCAA Gender-Equity Report*, National Collegiate Athletics Association, September 2006, http://www.ncaa.org/library/research/gender_equity_study/2003-04/2003-04_gender_equity_report.pdf (accessed July 27, 2007)

sports. These schools were also typically operating in the black in 2003; average expenses were $27.2 million, $2.2 million less than average revenue.

In 2003 football ($12.9 million in revenue and $7 million in expenses) and men's basketball ($4.3 million in revenue and $2.2 million in expenses) accounted for a huge share of both the spending and revenue in Division 1-A college sports, and both produced sizeable net financial gains. (See Table 6.16.) Figure 6.6 shows the trends in football and basketball spending and revenue from 1985 to 2003 in Division I-A. The amount of surplus revenue these sports generated grew substantially during this time span. The average football revenue at Division I-A schools grew from $4 million in 1985 to $11 million in 2001, whereas expenses only increased from $2.5 million to $7 million. Table 6.17 details where Division I-A schools' athletics revenue came from in 2003. Ticket sales were the biggest source, accounting for $8 million of the total revenue.

Academic Eligibility

Incoming student-athletes must meet a set of academic standards to participate in NCAA-sanctioned sports programs. These standards vary according to the division in which a school competes. According to the NCAA, in *Guide for the College-Bound Student-Athlete* (2007, http://www.ncaa.org/library/general/cbsa/2007-08/2007-08_cbsa.pdf), Division I academic eligibility rules through 2007 require that the student:

- Graduates from high school

- Completes fourteen core courses: four years of English; two of math; two of science; one extra year of English, math, or science; two years of social science; and three extra core courses of English, math, or science, or foreign language, nondoctrinal religion, or philosophy

- Achieves a minimum required GPA in core courses

- Achieves a combined SAT or ACT score that matches the student's GPA on a special NCAA chart

These requirements are scheduled to change beginning in the fall of 2008. The new requirements include an

FIGURE 6.3

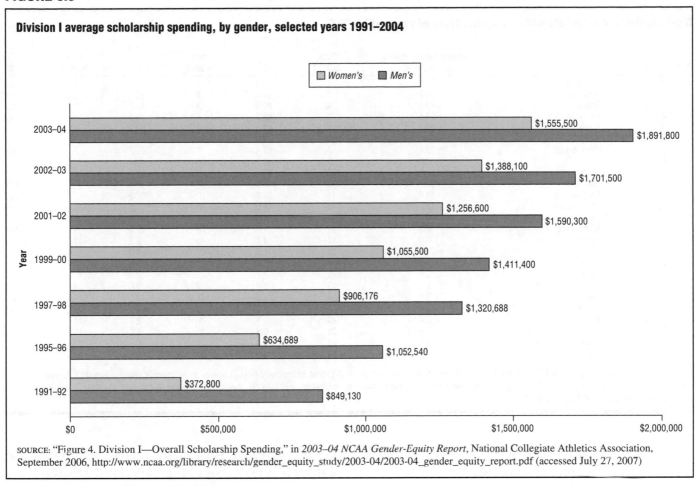

Division I average scholarship spending, by gender, selected years 1991–2004

Women's   Men's

Year	Women's	Men's
2003–04	$1,555,500	$1,891,800
2002–03	$1,388,100	$1,701,500
2001–02	$1,256,600	$1,590,300
1999–00	$1,055,500	$1,411,400
1997–98	$906,176	$1,320,688
1995–96	$634,689	$1,052,540
1991–92	$372,800	$849,130

SOURCE: "Figure 4. Division I—Overall Scholarship Spending," in *2003–04 NCAA Gender-Equity Report*, National Collegiate Athletics Association, September 2006, http://www.ncaa.org/library/research/gender_equity_study/2003-04/2003-04_gender_equity_report.pdf (accessed July 27, 2007)

additional year of math and an additional year of any of the previously mentioned courses. The requirements for Divisions II and III (also slated to change in 2008) are similar to those of Division I, though less stringent.

The *Guide for the College-Bound Student-Athlete* also outlines the rules for recruiting high school athletes, which vary somewhat by sport as well as by division. The recruiting rules for Division I are summarized in Table 6.18 and include regulations pertaining to phone contact, campus visits, and other forms of communication between coaches and prospective college athletes.

HIGH SCHOOL SPORTS

Participation

According to the U.S. Centers for Disease Control and Prevention, 56% of U.S. high school students played on a sports team in 2005. (See Table 6.19.) The percentage was higher among boys (61.8%) than girls (50.2%). Nearly 58% of white students played on a sports team. Minorities played sports in lesser proportions: 53.7% of non-Hispanic African-American students and 53% of Hispanic students played on sports teams.

Since 1971 the National Federation of State High School Associations (NFHS) has compiled data on sports participation from its member associations. The most recent data are published in the *2005–06 High School Athletics Participation Survey* (2006, http://www.nfhs.org/core/contentmanager/uploads/2005_06NFHSparticipationsurvey.pdf). Table 6.20 summarizes this NFHS data for 1971 through 2006. In 2005–06 the number of participants in high school sports reached 7.2 million. At about 3 million, participation among girls reached an all-time high in 2005–06. The total for boys, 4.2 million, was the second highest in the survey's history, trailing the nearly 4.4 million boys who participated in sports in 1977–78.

Table 6.21 shows the most popular high school sports for boys. More than one million boys participated in football in 2005–06. Boys' basketball had 546,335 participants, which was about half as many participants as football. Track and field (533,985), baseball (470,671), and soccer (358,935) were the third-, fourth-, and fifth-most popular boys' sports, respectively. Among high school girls, basketball was the most popular sport, with 452,929 participants, followed by outdoor track and field

TABLE 6.11

Most popular intercollegiate women's sports, selected years, 1977–2006

Rank in 2006		Percentage of schools offering sport	Rank in 2004	%	Rank in 2002	%	Rank in 1977	%
1.	Basketball	98.4	1	98.3	1	98.8	1	90.4
2.	Volleyball	95.2	2	94.6	2	95.4	2	80.1
3.	Soccer	89.4	4	88.6	3	87.9	20	2.8
4.	Cross country	89.2	3	88.8	5	86.5	8	29.4
5.	Softball	87.1	5	86.4	6	86.2	4	48.4
6.	Tennis	85.1	6	85.2	4	87.7	3	80.0
7.	Track & field	67.4	7	67.4	7	67.5	5	46.1
8.	Golf	52.2	8 tie	48.7	9	48.4	10	19.9
9.	Swimming	50.9	9 tie	48.7	8	52.0	6	41.0
10.	Lacrosse	30.6	10	28.5	11	26.7	11	13.0
11.	Field hockey	28.0	11	28.2	10	27.0	7	36.3
12.	Crew/rowing	15.2	12	14.0	12	16.2	13	6.9
13.	Ice hockey	9.7	14	8.8	14	8.5	24	1.3
14.	Gymnastics	9.5	13	11.0	13	12.0	9	25.9
Tie 15.	Fencing	5.9	17	4.6	16	5.8	12	9.8
Tie 16.	Water polo	5.9	15	6.5	15	6.0	—	—
17.	Skiing	5.7	16	5.8	17	5.0	16	3.6
18.	Sailing	3.8	21	3.2	20	3.1	21 tie	2.3
19.	Riding/equestrian	3.6	19	3.6	19	3.6	23	2.0
Tie 20.	Squash	3.4	18	3.8	21	3.1	21 tie	2.3
Tie 21.	Riflery	3.4	22	2.8	18	3.8	15	3.8
22.	Bowling	3.2	20	3.3	22	2.6	17	3.4
23.	Synchronized swimming	1.3	23	0.5	23	1.0	18	3.3
24.	Badminton	0.4	24	0.3	25	0.1	14	5.9
25.	Archery	0.2	25	0.2	24	0.5	19	3.0

SOURCE: Linda Jean Carpenter and R. Vivian Acosta, "Most Popular Sports in 2006 (Most Frequently Found Sports in Women's Intercollegiate Programs)," in *Women in Intercollegiate Sport: A Longitudinal, National Study—Twenty-Nine Year Update, 1977–2006*, Acosta/Carpenter, 2006, http://webpages.charter.net/womeninsport/ (accessed July 27, 2007)

(439,200), volleyball (390,034), fast-pitch softball (369,094), and soccer (321,555). (See Table 6.22.)

According to the NFHS, the state with the largest number of high school athletes in 2005–06 was Texas, with 742,341. Other leading states included California (678,019), New York (350,349), Illinois (323,703), Michigan (321,250), and Ohio (316,529).

Data from Lloyd D. Johnston et al.'s *Monitoring the Future, National Results on Adolescent Drug Use: Overview of Key Findings, 2006* (May 2007, http://www.monitoringthefuture.org/pubs/monographs/overview2006.pdf), an ongoing nationwide study of youth behavior and attitudes, suggest that the percentage of middle and high school students participating in school sports has generally declined over the past decade, although girls' participation has held fairly steady. A greater percentage of boys than girls have participated in school sports throughout this span. The national advocacy group Child Trends analyzed data on school sports participation from *Monitoring the Future* over several years, and its findings are summarized in Table 6.23. The analysis by Child Trends shows that participation in athletics among tenth-grade boys decreased from 69.8% in 1992 to 65.5% in 2004, whereas participation among tenth-grade girls increased slightly, from 56.6% in 1992 to 57.2% in 2004. This pattern was similar among twelfth graders. Child Trends finds that since 1991 the gender gap in high school sports participa-

tion has decreased substantially. Among tenth graders, the difference between boys and girls declined from seventeen percentage points in 1991 (boys, 69%, and girls, 52%) to nine percentage points in 2004 (boys, 66%, and girls, 57%). (See Figure 6.7.) Likewise, the gap for twelfth graders declined from eighteen percentage points in 1991 (boys, 65%, and girls, 47%) to nine percentage points in 2004 (boys, 60%, and girls, 51%).

Child Trends also finds a correlation between parents' education and students' participation in school athletics. Youth whose parents were better educated were more likely to participate than their peers whose parents had fewer years of education. In 2004, 73% of tenth graders with a parent who had attended graduate school participated in school sports, whereas participation among tenth graders whose parents did not finish high school was only 42%. (See Figure 6.8.)

Benefits of High School Sports Participation

In September 2005 the National Center for Education Statistics (NCES) published the report *What Is the Status of High School Athletes 8 Years after Their Senior Year?* (http://nces.ed.gov/pubs2005/2005303.pdf), which analyzes the status of former high school athletes in their midtwenties. The report was part of the National Education Longitudinal Study of 1988, which tracked a large sample of students who were seniors in 1992. This report examined their educational achievement, employment

TABLE 6.12

TABLE 6.13

Percentage of female coaches in women's intercollegiate sports, selected years, 1972–2006

Percentage of female coaches, by sport, 1977 and 2006

2006	42.4%	Women coaching women's teams
2004	44.1%	In 1972, the year Title IX was enacted, more than 90% of women's teams were coached by females.
2003	44.0%	
2002	44.0%	
2001	44.7%	By 1978, the year of mandatory Title IX compliance, the
2000	45.6%	percentage had dropped to 58.25. Some of the large
1999	46.3%	change in the early years from 1972 to 1978 was due
1998	47.4%	to the massive increase in the number of teams
1997	47.4%	offered for women (an increase from 2.5 in 1972
1996	47.7%	to 5.61 teams per school in 1978).
1995	48.3%	
1994	49.4%	Today, even though the number of women's teams is at
1993	48.1%	an all time high, the representation of females among
1992	48.3%	the coaching ranks of women's intercollegiate athletics
1991	47.7%	is at an all time low.
1990	47.3%	
1989	47.7%	Additionally, the representation of females among the
1988	48.3%	ranks of head coaches for MEN's teams remains at 2%
1987	48.8%	where it has been since before the passage of Title IX.
1986	50.6%	
1985	50.7%	When we look at intercollegiate coaching as an entire
1984	53.8%	workplace unit, we find that only 17.7% of
1983	56.2%	intercollegiate athletics teams have a female head
1982	52.4%	coach. Another way to say the same thing is to say
1981	54.6%	that 82.3% of all intercollegiate teams are coached
1980	54.2%	by males.
1979	56.1%	
1978	58.2%	
1972	90.0%+	Women coaching women's teams.

SOURCE: Linda Jean Carpenter and R. Vivian Acosta, "Percentage of Female Coaches All Division, All Sports, 2006," in *Women in Intercollegiate Sport: A Longitudinal, National Study—Twenty-Nine Year Update, 1977–2006*, Acosta/Carpenter, 2006, http://webpages.charter.net/womeninsport/ (accessed July 27, 2007)

	2006	1977
Archery	0.0%	83.4%
Badminton	0.0%	75.0%
Basketball	60.8%	79.4%
Bowling	50.0%	42.9%
Crew/rowing	40.0%	11.9%
Cross country	19.5%	35.2%
Fencing	24.2%	51.7%
Field hockey	94.2%	99.1%
Golf	36.8%	54.6%
Gymnastics	43.4%	69.7%
Ice hockey	35.2%	37.5%
Lacrosse	82.5%	90.7%
Riding	90.0%	75.0%
Riflery	26.3%	17.4%
Sailing	14.3%	7.1%
Skiing	9.4%	22.7%
Soccer	29.9%	29.4%
Softball	61.3%	83.5%
Squash	26.3%	71.4%
Swimming/diving	25.7%	53.6%
Synchronized swimming	100.0%	85.0%
Tennis	33.3%	72.9%
Track and field	19.4%	52.3%
Volleyball	53.5%	86.6%
Water polo	6.1%	—

SOURCE: Linda Jean Carpenter and R. Vivian Acosta, "Percentage of Female Coaches All Divisions, 1977 and 2006," in *Women in Intercollegiate Sport: A Longitudinal, National Study—Twenty-Nine Year Update, 1977–2006*, Acosta/Carpenter, 2007, http://webpages.charter.net/womeninsport/ (accessed July 27, 2007)

success, and health status as of 2000. The NCES finds that elite (those who were team captains or most valuable players) and varsity-level athletes were more likely than nonathletes to have received some postsecondary education and more likely to have earned a bachelor's degree. It also finds that elite athletes were more likely than nonathletes to be employed, and employed full time, in 2000. Elite and varsity athletes had higher incomes on average than those who did not participate in high school sports. In addition, the NCES finds that high school athletes were more likely than nonathletes to participate in fitness activities and group sports eight years after their senior year. Elite and varsity athletes were less likely to be daily smokers than their nonathletic peers. The only negative impact the NCES notes is that elite and varsity athletes were more likely than nonathletes to binge drink (i.e., these survey respondents reported having five or more alcoholic drinks on at least one occasion during the two weeks before the survey).

Money and High School Athletics

The perceived corruption of college sports by money appears to have seeped down to the high school level. A series of *New York Times* articles by Duff Wilson and

Pete Thamel in November and December 2005, including "The Quick Fix" (November 27) and "NCAA Calls for Investigation into Correspondence School" (December 2), reported on a Florida high school that was basically functioning as a diploma mill for elite athletes whose poor school performance threatened their chances to play at top-level universities. The school, the University High School in Miami, had no accreditation from the state, offered no classes for students to attend, and provided no real instruction. Students "attended" University High via correspondence courses, which essentially consisted of a series of open-book tests. Wilson and Thamel identified twenty-eight athletes who raised their sagging GPAs, often just enough to qualify for intercollegiate athletics, by enrolling in University High. Fourteen of them had already committed to attend NCAA Division I schools. Students paid about $400 to boost their grades in this way.

The vast sums of money involved in college sports have also led to extremely aggressive recruiting practices. According to Mark Schlabach, in "NCAA Cracks Down on Recruiting Practices" (*Washington Post*, August 6, 2004), high-profile recruiting scandals at two major colleges, the University of Colorado and the University of Miami, led to the creation of a special NCAA task force. The work of the task force culminated in new rules, approved by the NCAA Division I Board of Directors

TABLE 6.14

College athletes and ethnicity, 2004–05

Sport	American Indian/ Alaskan Native		Asian/ Pacific Islander		Black, Non-Hispanic		Hispanic		Nonresident alien		Other		White, Non-Hispanic	
	Men	Women	Men	Women	Men	Women	Men	Women	Men	Women	Men	Women	Men	Women
Archery		0.0		9.1		0.0		4.5		0.0		13.6		72.7
Badminton	0.0	0.0	0.0	26.1	0.0	8.7	0.0	0.0	0.0	17.4	0.0	13.0	0.0	34.8
Baseball	0.3	N/A	0.9	N/A	4.8	N/A	5.2	N/A	0.7	N/A	1.9	N/A	86.2	N/A
Basketball	0.4	0.5	0.6	1.2	42.2	28.5	2.3	2.6	2.7	2.5	2.1	2.1	49.6	62.7
Bowling	0.0	0.0	0.0	0.3	0.0	62.0	0.0	1.1	0.0	1.1	0.0	0.5	0.0	35.1
Cross country	0.5	0.3	1.4	1.5	9.0	10.3	5.4	4.3	2.4	2.0	2.7	3.0	78.6	78.6
Equestrian	0.0	0.5	2.3	1.0	4.5	0.6	2.3	1.8	2.3	0.2	0.0	2.5	88.6	93.4
Fencing	0.6	0.3	12.2	15.0	4.2	6.7	4.3	4.3	2.2	1.9	10.1	11.0	66.3	60.7
Field hockey	N/A	0.2	N/A	1.6	N/A	1.5	N/A	1.5	N/A	1.4	N/A	3.7	N/A	90.1
Football	0.3	N/A	1.2	N/A	32.7	N/A	2.5	N/A	0.2	N/A	2.1	N/A	60.9	N/A
Golf	0.3	0.3	1.9	4.4	2.4	3.3	1.7	2.9	5.0	6.9	1.7	1.9	87.0	80.3
Gymnastics	1.1	0.2	8.5	5.4	4.8	3.4	4.0	2.3	2.3	3.2	1.7	3.3	77.6	82.1
Ice hockey	0.3	0.2	0.6	1.3	0.4	0.5	0.4	0.4	14.6	14.5	3.3	4.5	80.3	78.5
Lacrosse	0.3	0.2	0.8	1.4	2.0	2.1	1.2	1.2	1.1	0.5	3.9	3.7	90.7	90.9
Rifle	0.4	0.9	3.9	5.6	0.8	5.1	3.1	3.7	0.4	0.9	2.7	2.3	88.6	81.3
Rowing		0.5		3.6		1.9		3.5		2.1		6.4		82.0
Rugby														
Sailing		N/A		N/A		N/A		N/A		N/A		N/A		N/A
Skiing	0.7	0.0	0.6	1.3	0.0	0.4	0.0	0.4	5.4	8.0	3.4	3.6	89.9	86.2
Soccer	0.2	0.2	1.8	1.8	6.2	3.8	6.9	3.9	5.6	2.2	3.2	2.4	76.1	85.6
Softball	N/A	0.6	N/A	1.3	N/A	5.9	N/A	4.8	N/A	0.8	N/A	1.9	N/A	84.8
Squash		0.0		9.3		1.1		4.4		3.8		15.0		66.5
Swimming/diving	0.3	0.3	2.5	2.6	1.6	1.2	3.2	2.6	3.9	2.6	4.1	3.3	84.6	87.3
Synchronized swimming	N/A	1.0	N/A	7.7	N/A	1.0	N/A	3.8	N/A	4.8	N/A	1.9	N/A	79.8
Team handball	N/A	0.0	N/A	0.0	N/A	0.0	N/A	0.0	N/A	0.0	N/A	0.0	N/A	0.0
Tennis	0.2	0.2	5.4	5.0	4.8	5.8	4.6	3.9	14.7	11.5	4.2	3.4	66.1	70.2
Track, indoor	0.3	0.3	1.4	1.4	20.5	21.1	3.4	2.7	2.4	2.5	3.1	3.1	68.9	68.9
Track outdoor	0.3	0.3	1.5	1.4	20.8	20.9	4.2	3.3	2.3	2.5	3.0	3.3	67.9	68.3
Volleyball	0.3	0.4	4.4	2.2	7.7	8.8	11.8	3.9	2.8	2.5	3.1	2.3	70.0	79.9
Water polo	0.9	0.7	4.6	4.4	0.6	0.9	5.3	7.4	5.0	3.3	10.0	6.2	73.6	77.2
Wrestling	0.6	N/A	1.7	N/A	5.4	N/A	5.1	N/A	0.2	N/A	3.4	N/A	83.6	N/A
All sports	0.3	0.3	1.5	2.1	18.0	10.9	3.8	3.3	2.6	2.8	2.7	3.0	71.1	77.5

N/A=Not applicable.
Empty cells indicate the data are unavailable.

SOURCE: Roberto Vincente, "2004–05 Student-Athlete Race/Ethnicity Percentages for Divisions I, II and III Overall," in *1999–00—2004–05 NCAA Student-Athlete Race and Ethnicity Report*, National Collegiate Athletic Association, June 2006, http://www.ncaa.org/library/research/ethnicity_report/2004-05/2004-05_race_ethnicity_report.pdf (accessed July 27, 2007)

in August 2004, aimed at eliminating what Brand calls a "culture of entitlement." Previously, colleges were wooing prospects with high-priced meals and stays in luxury hotels, often transporting them to campus in expensive chartered planes and limousines. Schlabach also mentions widely reported earlier charges that colleges were plying top high-school athletes with sex and alcohol. The revised rules prohibit schools from employing any of these practices, requiring that prospects be transported from airports in standard vehicles and fed "standard meals similar to those offered on campus." They also require schools to establish policies explicitly forbidding illegal actions during recruiting, such as underage drinking and sex for hire.

FIGURE 6.4

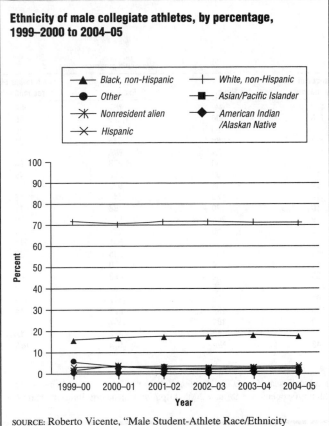

Ethnicity of male collegiate athletes, by percentage, 1999–2000 to 2004–05

SOURCE: Roberto Vicente, "Male Student-Athlete Race/Ethnicity Percentages for Divisions I, II and III Overall," in *1999–00—2004–05 NCAA Student-Athlete Race and Ethnicity Report*, National Collegiate Athletic Association, June 2006, http://www.ncaa.org/library/research/ethnicity_report/2004-05/2004-05_race_ethnicity_report.pdf (accessed July 27, 2007)

FIGURE 6.5

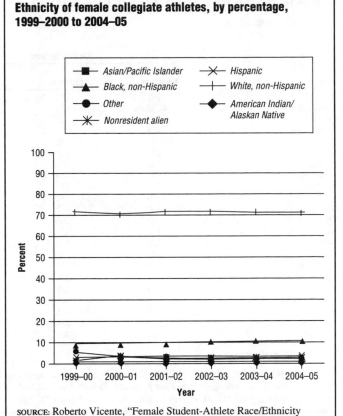

Ethnicity of female collegiate athletes, by percentage, 1999–2000 to 2004–05

SOURCE: Roberto Vicente, "Female Student-Athlete Race/Ethnicity Percentages for Divisions I, II and III Overall," in *1999–00—2004–05 NCAA Student-Athlete Race and Ethnicity Report*, National Collegiate Athletic Association, June 2006, http://www.ncaa.org/library/research/ethnicity_report/2004-05/2004-05_race_ethnicity_report.pdf (accessed July 27, 2007)

TABLE 6.15

NCAA sports participation, by ethnicity, 1999–00 to 2004–05

Year	American Indian/ Alaskan Native		Asian/ Pacific Islander		Black non-Hispanic		Hispanic		Nonresident alien		Other		White, non-Hispanic	
	Men	Women	Men	Women	Men	Women	Men	Women	Men	Women	Men	Women	Men	Women
1999–00*	0.3	0.3	1.2	1.5	16.3	9.4	3.0	2.4	1.8	1.5	6.0	6.8	71.6	78.1
2000–01*	0.3	0.4	1.3	1.7	17.2	10.2	3.3	2.7	4.1	4.5	3.3	3.7	70.4	77.0
2001–02*	0.3	0.3	1.4	1.7	17.7	10.4	3.5	2.8	2.5	2.4	3.1	3.2	71.6	79.1
2002–03*	0.3	0.3	1.4	1.9	17.9	10.5	3.5	3.0	2.6	2.6	2.7	2.9	71.6	78.9
2003–04*	0.4	9.3	1.4	2.0	18.1	10.6	3.5	3.2	2.7	2.9	2.5	2.8	71.4	78.2
2004–05*	0.3	0.3	1.5	2.1	18.0	10.9	3.8	3.3	2.6	2.8	2.7	3.0	71.1	77.5

*Provisional members are included in these numbers.

SOURCE: Roberto Vicente, "Student-Athlete Race and Ethnicity Percentages for Divisions I, II and III Overall, All Sports," in *1999–00—2004–05 NCAA Student-Athlete Race and Ethnicity Report*, National Collegiate Athletic Association, June 2006, http://www.ncaa.org/library/research/ethnicity_report/2004-05/2004-05_race_ethnicity_report.pdf (accessed July 27, 2007)

TABLE 6.16

Division I-A revenue and expenses, by sport, fiscal year 2003

[Dollar amounts in thousands]

Sport	Men's programs			Women's programs		
	Revenues	Expenses	Number of respondents	Revenues	Expenses	Number of respondents
Baseball	367	760	102	N/A	N/A	N/A
Basketball	4,252	2,227	116	506	1,279	115
Fencing	39	133	8	50	165	10
Field hockey	N/A	N/A	N/A	166	535	24
Football	12,969	7,046	115	N/A	N/A	N/A
Golf	102	251	107	80	263	94
Gymnastics	110	331	17	163	593	46
Ice hockey	1,522	1,169	12	104	923	4
Lacrosse	270	664	14	176	545	18
Rifle	9	43	10	20	68	14
Rowing	264	472	9	206	682	39
Skiing	52	205	5	50	227	5
Soccer	130	454	57	156	531	111
Softball	N/A	N/A	N/A	151	545	93
Squash	20	80	1	0	0	0
Swimming	120	418	65	132	492	86
Synchronized swimming	N/A	N/A	N/A	55	289	3
Tennis	83	285	91	90	317	110
Track & field/cross country	121	496	108	157	623	114
Volleyball	221	416	9	181	597	113
Water polo	102	287	7	68	312	12
Wrestling	164	460	42	N/A	N/A	N/A

Note: N/A=not applicable

SOURCE: Daniel L. Fulks, "Table 3.29. Total Revenues and Expenses by Sport, Division I-A, Fiscal Year 2003," in *2002–03 NCAA Revenues and Expenses of Divisions I and II Intercollegiate Athletics Programs Report*, National Collegiate Athletic Association, February 2005, http://www.ncaa.org/library/research/i_ii_rev_exp/2003/2002–03_d1_d2_rev_exp.pdf (accessed August 23, 2007)

FIGURE 6.6

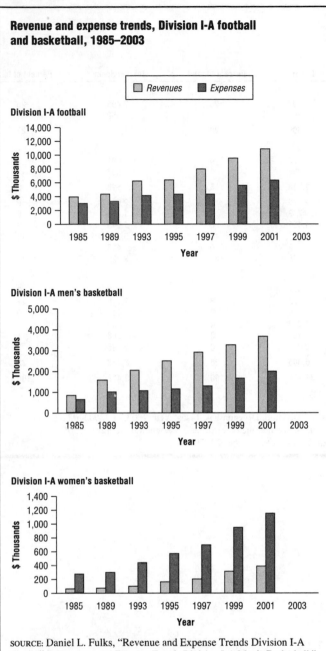

Revenue and expense trends, Division I-A football and basketball, 1985–2003

Division I-A football

Division I-A men's basketball

Division I-A women's basketball

SOURCE: Daniel L. Fulks, "Revenue and Expense Trends Division I-A Football," "Revenue and Expense Trends Division I-A Men's Basketball," and "Revenue and Expense Trends Division I-A Women's Basketball," in *2002–03 NCAA Revenues and Expenses of Divisions I and II Intercollegiate Athletics Programs Report*, National Collegiate Athletic Association, February 2005, http://www.ncaa.org/library/research/ i_ii_rev_exp/2003/2002-03_d1_d2_rev_exp.pdf (accessed August 23, 2007)

TABLE 6.17

Sources of revenue, NCAA Division I-A, fiscal year 2003

[Dollar amounts in thousands]

Category	Public	Percent of total	Private	Percent of total	Total division	Percent of total
Ticket sales						
Public/faculty/staff	7,686	26	6,298	20	7,495	26
Students	384	1	202	1	359	1
Total ticket sales	**8,070**	**28**	**6,500**	**20**	**7,854**	**27**
Postseason compensation						
Bowl games	613	2	1,180	4	691	2
Tournaments	183	1	358	1	207	1
Total postseason	**796**	**3**	**1,538**	**5**	**898**	**3**
NCAA and conference distributions	2,723	9	2,126	7	2,641	9
Student activity fees	2,038	7	703	2	1,854	6
Guarantees and options	978	3	1,455	5	1,043	3
Cash contributions from alumni and others	5,301	18	5,081	16	5,271	18
Direct government support	482	2	2	0	416	1
Institutional support	2,239	8	7,968	25	3,029	10
Other						
Concessions	576	2	401	1	552	2
Radio/television	2,061	7	2,473	8	2,118	7
Program sales/advertising	111	0	155	0	117	0
Sign age/sponsorship	1,259	4	1,262	4	1,259	4
Sports camps	294	1	101	0	268	1
Miscellaneous	2,110	7	2,013	6	2,096	7
Total other	**6,411**	**22**	**6,405**	**20**	**6,410**	**22**
Total	**29,038**	**100**	**31,778**	**100**	**29,416**	**100**

Notes: Total public institutions reporting=97. Total private institutions reporting=17.

SOURCE: Daniel L. Fulks, "Table 3.27. Sources of Total Revenues—Public, Private, Total Division, Division I-A, Fiscal Year 2003," in *2002–03 NCAA Revenues and Expenses of Divisions I and II Intercollegiate Athletics Programs Report*, National Collegiate Athletic Association, February 2005, http://www.ncaa.org/library/research/i_ii_rev_exp/2003/2002–03_d1_d2_rev_exp.pdf (accessed September 22, 2005)

TABLE 6.18

Summary of NCAA Division I recruiting rules, 2007–08

| | Sophomore year | | | |
Recruiting method	Men's basketball	Women's basketball	Football	Other sports
Recruiting materials	• You may receive brochures for camps and questionnaires. • You may begin receiving recruiting materials June 15 after your sophomore year.	• You may receive brochures for camps and questionnaires.	• You may receive brochures for camps and questionnaires.	• You may receive brochures for camps and questionnaires.
Telephone calls	• You may make calls to coach at your expense. • College may accept collect calls from you at end of your sophomore year. • College coach cannot call you.	• You may make calls to coach at your expense only. • College coach cannot call you.	• You may make calls to coach at your expense only. • College coach cannot call you.	• You may make calls to coach at your expense only. • College coach cannot call you. • Women's ice hockey—if you are an international prospect, a college coach may call you once in July after sophomore year
Off-campus contact	• None allowed.	• None allowed.	• None allowed.	• None allowed.
Official visit	• None allowed.	• None allowed.	• None allowed.	• None allowed.
Unofficial visit	• You may make an unlimited number of unofficial visits.	• You may make an unlimited number of unofficial visits.	• You may make an unlimited number of unofficial visits.	• You may make an unlimited number of unofficial visits.
	Junior year			
Recruiting materials	• Allowed. • You may begin receiving recruiting materials June 15 after your sophomore year.	• You may begin receiving September 1 of junior year.	• You may begin receiving September 1 of junior year.	• You may begin receiving September 1 of junior year. • Men's ice hockey—you may begin receiving recruiting materials June 15 after your sophomore year.
Telephone calls	• You may make calls to the coach at your expense.	• You may make calls to the coach at your expense.	• You may make calls to the coach at your expense.	• You may make calls to the coach at your expense.
College coaches may call you	• Once per month beginning June 15, before your junior year, through July 31 after your junior year.	• Once per month in April, May and June 1–20. • Once between June 21 and June 30 after your junior year. • Three times in July after your junior year.	• Once from April 15 to May 31 of your junior year.	• Once per week starting July 1 after your junior year. • Men's ice hockey—once per month beginning June 15, before your junior year, through July 31 after your junior year.
Off-campus contact	None allowed.	None allowed.	None allowed.	• Allowed starting July 1 after your junior year. • For gymnastics—allowed after July 15 after your junior year.
Official visit	• None allowed.	• None allowed.	• None allowed.	• None allowed.
Unofficial visit	• You may make an unlimited number of unofficial visits.	• You may make an unlimited number of unofficial visits.	• You may make an unlimited number of unofficial visits.	• You may make an unlimited number of unofficial visits.

TABLE 6.18

Summary of NCAA Division I recruiting rules, 2007–08 [CONTINUED]

Recruiting method	Senior year			
	Men's basketball	Women's basketball	Football	Other sports
Recruiting materials	• Allowed.	• Allowed.	• Allowed.	• Allowed.
Telephone calls	• You may make calls to the coach at your expense.	• You may make calls to the coach at your expense.	• You may make calls to the coach at your expense.	• You may make calls to the coach at your expense.
College coaches may call you	• Twice per week beginning August 1.	• Once per week beginning August 1.	• Once per week beginning September 1.	• Once per week beginning July 1. • Men's ice hockey— once per week beginning August 1.
Off-campus contact	• Allowed beginning September 9.	• Allowed beginning September 16.	• Allowed beginning November 25.	• Allowed.
Official visit	• Allowed beginning opening day of classes your senior year. • You are limited to one official visit per college up to a maximum of five official visits to divisions I and II colleges.	• Allowed beginning opening day of classes your senior year. • You are limited to one official visit per college up to a maximum of five official visits to divisions I and II colleges.	• Allowed beginning opening day of classes your senior year. • You are limited to one official visit per college up to a maximum of five official visits to divisions I and II colleges.	• Allowed beginning opening day of classes your senior year. • You are limited to one official visit per college up to a maximum of five official visits to divisions I and II colleges.
Unofficial visit	• You may make an unlimited number of unofficial visits.	• You may make an unlimited number of unofficial visits.	• You may make an unlimited number of unofficial visits.	• You may make an unlimited number of unofficial visits.
Evaluation and contacts	• Up to seven times during your senior year.	• Up to five times during your senior year.	• Up to six times during your senior year.	• Up to seven times during your senior year.
How often can a coach see me or talk to me off the college's campus?	• A college coach may contact you or your parents/legal guardians not more than three times during your senior year.	• A college coach may contact you or your parents/legal guardians not more than three times during your senior year.	• A college coach may contact you or your parents/legal guardians (including evaluating you off the college's campus), six times. • One evaluation during September, October and November.	• A college coach may contact you or your parents/legal guardians not more than three times during your senior year.

SOURCE: "Summary of Recruiting Rules for Each Sport—Division I," in *2007–08 Guide for the College-Bound Student-Athlete*, National Collegiate Athletic Association, 2007, http://www.ncaa.org/library/general/cbsa/2007–08/2007–08_cbsa.pdf (accessed July 30, 2007)

TABLE 6.19

High school students engaged in organized physical activity, by sex, race, and Hispanic origin, 2005

Characteristic	Total	Enrolled in physical education class		Played on a sports team	Watched three or more hours/ day of TV
		Attended daily	Exercised 20 minutes or more per class*		
All students	54.2	33.0	84.0	56.0	37.2
Male	60.0	37.1	87.2	61.8	38.0
Grade 9	72.8	46.5	86.3	64.7	42.4
Grade 10	65.4	39.0	88.0	63.4	42.7
Grade 11	51.1	33.5	87.5	61.0	34.1
Grade 12	45.9	26.1	87.3	57.3	30.3
Female	48.3	29.0	80.3	50.2	36.3
Grade 9	70.3	43.1	80.3	56.1	42.4
Grade 10	53.0	31.5	81.0	52.3	37.4
Grade 11	32.9	19.4	79.5	48.9	31.7
Grade 12	32.0	18.8	79.7	41.3	32.4
White, non-Hispanic	52.1	31.7	86.3	57.8	29.2
Male	58.1	36.7	89.3	61.5	30.2
Female	46.1	26.6	82.5	53.9	28.1
Black, non-Hispanic	55.8	34.4	78.7	53.7	64.1
Male	61.7	37.5	83.8	64.6	63.5
Female	50.5	31.6	73.1	43.6	64.5
Hispanic	61.5	38.3	81.6	53.0	45.8
Male	65.9	38.1	85.0	62.0	45.8
Female	57.1	38.6	77.5	43.8	45.8

*For students enrolled in physical education classes.

SOURCE: "Table 1231. High School Students Engaged in Organized Physical Activity by Sex, Race and Hispanic Origin: 2005," in "Youth Risk Behavior Surveillance—United States, 2005," *Morbidity and Mortality Weekly Report*, vol. 55, no. SS-1, June 9, 2006, http://www.census.gov/compendia/statab/tables/07s1231.xls (accessed July 30, 2007)

TABLE 6.20

Participation in high school athletic programs, by sex, 1971–72 to 2005–06

Year	Boys	Girls	Total
1971–72	3,666,917	294,015	3,960,932
1972–73	3,770,621	817,073	4,587,694
1973–74	4,070,125	1,300,169	5,370,294
1975–76	4,109,021	1,645,039	5,754,060
1977–78	4,367,442	2,083,040	6,450,482
1978–79	3,709,512	1,854,400	5,563,912
1979–80	3,517,829	1,750,264	5,268,093
1980–81	3,503,124	1,853,789	5,356,913
1981–82	3,409,081	1,810,671	5,219,752
1982–83	3,355,558	1,779,972	5,135,530
1983–84	3,303,599	1,747,346	5,050,945
1984–85	3,354,284	1,757,884	5,112,168
1985–86	3,344,275	1,807,121	5,151,396
1986–87	3,364,082	1,836,356	5,200,438
1987–88	3,425,777	1,849,684	5,275,461
1988–89	3,416,844	1,839,352	5,256,196
1989–90	3,398,192	1,858,659	5,256,851
1990–91	3,406,355	1,892,316	5,298,671
1991–92	3,429,853	1,940,801	5,370,654
1992–93	3,416,389	1,997,489	5,413,878
1993–94	3,472,967	2,130,315	5,603,282
1994–95	3,536,359	2,240,461	5,776,820
1995–96	3,634,052	2,367,936	6,001,988
1996–97	3,706,225	2,474,043	6,180,268
1997–98	3,763,120	2,570,333	6,333,453
1998–99	3,832,352	2,652,726	6,485,078
1999–00	3,861,749	2,675,874	6,537,623
2000–01	3,921,069	2,784,154	6,705,223
2001–02	3,960,517	2,806,998	6,767,515
2002–03	3,988,738	2,856,358	6,845,096
2003–04	4,038,253	2,865,299	6,903,552
2004–05	4,110,319	2,908,390	7,018,709
2005–06	4,206,549	2,953,355	7,159,904

SOURCE: "Athletic Participation Survey Totals," in *2005–06 High School Athletics Participation Survey*, National Federation of State High School Associations, 2006, http://www.nfhs.org/core/contentmanager/uploads/2005_06NFHSparticipationsurvey.pdf (accessed July 30, 2007)

TABLE 6.21

Most popular high school sports for boys, by number of schools and number of participants, 2005–06

Schools		Participants	
1. Basketball	17,535	1. Football–11-player	1,071,775
2. Track and field–outdoor	15,497	2. Basketball	546,335
3. Baseball	15,290	3. Track and field–outdoor	533,985
4. Football–11-player	13,727	4. Baseball	470,671
5. Golf	13,267	5. Soccer	358,935
6. Cross country	13,110	6. Wrestling	251,534
7. Soccer	10,580	7. Cross country	208,303
8. Wrestling	9,744	8. Golf	161,284
9. Tennis	9,706	9. Tennis	153,006
10. Swimming & diving	6,224	10. Swimming & diving	107,468

SOURCE: "Ten Most Popular Boys Programs," in *2005–06 High School Athletics Participation Survey*, National Federation of State High School Associations, 2006, http://www.nfhs.org/core/contentmanager/uploads/2005_06NFHSparticipationsurvey.pdf (accessed July 30, 2007)

TABLE 6.22

Most popular high school sports for girls, by number of schools and number of participants, 2005–06

Schools		Participants	
1. Basketball	17,275	1. Basketball	452,929
2. Track and field–outdoor	15,417	2. Track and field–outdoor	439,200
3. Softball–fast pitch	14,710	3. Volleyball	390,034
4. Volleyball	14,578	4. Softball–fast pitch	369,094
5. Cross country	12,989	5. Soccer	321,555
6. Soccer	9,970	6. Cross country	175,954
7. Tennis	9,816	7. Tennis	173,753
8. Golf	8,816	8. Swimming & diving	147,413
9. Swimming & diving	6,559	9. Competitive spirit squad	98,570
10. Competitive spirit squad	3,914	10. Golf	64,195

SOURCE: "Ten Most Popular Girls Programs," in *2005–06 High School Athletics Participation Survey*, National Federation of State High School Associations, 2006, http://www.nfhs.org/core/contentmanager/uploads/2005_06NFHSparticipationsurvey.pdf (accessed July 30, 2007)

TABLE 6.23

Participation in school athletics, 1991–2004

	1991	1992	1993	1994	1995	1996	1997	1998	1999	2000	2001	2002	2003	2004
Eighth grade	**69.6**	**67.3**	**66.6**	**66.5**	**68.1**	**67.4**	**66.7**	**68.7**	**67.7**	**67.3**	**69.1**	**67.2**	**65.3**	**65.7**
Gender														
Male	73.4	71.0	71.1	70.2	72.5	69.8	68.0	71.7	69.0	69.2	70.8	68.3	68.0	66.6
Female	66.2	64.0	62.7	63.2	64.3	65.6	65.5	65.8	66.6	65.8	67.5	66.1	62.9	64.9
Race														
White	71.1	68.7	70.0	69.8	69.5	70.7	70.1	71.2	70.0	70.2	72.6	71.9	67.5	68.0
Black	73.8	68.4	61.8	62.4	69.7	64.5	63.0	64.9	69.5	63.4	67.3	65.9	67.2	64.5
Parental education*														
Less than high school	54.3	47.7	49.9	51.0	50.5	53.4	52.3	53.0	55.0	47.5	53.3	55.5	51.3	48.8
Completed high school	66.1	63.7	62.5	63.9	64.8	64.2	61.5	63.0	63.3	64.3	64.1	63.0	64.4	58.1
Some college	73.3	67.6	69.7	69.5	73.8	69.4	70.5	70.2	69.6	69.8	69.1	66.8	65.0	67.0
Completed college	73.6	75.5	72.7	72.3	71.3	75.3	71.6	74.0	74.1	74.0	77.0	72.5	69.7	74.0
Graduate school	76.6	76.7	76.3	74.4	74.9	77.7	74.8	76.6	75.4	75.8	78.7	76.9	76.2	74.8
College plans														
None or under 4 years	49.9	46.9	47.9	51.0	51.3	50.5	50.2	49.4	46.8	46.8	46.5	49.0	41.4	45.7
Complete four years	72.7	70.4	69.0	68.7	70.3	70.0	68.9	70.9	70.2	69.5	71.6	68.7	67.8	67.9
Tenth grade	**60.2**	**62.9**	**62.0**	**61.8**	**62.6**	**61.5**	**61.7**	**61.6**	**62.2**	**61.5**	**62.9**	**61.1**	**60.2**	**61.1**
Gender														
Male	68.7	69.8	68.0	69.2	68.2	65.5	66.0	67.8	68.1	65.5	66.3	64.3	63.4	65.5
Female	51.9	56.6	56.5	54.9	57.5	57.7	57.5	56.1	57.4	58.3	60.0	57.8	57.0	57.2
Race														
White	61.8	64.6	64.1	64.0	63.6	63.5	63.3	63.6	65.4	63.8	65.2	62.8	62.8	64.3
Black	55.7	62.8	59.9	57.2	62.3	56.5	62.5	58.8	57.2	55.7	60.9	64.8	58.5	57.0
Parental education*														
Less than high school	44.5	40.1	42.5	42.7	40.9	42.7	44.2	46.7	44.0	45.9	48.3	40.2	44.0	42.0
Completed high school	54.4	56.8	58.2	53.2	54.3	53.7	56.3	53.6	54.0	51.7	56.5	54.7	50.9	54.2
Some college	59.8	63.6	62.9	62.0	62.6	62.4	60.5	64.7	65.2	61.4	63.0	60.9	61.8	60.8
Completed college	67.2	72.6	67.3	70.3	71.8	68.3	68.8	68.1	70.0	69.9	68.9	70.6	66.4	67.7
Graduate school	70.9	74.6	75.1	74.0	74.9	73.5	72.7	72.9	71.9	75.9	75.5	72.0	74.4	73.0
College plans														
None or under 4 years	38.9	42.7	41.3	39.9	39.9	40.3	42.0	45.5	39.0	39.4	41.1	37.5	40.6	38.6
Complete four years	64.6	66.9	66.0	66.5	66.2	65.1	64.8	64.4	66.0	65.0	66.4	64.9	63.1	64.0

TABLE 6.23

Participation in school athletics, 1991–2004 [CONTINUED]

	1991	1992	1993	1994	1995	1996	1997	1998	1999	2000	2001	2002	2003	2004
Twelfth grade	56.2	55.6	55.7	56.3	55.1	55.1	55.5	55.9	54.3	55.0	55.0	54.0	53.3	54.8
Gender														
Male	64.9	63.8	65.5	66.1	62.4	62.7	63.4	63.0	62.3	64.2	61.9	60.2	58.9	59.5
Female	47.0	48.0	46.2	47.5	48.1	48.0	48.4	48.7	47.3	46.9	48.6	48.7	48.0	51.3
Race														
White	57.0	57.3	56.7	57.7	54.9	56.8	56.3	57.7	56.5	57.4	57.5	56.3	55.4	56.5
Black	56.2	50.9	52.9	59.7	56.7	53.1	52.9	54.1	50.1	55.4	57.9	48.4	50.5	53.2
Parental education*														
Less than high school	41.3	46.7	44.4	41.7	38.7	35.3	37.2	41.3	43.5	33.2	38.0	39.7	42.6	41.9
Completed high school	50.3	49.1	52.8	51.2	48.4	50.1	50.2	52.5	49.5	53.5	50.1	47.0	49.1	48.5
Some college	60.3	54.9	55.8	57.1	53.2	54.3	55.5	57.4	54.6	56.8	56.1	53.3	51.5	55.0
Completed college	61.7	63.8	60.8	61.8	62.2	62.1	60.6	59.1	57.3	58.6	62.1	62.1	57.8	60.8
Graduate school	66.4	67.5	66.4	68.4	68.0	64.6	66.7	66.2	65.8	63.0	63.5	62.6	66.7	63.8
College plans														
None or under 4 years	42.6	41.0	40.0	44.0	41.2	41.6	39.8	42.2	43.3	42.0	40.7	41.6	40.9	40.2
Complete four years	61.5	60.7	60.4	60.0	58.8	59.0	60.3	59.9	57.8	58.4	58.8	57.7	56.2	58.8

*Parental education is calculated by the Institute of Social Research as the average of the mother's and father's education. Child Trends has relabeled these results to reflect the education level of the most educated parent. In those circumstances where the gap between mothers' and fathers' education is more than one level, this results in an underestimate of the most educated parent's education level.

SOURCE: "Table 1. Participation in School Athletics, 1991–2004," in *Participation in School Athletics*, Child Trends, November 2006, http://www.childtrendsdatabank.org/pdf/37_PDF.pdf (accessed July 30, 2007)

FIGURE 6.7

Percentage of students who participated in school athletics, by gender, 1991 and 2004

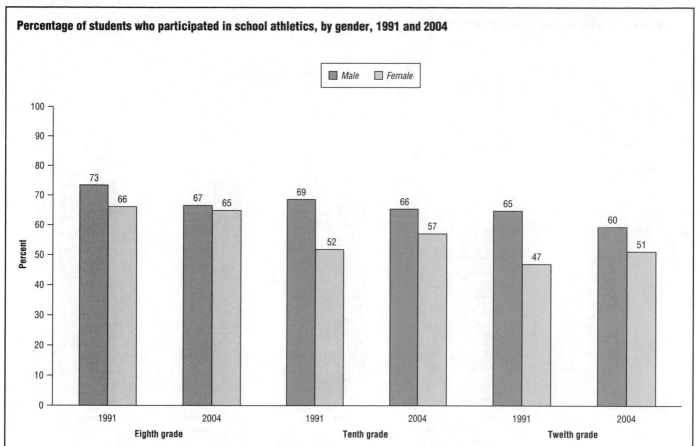

Note: Participation in school athletics includes all students who have participated to any degree in school athletic teams during the current school year.

SOURCE: "Figure 1. Percentage of Students in Grades 8, 10, and 12 Who Participate in School Athletics, by Gender, 1991 and 2004," in *Participation in School Athletics*, Child Trends, November 2006, http://www.childtrendsdatabank.org/pdf/37_PDF.pdf (accessed July 30, 2007)

FIGURE 6.8

Percentage of students who participated in school athletics, by parents' education, 2004

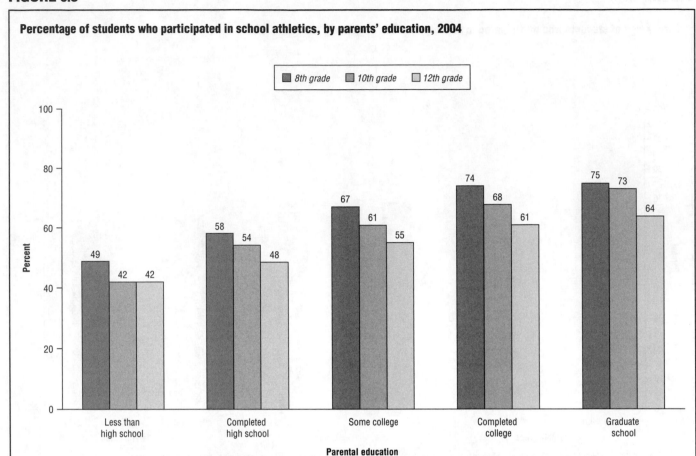

Notes: Participation in school athletics includes all students who have participated to any degree in school athletic teams during the current school year. Parental education is calculated by the Institute of Social Research as the average of the mother's and father's education. Child Trends has relabeled these results to reflect the education level of the most educated parent. In those circumstances where the gap between mother's and father's education is more than one level, this results in an underestimate of the most educated parent's education level.

SOURCE: "Figure 2. Percentage of Students in Grades 8, 10 and 12 Who Participate in School Athletics, by Parents' Education, 2004," in *Participation in School Athletics*, Child Trends, November 2006, http://www.childtrendsdatabank.org/pdf/37_PDF.pdf (accessed July 30, 2007)

CHAPTER 7
THE OLYMPICS

If professional team sports in the United States epitomize the corporatization of athletics, the Olympics, at least in theory, exemplify the opposite: global goodwill and celebration that surround the pursuit of athletic excellence for its own sake. This does not, however, diminish the fact that vast sums of money change hands via the Olympics. Nor does it prevent the pursuit of these vast sums, or political grandstanding, from sometimes overshadowing the Olympic ideal.

The XXVIII Olympiad took place over seventeen days in August 2004. These Summer Olympics were held in Athens, Greece, the birthplace of Olympic athletic events. According to the International Olympic Committee (IOC), in "Olympic Games" (2007, http://www.olympic.org/uk/games/index_uk.asp), 10,625 athletes representing 201 countries competed in 28 sports. Medals were awarded in 301 separate events. The 2008 summer games will take place in Beijing, China. These games will feature 302 medal events, one more than in the 2004 Athens games. Table 1.5 in Chapter 1 shows the list of Olympic sports as of the 2004 summer games and the 2006 winter games.

The winter games are much smaller than the summer games. For example, at the 2006 winter games in Turin, Italy, the IOC (2007, http://www.olympic.org/uk/games/past/index_uk.asp?OLGT=2&OLGY=2006) reports that there were 2,508 athletes from 80 countries. They competed in eighty-four total events in seven sports.

The IOC regularly reviews which sports are to be included in the Olympic games. A number of factors are taken into consideration, most prominently popularity and cost. For example, beach volleyball made its Olympic debut in 1996. Snowboarding was added to the winter games program in 1998. The IOC has also decided to eliminate baseball and softball as of 2012. The Olympic Charter limits the number of sports that can take place at the Olympics; therefore, sports must be cut to accommodate the addition of new ones. In "Olympic Sports of the Past" (2007, http://www.olympic.org/uk/sports/past/index_uk.asp), the IOC notes that sports have come and gone from the lineup over the decades, including tug-of-war (1900–20), golf (1900–04), rugby (1900, 1908, and 1920–24), and polo (1900, 1908, 1920–24, and 1936). For the 2008 summer games, women's boxing was eliminated, whereas open-water swimming and women's steeplechase were added.

Before the 1996 games the Olympics sometimes included demonstration sports, the purpose of which was to showcase an emerging or locally popular sport before a global audience. Winners in these sports were not officially recognized as Olympic champions. Some of these sports, such as flat-water canoeing and kayaking, were later added as regular Olympic events at subsequent games. Winter sports that have been demonstrated include speed skiing, curling, and freestyle aerial skiing.

HISTORY OF THE OLYMPICS

In "The Ancient Olympic Games, 776 B.C.–393 A.D." (2007, http://www.olympic.org/uk/games/ancient/index_uk.asp), the IOC explains that the roots of the Olympic games are in ancient Greece. Exactly when the ancient Olympics started is unknown, but the first recorded games took place in the city of Olympia in 776 BC. The games grew in importance over the next few centuries, reaching their peak in the fifth and sixth centuries BC. By that time, they had grown from a single event—a two-hundred-yard foot race called the stadion—to twenty events spread over several days. Like today, the Greek Olympic games were held every four years.

As the Roman Empire rose to power in the region and subsequently adopted Christianity as its official religion, the Olympic games declined in stature. The games, which had always been a religious as much as an athletic celebration, were eventually outlawed in AD 393 by the emperor Theodosius (c. 346–395).

TABLE 7.1

Summer Olympic games sites

1896–Athens, Greece
1900–Paris, France
1904–St. Louis, United States
1908–London, United Kingdom
1912–Stockholm, Sweden
1920–Antwerp, Belgium
1924–Paris, France
1928–Amsterdam, Netherlands
1932–Los Angeles, United States
1936–Berlin, Germany
1948–London, United Kingdom
1952–Helsinki, Finland
1956–Melbourne, Australia
1960–Rome, Italy
1964–Tokyo, Japan
1968–Mexico City, Mexico
1972–Munich, West Germany
1976–Montreal, Canada
1980–Moscow, U.S.S.R.
1984–Los Angeles, United States
1988–Seoul, South Korea
1992–Barcelona, Spain
1996–Atlanta, United States
2000–Sydney, Australia
2004–Athens, Greece
2008–Beijing, China
2012–London, United Kingdom

SOURCE: Created by Robert Jacobson for The Gale Group, 2007

TABLE 7.2

Winter Olympic games sites

1924–Chamonix, France
1928–St. Moritz, Switzerland
1932–Lake Placid, N.Y., United States
1936–Garmisch-Partenkirchen, Germany
1948–St. Moritz, Switzerland
1952–Oslo, Norway
1956–Cortina d'Ampezzo, Italy
1960–Squaw Valley, California, United States
1964–Innsbruck, Austria
1968–Grenoble, France
1972–Sapporo, Japan
1976–Innsbruck, Austria
1980–Lake Placid, New York, United States
1984–Sarajevo, Yugoslavia (now Bosnia and Herzegovina)
1988–Calgary, Alberta, Canada
1992–Albertville, France
1994–Lillehammer, Norway
1998–Nagano, Japan
2002–Salt Lake City, Utah, United States
2006–Torino (Turin), Italy
2010–Vancouver, Canada
2014–Sochi, Russia

SOURCE: Created by Robert Jacobson for The Gale Group, 2007

Interest in the Olympics was revived in the mid-nineteenth century, when modern archaeologists began to unearth the ruins of ancient Olympia. In 1890 the French historian and educator Pierre de Coubertin (1862–1937) developed the idea of holding an international competition of young athletes as a way to promote peace and cooperation among nations. He presented his ideas at the Sorbonne University in Paris in 1894, and two years later the first modern Olympic games were held in Athens, Greece.

The IOC states in "Olympic Games" that the inaugural Olympic games of 1896 featured 241 athletes from 14 countries competing in 43 events—the largest international sporting event ever held up to that time. The event was repeated in Paris in 1900 and again in St. Louis, Missouri, in 1904. (See Table 7.1.)

Winter Olympics History

By 1908, movement toward establishing a winter version of the Olympics had begun. That year, figure skating was introduced during the summer games in London. A cluster of winter events was scheduled to be added for 1916, but the games were canceled because of the outbreak of World War I (1914–1918). When the Olympics resumed in 1920, they included figure skating and ice hockey as medal events. In "Olympic Games," the IOC indicates that over the objections of Coubertin and the organizers of an Olympic-style Scandinavian winter competition that had been held periodically since

1901, the committee approved an eleven-day International Winter Sports Week that featured Nordic skiing, speed skating, figure skating, hockey, and bobsledding in Chamonix, France, in 1924. These games were a success and were retroactively dubbed the first Winter Olympics by the IOC in 1926. The winter games took place during regular Olympic years until 1992. Beginning with the 1994 games in Lillehammer, Norway, the winter games have been held every four years, alternating with the summer games. Table 7.2 shows the sites at which all the Winter Olympics have been held.

Politics and the Olympics

Coubertin's dream of a world made more peaceful through sport did not materialize. Moreover, wars and other political complications crippled the Olympic movement at several points during the twentieth century. The 1916 games were a casualty of World War I, and World War II (1939–1945) claimed the 1940 and 1944 Olympics.

Twice the Olympics have been the scene of violent acts of terrorism. In "When the Terror Began" (*Sports Illustrated*, August 26, 2002), Alexander Wolff states that at the 1972 summer games in Munich, West Germany, Palestinian terrorists took eleven members of the Israeli team hostage. An attempt to rescue the hostages was bungled, and as a result all eleven hostages, five terrorists, and a police officer died.

Shaila Dewan reports in "Bomber Offers Guilty Pleas, and Defiance" (*New York Times*, April 14, 2005) that two people were killed and 150 injured when a bomb exploded on a crowded Centennial Olympic Park at the 1996 summer games in Atlanta, Georgia. The perpetrator,

Eric Robert Rudolph (1966–)—a member of a radical Christian group violently opposed to abortion and homosexuality—was not arrested until 2003. In 2005 he pleaded guilty and was sentenced to four consecutive life sentences without parole.

BOYCOTTS. Even when the Olympics have taken place on schedule, they have sometimes been used to make political statements. Boycotts have been a frequent occurrence. The IOC notes in "Olympic Games" that the 1956 games in Melbourne, Australia, were the scene of two different boycotts: by the Netherlands, Spain, and Switzerland in response to the Soviet Union's brutal handling of that year's Hungarian uprising; and by Egypt, Lebanon, and Iraq in protest of British and French involvement in the Suez crisis in the Middle East. Several African nations threatened to boycott the Olympics in 1968, 1972, and 1976, in protest of South African and Rhodesian racial policies. The IOC bowed to this pressure and banned South Africa and Rhodesia from participating in the 1968 and 1972 Olympics. In 1980 and 1984 the two major cold war powers traded boycotts. The United States and sixty-four other Western nations stayed home from the 1980 Olympics in Moscow in protest of the Soviet invasion of Afghanistan. Four years later the Soviet Union and fourteen of its allied nations retaliated by boycotting the Los Angeles games of 1984, on the grounds that the American hosts could not guarantee their safety. In 1988 North Korea boycotted the Olympics in South Korea, arguing that the two countries should have been named co-hosts.

SCANDAL. Christopher Clarey reports in "Despite Disputes, Games Still Glow as the Flame Dies Out" (*International Herald Tribune*, February 27, 2002) that in 1998 information was uncovered revealing that several members of the IOC had accepted gifts from the 2002 Salt Lake City Winter Olympics organizing committee in exchange for their site selection votes. Ten IOC members were forced off of the committee as a result, and in the aftermath of the scandal changes were made in the process for selecting host cities. Questions remain whether the reforms have really eliminated the possibility of bribery in the Olympic site selection process. An August 2004 BBC documentary, *Panorama: Buying the Games* (http://news.bbc.co.uk/1/hi/programmes/panorama/3937425.stm), used hidden cameras and journalists posing as agents interested in securing the games for London to reveal that the IOC was still ripe for corruption.

STRUCTURE OF THE OLYMPIC MOVEMENT

The Olympics are run by a complex array of organizations known primarily by their initials. At the center of the structure is the IOC, based in Lausanne, Switzerland. The IOC (2007, http://www.olympic.org/uk/organisation/ioc/organisation/index_uk.asp) is the "supreme authority of the Olympic Movement." Its role is to "promote top-level sport as well as sport for all in accordance with the Olympic Charter. It ensures the regular celebration of the Olympic games and strongly encourages, by appropriate means, the promotion of women in sport, that of sports ethics and the protection of athletes."

According to the IOC (2007, http://www.olympic.org/uk/organisation/if/index_uk.asp), the next layer of Olympic oversight, the International Federations (IFs), coordinates international competition within a particular sport. Track and field, for example, is governed by the International Amateur Athletics Federation. In 2007 there were twenty-eight IFs involved in the summer games and another seven that presided over sports in the winter games. These federations make all the rules that pertain to their sport and run the world championships and other international competitions within their realm. Each country that competes in a sport at the international level has a national governing body (NGB), which coordinates the sport domestically.

International Olympic Committee

The IOC (2007, http://www.olympic.org/uk/organisation/ioc/index_uk.asp) was created by the International Athletic Congress of Paris on June 23, 1894, convened by Coubertin, who is generally considered the father of the modern Olympic movement. The original committee in 1894 consisted of fourteen members plus Coubertin. Coubertin remained at the helm of the IOC through the 1924 Olympics. The IOC was charged with the control and development of the modern Olympic games. Membership in the IOC is limited to one member from most countries, and two members from the largest and most active member countries, or countries that have hosted the Olympics. Members must speak French or English and be citizens and residents of a country with a recognized national Olympic committee (NOC).

The IOC runs the Olympic movement according to the terms of the Olympic Charter (September 1, 2004, http://multimedia.olympic.org/pdf/en_report_122.pdf). The charter outlines the six Fundamental Principles of Olympism. These principles, as written in the charter, are:

1. Olympism is a philosophy of life, exalting and combining in a balanced whole the qualities of body, will and mind. Blending sport with culture and education, Olympism seeks to create a way of life based on the joy of effort, the educational value of good example and respect for universal fundamental ethical principles.

2. The goal of Olympism is to place sport at the service of the harmonious development of man, with a view to promoting a peaceful society concerned with the preservation of human dignity.

3. The Olympic Movement is the concerted, organised, universal and permanent action, carried out under the supreme authority of the IOC, of all individuals and entities who are inspired by the values of Olympism. It covers the five continents. It reaches its peak with the bringing together of the world's athletes at the great sports festival, the Olympic Games. Its symbol is five interlaced rings.

4. The practice of sport is a human right. Every individual must have the possibility of practising sport, without discrimination of any kind and in the Olympic spirit, which requires mutual understanding with a spirit of friendship, solidarity and fair play. The organisation, administration and management of sport must be controlled by independent sports organizations.

5. Any form of discrimination with regard to a country or a person on grounds of race, religion, politics, gender or otherwise is incompatible with belonging to the Olympic Movement.

6. Belonging to the Olympic Movement requires compliance with the Olympic Charter and recognition by the IOC.

The IOC has a maximum of 115 members, who meet at least once per year. During this session the committee elects a president for a term of eight years (renewable for another four), and an executive board, whose members serve for four years. The IOC (2007, http://www.olympic.org/uk/organisation/commissions/index_uk.asp) is administered by a director general, with the assistance of the directors of the IOC's various units, which include International Relations; Coordination Commissions for the Olympic Games; Finance; Marketing; Juridical; Radio and Television; and Medical.

U.S. Olympic Committee

In the United States, building a team to represent the nation at the Olympics is the responsibility of the U.S. Olympic Committee (USOC). Julia Cantone indicates in "General Olympic FAQ" (October 7, 2003, http://www.usolympicteam.com/19116_18922.htm) that the USOC comprises seventy-two member organizations. Thirty-nine of them are NGBs—such as USA Gymnastics and USA Track and Field—each of which supports a particular sport. Other USOC members include community- and education-based multisport organizations, U.S. Armed Forces sports, and organizations involved in sports for people with disabilities. Besides the Olympics, the USOC is the driving force for U.S. sports that are part of the Pan American Games program. The Pan American Games are an international goodwill sports competition featuring athletes from the Americas; they take place every four years in the year preceding the Olympics. In the United States the NGBs are responsible for selecting the athletes who will represent their country in their sport at the Olympics. In most events this is done at national competitions called Olympic Trials.

Besides its role in developing the U.S. Olympic team, the USOC is instrumental in U.S. cities' bids to host the Winter or Summer Olympics or the Pan American Games. The USOC may vote on and endorse a particular city's bid to serve as host. All U.S. Olympic Trial site selections also go through the USOC. According to *The Business of Sports* (2004), edited by Scott R. Rosner and Kenneth L. Shropshire, the USOC gets much of its funding from the IOC; in fact, 25% of the IOC's broadcast revenue ends up with the USOC. Of the money the National Broadcasting Corporation (NBC) will have spent for televising the Olympics between 2000 and 2008, the USOC will bank $418 million. The *Business of Sports* notes that the USOC also receives a large share of what the IOC takes in from corporate sponsorships—more than the other 198 NOCs combined. Besides these sources, the USOC also earns nearly $200 million per year through its own domestic sponsorships, licensing fees, and other joint ventures.

In "The Olympic Family" (1997, http://www.usa-gymnastics.org/organization/olympic-family.html), USA Gymnastics explains that the USOC was created as a small, informal organization in 1896 by James E. Sullivan (1860–1914), the founder of the Amateur Athletic Union. The first elected president of the USOC was Albert G. Spalding (1850–1915), a well-known sporting goods manufacturer. The committee became a formal entity, called the American Olympic Association, in 1921. The name was changed twice in the 1940s—to the United States of America Sports Federation in 1940 and to the U.S. Olympic Association (USOA) in 1945. The USOA received its federal charter as a private nonprofit corporation in 1950. The USOC took its current name in 1961.

In 1978 the USOC acquired its status as the legal coordinating body for the Olympic and Pan American Games through the passage of the Amateur Sports Act. The act also recognized the authority of the NGBs to oversee development within their own sports. In addition, the act mandated that 20% of membership and voting power within both the USOC and the sport-specific agencies be held by "recent or active" athletes. That year, the USOC moved its headquarters from New York City to Colorado Springs, Colorado.

As of 2007 the USOC operated three training centers, located in Colorado Springs; Lake Placid, New York; and Chula Vista, California. The USOC also maintains an Olympic Education Center in Marquette, Michigan, where athletes can pursue an academic degree without interrupting their training.

The *Business of Sports* indicates that the USOC has struggled financially in recent years, its nonprofit status notwithstanding. Its administrative costs and overhead are high, and it provides more than $80 million per year in monetary support to American athletes and NGBs. In addition, unlike most NOCs around the world, the USOC does not receive direct financial support from the government.

THE FLOW OF OLYMPIC MONEY

All the symbols, images, phrases, and other intellectual property associated with the Olympics belong to the IOC. In *2006 Marketing Fact File* (July 15, 2005, http://multimedia.olympic.org/pdf/en_report_344.pdf), the IOC explains that the Olympic movement generates marketing revenue through five major channels: broadcasting, the Olympic Partners worldwide sponsorship program, domestic sponsorships, ticketing, and licensing. The IOC manages the first two; the others are managed by the Organizing Committees for the Olympic Games (OCOGs) within the host country, under the IOC's direction. The IOC indicates that the total marketing revenue for the 2001–04 quadrennium was nearly $4.2 billion, up from $3.8 billion in the previous four-year period and $2.6 billion in 1993–96. The IOC reports in *Marketing Report: Torino 2006* (March 29, 2007, http://www.olympic.org/uk/utilities/reports/level2_uk.asp?HEAD2=176&HEAD1=8) that the 2006 Winter Olympics in Turin generated another $833 million in broadcasting revenue alone, and well over $100 million more in ticket and licensing revenue.

As with the major professional sports in the United States, the biggest financial driver of the Olympics is television, with a startling growth in revenue generated through television broadcasts of the Olympics. The IOC states in the *Marketing Fact File* that for the Olympic cycle running from 2001 to 2004, worldwide broadcast rights netted the IOC $2.2 billion, about half of its total revenue. About three-quarters of the total came from the United States, specifically from NBC, which paid $793.5 million to broadcast the 2004 Athens Olympics. European networks contributed another 18%. The rest of the world contributed the remainder. These proportions are not likely to change for the next several years; Richard Sandomir reports in "Ebersol Proud as a Peacock over NBC and the Games" (*New York Times*, July 6, 2005) that as of 2005 NBC had a $4.5 billion deal to broadcast the Olympics in the United States through the 2012 games. Broadcast revenue in the previous quadrennium was $1.8 billion, and the 1993–96 total was $1.3 billion.

The *Marketing Fact File* reports that 49% of the broadcast rights fees for each Olympics is distributed to the OCOGs responsible for that particular Olympics. The OCOGs consist of top officials from the NOC of the host nation and other key representatives of the host city and country. The other half of the broadcast revenue goes to the Olympic movement. NBC (2007, http://www.nbcunicom/About_NBC_Universal/Company_Overview/overview02.shtml) reports that 203 million viewers watched at least some part of its broadcast of the 2004 Summer Olympics, a new record for Olympic viewing. According to the *Marketing Fact File*, the 2004 summer games were watched for a total of 34.4 billion viewer hours, down slightly from the 36.1 billion during the 2000 summer games. The *Marketing Report: Torino 2006* states that the total viewer hours for the 2006 winter games were 10.6 billion.

A second key revenue source is the IOC's corporate sponsorship program, known officially as the Olympic Partners (TOP) program. The IOC (2007, http://www.olympic.org/uk/organisation/facts/programme/sponsors_uk.asp) notes that the TOP program consists of twelve international corporations, which in return for their money are ensured exclusive sponsorship in their business category. For example, as long as Coca-Cola remains a TOP sponsor, Pepsi will not be one. As with broadcast rights, the United States dominates the TOP program; seven of the TOP sponsors are U.S. based. The *Business of Sports* notes that sponsorships accounted for about 40% of the IOC's revenues from 2001 to 2004. According to the *Marketing Fact File*, the TOP program brought in $663 million during the 2001–04 quadrennium. For the 2006 Winter Olympics, the *Marketing Report: Torino 2006* states that the sponsorship revenue totaled 269.8 million euros ($372 million at the August 2007 exchange rate).

The *Marketing Fact File* indicates that the IOC received another $411 million, representing 10% of its total revenue, from ticket sales to the events and opening and closing ceremonies of the Olympics during the 2001–04 quadrennial. The other major revenue source, the sale of licensed merchandise bearing Olympic logos and other trademarks, including Olympic coins and stamps, generated the remaining 2% of the IOC's revenue, or about $87 million. According to the *Marketing Report: Torino 2006*, ticket sales for the 2006 winter games generated 66 million euros ($91 million), and another 16.7 million euros ($23 million) in licensing revenue.

About 92% of IOC revenue is subsequently distributed to the other organizations that collectively make up the Olympic movement, including: OCOGs, which, as noted earlier, are the committees formed to run the Olympics within the country that has been selected to host the games; NOCs, whose main role within each of the 199 countries in the Olympic family is to field their country's Olympic team; and IFs, which coordinate and monitor international competition within their specific sport or family of sports. The IOC retains only about 8% of its overall revenue. These funds are used to cover the organization's operating and administrative costs.

According to the *2006 Marketing Fact File*, the summer and winter OCOGs for each four-year period share about half of the TOP program revenue and in-kind contributions. Before 2004 the IOC contributed 60% of broadcast revenue for each Olympic games to the OCOGs; since 2004 it has contributed 40%.

In contrast to the IOC, IFs, NOCs, and NGBs, the OCOGs are temporary agencies. They disband once the games they were created to organize are over. The OCOGs are highly dependent on the IOC for their funding, receiving a substantial share of the IOC's revenue from sponsorships and broadcasting. OCOGs also generate revenue of their own through sponsorship, ticket sales, and licensing of merchandise. In the fact sheet "Revenue Generation and Distribution" (December 2005, http://multimedia.olympic.org/pdf/en_report_845.pdf), the IOC explains that even though the IOC turns over most of its revenue to other organizations, the OCOGs give only 5% of the revenue they generate to the IOC and retain the other 95%, most of which is spent on facility rentals and the construction and removal of temporary facilities.

The vast commercial activity that fuels the Olympic flame would seem to conflict with the philosophical groundings of the Olympic movement, which value the noble spirit of competition above financial matters. The Olympic Charter acknowledges this apparent contradiction, and the IOC has implemented policies designed to address it. No advertising is allowed in the venues where events take place, or on the uniforms of athletes, coaches, or officials. The TOP program is designed to generate the maximum amount of support with a minimum number of corporate sponsors, and images of Olympic events are not allowed to be used for commercial purposes.

SELECTION OF OLYMPIC SITES

One of the IOC's (2007, http://www.olympic.org/uk/organisation/missions/cities_uk.asp) chief responsibilities is to select the cities that will host the Olympics. Olympic site selection is a two-phase procedure. The first phase is called Applicant Cities. Applicant cities must be proposed to the IOC by their NOC. They must then complete a questionnaire that outlines how they plan to carry out the monumental task of hosting the games. The IOC assesses the applications with regard to the cities' ability to organize the games. Criteria include technical capacity, government support, public opinion, general infrastructure, security, venues, accommodations, and transportation. The IOC then accepts a handful of these applicants for the next phase, called Candidate Cities.

In the second phase, candidate cities must provide the IOC with a candidature file. These files are analyzed by the IOC Evaluation Commission, which consists of IOC members, representatives of the IFs, NOCs, the IOC Athletes' Commission, the International Paralympics Committee, and other experts. The Evaluation Commission also physically inspects the candidate cities. It then issues a report, on whose basis the IOC Executive Board prepares a list of final candidates. This list is submitted to the IOC session for a vote.

OLYMPIC ATHLETES: PROFESSIONALS OR AMATEURS?

Early on, the Olympics were considered an arena for strictly amateur competition. Professional athletes were not allowed to participate. This led to a number of controversies and disqualifications over the years, the most famous being the disqualification of the 1912 Olympic pentathlon and decathlon champion Jim Thorpe (1888–1953), who was stripped of his gold medals when it was discovered that he had played semiprofessional baseball.

Eventually, the rigid rules regarding professionalism became less practical. Many countries were supporting their athletes financially, allowing them to train full time and making a mockery of their "amateur" status. This put athletes in other countries at a competitive disadvantage. The regulations prohibiting professional athletes from participating in the Olympics were relaxed in the 1980s and eliminated entirely in the 1990s. This change allowed, for example, the development of the U.S. basketball "Dream Team," featuring a number of top National Basketball Association players, and the participation of National Hockey League players on Winter Olympics hockey teams.

DOPING

Almost from the beginning, the use of performance-enhancing substances, known as doping, has plagued the Olympics. An early example was Thomas J. Hicks, winner of the 1904 marathon, who was given strychnine and brandy. Doping methods improved over time, sometimes with disastrous results. The Danish cyclist Knut Jensen died after falling from his bicycle during the 1960 games. He was found to have taken amphetamines. The international sports federations and the IOC banned doping in the 1960s, but for most of the time since then officials have lacked the tools to adequately police the use of illicit substances. Until recently, the highest-profile Olympic athlete to be disqualified for doping was the Canadian sprinter Ben Johnson (1961–), winner of the one-hundred-meter race in 1988. A few years later, it was revealed that East German sports officials had doped female athletes for years without the IOC's knowledge. As the problem of doping grew out of control in the

1990s, the international sports community responded by forming the World Anti-Doping Agency (WADA) in 1999. WADA oversees the monitoring and enforcing of doping regulations at the Olympics.

WADA's creation did not, however, solve the problem entirely. Athletes in every Olympic games since its formation have been found to be in violation of anti-doping rules. In "Doping Cases Hit Record" (*USA Today*, August 29, 2004), Tom Weir reports that twenty-four athletes were ousted from the Athens Olympics for drug-related violations. The list included no American athletes. The last U.S. competitors to test positive for banned substances at the Olympics were the shot putter Bonnie Dasse and the hammer thrower Jud Logan, both in 1992. Since then, however, several Americans who appeared headed for the Olympics have been barred, or have come under a cloud of suspicion. In the wake of the BALCO scandal (see Chapter 9 for more information), the sprinter Kelli White received a two-year ban that kept her out of the 2004 Olympics. The sprinter Tim Montgomery (1975–), also implicated in the BALCO affair, failed to qualify for the 2004 games, but in 2005 he received a two-year ban from competing and was stripped of a number of his past medals and results, including a former world-record performance in the one-hundred-meter dash. Perhaps the highest-profile Olympic athlete embroiled in BALCO was the sprinter Marion Jones (1975–). Jones, however, proclaimed her innocence throughout the investigation. In "Doping Test Criticized, Defended after Jones Cleared" (*USA Today*, September 8, 2006), Dick Patrick notes that she was finally cleared of the charges in 2006, after the results of further testing turned up negative. However, the article "Marion Jones Running out of Money" (*Boston Globe*, June 25, 2007) reports that the ordeal cost Jones hundreds of thousands of dollars in endorsements and appearance fees, and thousands more in legal expenses, bringing her to the brink of financial ruin. In October 2007 Jones admitted to having used illegal performance-enhancing drugs during the 2000 Olympics in Sydney, Australia, in which she won three gold medals and two bronze. Facing pressure from the U.S. Olympic Committee, she surrendered her Olympic medals and was retroactively disqualified from all events dating back to September 1, 2000.

OTHER OLYMPIC GAMES

Special Olympics

Special Olympics is a global nonprofit organization that provides opportunities for athletic training and competition for people with developmental disabilities. According to the Special Olympics, in "From Backyard Camp to Global Movement: The Beginnings of Special Olympics" (2007, http://www.specialolympics.org/Special+Olympics+Public +Website/English/About_Us/History/default.htm), the organization serves more than 2.5 million athletes in at least 165 countries. Participants may train or compete in any of thirty Olympic-style summer and winter sports.

The Special Olympics movement began in the summer of 1968, when the First International Special Olympics were held at Soldier Field in Chicago, Illinois, home of the National Football Leagues's Chicago Bears. The roots of the Special Olympics go back to 1962, when Eunice Mary Kennedy Shriver (1920–), the sister of President John F. Kennedy (1917–1963), started a day camp for developmentally disabled children. In June of that year Shriver invited thirty-five boys and girls to Camp Shriver at Timberlawn, her home in Rockville, Maryland. Her idea was that children who were cognitively impaired were capable of accomplishing much more than was generally believed at the time, if they were given opportunities to do so. Building on Camp Shriver, Shriver began to actively promote the notion of involving people with disabilities in physical activities and competition. Through the Kennedy Foundation, she targeted grants to universities, community centers, and recreation departments that created such opportunities. The foundation helped fund eleven camps similar to Camp Shriver across the country in 1963. By 1969 thirty-two camps serving ten thousand children were being supported by the foundation.

In 1967 the Kennedy Foundation worked with the Chicago Park District to organize a citywide track meet for mentally disabled people that was modeled on the Olympics. The first Special Olympics at Soldier Field attracted one thousand athletes from twenty-six states and Canada, who competed in track and field, floor hockey, and aquatics.

In "World Games: List of Special Olympics World Games" (2007, http://www.specialolympics.org/Special +Olympics+Public+Website/English/Compete/World _Games/List+of+World+Games.htm), the Special Olympics states that by the Fourth International Special Olympics Summer Games, which took place at Central Michigan University in August 1975, the number of participants had more than tripled to thirty-two hundred, representing ten countries. The games were broadcast to a nationwide audience on the television show *CBS Sports Spectacular*. The Special Olympics Winter Games were launched two years later, with about five hundred athletes competing in skating and skiing events at Steamboat Springs, Colorado. The Tenth Special Olympics World Summer Games, held from June to July 1999 in Raleigh-Durham and Chapel Hill, North Carolina, attracted 7,000 athletes from 150 countries. The games featured nineteen sports by this time. In the press release "The 2007 Special Olympics World Summer Games Set to Take Place in Shanghai, China" (September 21, 2007, http://www.specialolympics.org/), the Special Olympics notes that the 2007 Special Olympics World Summer Games in Shanghai, China (October 2–11, 2007), was expected to serve nearly 7,500 athletes from 165 countries. The Special Olympics World Winter Games will take place in February 2009 in Boise, Idaho.

In "Celebrating Growth: Adding It Up" (2007, http://www.specialolympics.org/Special+Olympics+Public+Website/English/About_Us/Campaign_Celebration/Adding+It+Up.htm), Andrei Chursov of the Special Olympics reports that by December 2005 nearly 2.3 million Special Olympics athletes actively participated in training sessions and athletic competitions across the world. This represented a 129 percent growth rate between 2000 and 2005. For the last few years, the fastest growth in Special Olympics participation has taken place in Africa, East Asia, the Asian Pacific, and the Middle East.

In 1988 the IOC formally recognized the Special Olympics, signing an agreement proclaiming its support. The Special Olympics also has a formal relationship with the USOC and has been designated as the National Governing Body/Disabled Sports Organization for athletes with intellectual disabilities. The Special Olympics has other relationships, some of them formal, others less so, with the NOCs of many other nations. Furthermore, the Special Olympics has links with the IFs and NGBs that govern individual sports. Competition must be in accordance with the rules of these organizations, except in cases where they conflict with the Special Olympics' own rules; in such instances, Special Olympics rules take precedence.

Paralympics

While the Special Olympics serves people with mental disabilities, athletes with physical disabilities, including mobility limitations, amputees, and people with visual disabilities and cerebral palsy, may compete in the Paralympics. The International Paralympic Committee (IPC; September 25, 2007, http://www.paralympic.org/release/Main_Sections_Menu/Paralympic_Games/) notes that the concept for the Paralympics grew out of a 1948 event called the Stoke Mandeville Games, a competition for World War II veterans with spinal cord injuries. The first Olympic-style competition for people with physical disabilities took place in 1960 in Rome. These became the Paralympic games. The Winter Paralympics were added in 1976.

Unlike the Special Olympics, the Paralympics have always been held in the same year as the Olympic games.

Since the 1988 summer games in Seoul, South Korea, and the 1992 winter games in Albertville, France, the Paralympics have been held in the same venues as well. This arrangement has been cemented in place by an agreement reached with the IOC in 2001. Since the 2002 games in Salt Lake City, both the Olympic and Paralympic games have been set up by the same organizing committee as well. Paralympic athletes live in the same Olympic village with the same food and medical facilities as their Olympic counterparts, and the ticketing, technology, and transportation systems are shared. A total of 3,806 athletes representing 136 countries competed in the 2004 Summer Paralympics in Athens, Greece. In the 2006 Winter Paralympics in Turin, 474 athletes competed. There were fifty-eight medal events in the sports of alpine skiing, ice sledge hockey, Nordic skiing, and wheelchair curling. In the brochure *Spirit in Motion* (2003, http://www.paralympic.org/release/Main_Sections_ Menu/IPC/IPC_Brochure.pdf), the IPC explains that it oversees the Paralympics, performing much the same role as the IOC does for the Olympics. The IPC consists of 160 national Paralympic committees and five disability-specific international sports federations, similar to the IFs that oversee specific Olympic sports. The national Paralympics organization for the United States is U.S. Paralympics, which is a division of the USOC.

Deaflympics

Besides the Special Olympics and the Paralympics, the IOC also sanctions the Deaflympics, which have existed since 1924—almost as long as the Olympics themselves. The first Deaflympics, organized by the International Committee of Sports for the Deaf (ICSD; 2007, http://www.deaflympics.com/about/), were held in Paris that year. The winter games were added in 1949.

According to the ICSD (2007, http://www.deaflympics.com/games/), 2,150 deaf athletes from 70 countries participated in the Twentieth Summer Games, held in Melbourne, Australia, in January 2005. The Sixteenth Winter Games, held in Salt Lake City in 2007, were expected to host 298 athletes from 23 different nations. The ICSD (2007, http://www.deaflympics.com/athletes/?ID=239) explains that athletes must have a hearing loss of at least fifty-five decibels in their better ear to qualify for the Deaflympics. To ensure a level playing field, hearing aids, cochlear implants, and other devices that augment hearing are not used during the competition.

CHAPTER 8
SPORTS AND HEALTH

Sport is a preserver of health.

—Hippocrates (460?–377? BC)

The truth of Hippocrates's assertion has been nearly universally accepted for centuries, but only since the twentieth century have researchers worked to quantify the impact of physical activity, or the lack thereof, on physical and mental well-being. In *Focus Area 22: Physical Activity and Fitness Progress Review* (April 14, 2004, http://www.cdc.gov/nchs/ppt/hpdata2010/focusareas/fa22_progress_review.ppt), the Centers for Disease Control and Prevention (CDC) reports that about 1.2 million, or 48%, of the nation's 2.4 million deaths in 2000 were preventable; and of those preventable deaths, 400,000, or 17%, were due to poor diet and physical activity.

Hippocrates may not have appreciated as fully the other side of the sports-health nexus. As sports become a bigger business and as the pressure to perform becomes increasingly intense, greater attention is being given to the potential negative health impact of sports participation, especially on children and youth.

BENEFITS OF PHYSICAL ACTIVITY

The CDC's *Focus Area 22* is a progress report on one area of a broader initiative called Healthy People 2010 (http://www.healthypeople.gov/). It lists several benefits of physical activity and fitness:

- Builds and maintains healthy bones and muscles, controls weight, builds lean muscle, reduces fat and blood pressure, and improves blood glucose control.

- Decreases the risk of obesity and chronic diseases (coronary heart disease, high blood pressure, diabetes, colon cancer, and osteoporosis).

- Reduces feelings of depression and anxiety and promotes psychological well-being.

- Relates to functional independence of older adults and quality of life of people of all ages.

The specific health benefits of sports participation depend on the sport. Speed walking, jogging, cycling, swimming, and skiing have been shown to build cardiovascular endurance. Sports that involve gentle bending or stretching, including bowling, golf, and tai chi, are identified as promoting flexibility, which in turn may reduce the risk of injury. Other sports, such as those involving weightlifting or throwing, build strength. One important result of building strong muscles and, especially, bones is that it helps stave off osteoporosis by increasing the mineral content of bones. In "Lifestyle Factors and the Development of Bone Mass and Bone Strength in Young Women" (*Journal of Pediatrics*, June 2004), Tom Lloyd et al. of Pennsylvania State University report that exercise is more important than taking calcium supplements in promoting strong bones and that exercise was responsible for between 16% and 22% of the variation in hip bone mineral density in the eighty women they studied over ten years.

Coronary heart disease, diabetes, colon cancer, and high blood pressure can all be prevented or improved through regular physical activity. The CDC, in *Physical Activity and Good Nutrition: Essential Elements to Prevent Chronic Diseases and Obesity, 2007* (April 2007, http://www.cdc.gov/nccdphp/publications/aag/pdf/dnpa.pdf), points to an obesity epidemic as the key factor in these chronic health problems. According to the CDC, the prevalence of obesity among adults between twenty and seventy-four years of age increased from 15% in 1976–80 to 32.9% in 2003–04. The obesity rate among teenagers more than tripled during this span, increasing from 5% to 17.4% for those in the twelve to nineteen age group. Youfa Wang and May A. Beydoun of the Johns Hopkins Bloomberg School of Public Health, in "The Obesity Epidemic in the United States—Gender, Age, Socioeconomic, Racial/Ethnic, and Geographic Characteristics: A Systematic Review and Meta-regression Analysis" (*Epidemiologic Reviews*, vol. 29, August 2007), project that by 2015, 41% of American adults will be obese.

TABLE 8.1

Time required to burn 150 calories through selected sports and other physical activities[a]

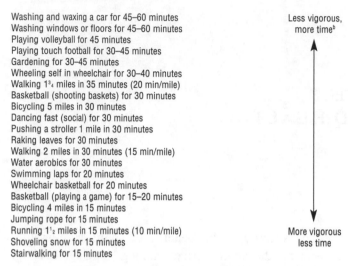

Washing and waxing a car for 45–60 minutes — Less vigorous, more time[b]
Washing windows or floors for 45–60 minutes
Playing volleyball for 45 minutes
Playing touch football for 30–45 minutes
Gardening for 30–45 minutes
Wheeling self in wheelchair for 30–40 minutes
Walking 1¾ miles in 35 minutes (20 min/mile)
Basketball (shooting baskets) for 30 minutes
Bicycling 5 miles in 30 minutes
Dancing fast (social) for 30 minutes
Pushing a stroller 1 mile in 30 minutes
Raking leaves for 30 minutes
Walking 2 miles in 30 minutes (15 min/mile)
Water aerobics for 30 minutes
Swimming laps for 20 minutes
Wheelchair basketball for 20 minutes
Basketball (playing a game) for 15–20 minutes
Bicycling 4 miles in 15 minutes
Jumping rope for 15 minutes
Running 1½ miles in 15 minutes (10 min/mile) — More vigorous less time
Shoveling snow for 15 minutes
Stairwalking for 15 minutes

[a]A moderate amount of physical activity is roughly equivalent to physical activity that uses approximately 150 calories of energy per day, or 1,000 calories per week.
[b]Some activities can be performed at various intensities; the suggested durations correspond to expected intensity of effort.

SOURCE: "Table IV-4. Examples of Moderate Amounts of Activity," in *Clinical Guidelines on the Identification, Evaluation, and Treatment of Overweight and Obesity in Adults: The Evidence Report*, National Institutes of Health, National Heart, Lung, and Blood Institute in cooperation with The National Institute of Diabetes and Digestive and Kidney Diseases, September 1998, http://www.nhlbi.nih.gov/guidelines/obesity/ob_gdlns.htm (accessed August 23, 2007)

Sports participation helps control weight by burning calories that would otherwise be stored as fat. The more vigorous the sport and the more frequent the participation, the more calories are burned. The article "How Many Calories Have You Burned?" (*USA Today*, February 26, 2007) reports on the number of calories that are burned in one hour of physical activity for those weighing 120, 154, and 170 pounds. For someone weighing 154 pounds, cross-country skiing for one hour would burn 559 calories; tennis, 489 calories; playing basketball, 440 calories; and bowling, 210 calories. Table 8.1 shows the time required to burn 150 calories doing a variety of sports and other physical activities. For example, playing a game of basketball for fifteen to twenty minutes burns 150 calories, the same number as playing volleyball for forty-five minutes, playing touch football for thirty to forty-five minutes, or swimming laps for twenty minutes.

Sports Participation and Mental Health

Besides the obvious physical benefits of sports participation, there appear to be psychological benefits as well. The press release "Univ. of Fla. Study: Sports Participation Has Mental Perks for All" (March 7, 2001, http://news.ufl.edu/2001/03/07/body-image/) reports that a 2001 survey conducted by University of Florida researchers found that athletes have a better image of their own body than nonathletes. The effect is visible without regard to sport, gender, or level of expertise. According to the press release, Heather Hausenblas, the study's lead author, posits that the effect is part of a broader improvement in self-esteem that accompanies sports participation. Based on Hausenblas's review of more than eighty other studies, athletes are 20% more likely than nonathletes to have a positive self-image. Competitive athletes have a better body image than casual athletes, and casual athletes have a better body image than nonathletes. The press release also quotes John Russell, the president of the American Fitness Association, as saying that even small doses of exercise can benefit people beyond the well-documented cardiovascular effects. Exercise, he said, can alter one's mood by releasing the brain chemical called endorphins. He speculates that endorphins, by putting the exerciser in a better mood, may indirectly improve an athlete's body image.

The idea that sports participation can help improve one's mood is well supported by other scientific research. For example, Rosemarie Kobau et al. report in "Sad, Blue, or Depressed Days: Health Behaviors and Health-Related Quality of Life, Behavioral Risk Factor Surveillance System, 1995–2000" (*Health and Quality of Life Outcomes*, July 30, 2004) that individuals who do not exercise tend to experience more days in which they feel sad. Another study, "Adolescent Women's Sports Involvement and Sexual Behavior/Health: A Process-Level Investigation" (*Journal of Youth and Adolescence*, 2004) by Stephanie Jacobs Lehman and Susan Silverberg Koerner, finds evidence of a link between girls' involvement in organized sports and positive sexual health and behavior. This study links participation in organized sports with positive behavior related to sexual risk-taking, sexual/reproductive health, and sexual/reproductive health-seeking behavior. This effect is connected to self-empowerment and a positive view of one's own body.

Youth Sports Participation as an Indicator of Adult Behavior

Participating in sports as a child or adolescent also increases the likelihood that a person will participate as an adult. In "Childhood and Adolescent Sports Participation as Predictors of Participation in Sports and Physical Fitness Activities during Young Adulthood" (*Youth and Society*, vol. 35, no. 4, 2004), Daniel F. Perkins et al. analyze data from the Michigan Study of Adolescent Life Transitions longitudinal study to examine the connection between sports participation in childhood and physical fitness into young adulthood. The researchers examine survey responses about sports participation from more than six hundred respondents when they were twelve, seventeen, and twenty-five years old and find that childhood sports participation is an excellent predictor of both fitness and participation years later.

Even though many of the previously cited studies highlight the value of sports participation for young people, the benefits of sports are truly multigenerational. According to the Gerontological Society of America, physical activity yields a number of benefits for the elderly as well as for the young. Exercise has been shown to be the key to maintaining mobility in older adults. This activity could be as simple as walking regularly.

HEALTH RISKS OF SPORTS PARTICIPATION
Injuries

TYPES OF INJURIES. In *Sports Injuries* (April 2004, http://www.niams.nih.gov/Health_Info/Sports_Injuries/sports _Injuries_hoh.pdf), Mary Anne Dunkin of the National Institute of Arthritis and Musculoskeletal and Skin Diseases details the kinds of injuries athletes are likely to sustain and the activities in which they sustain them. Dunkin lists muscle sprains and strains, ligament and tendon tears, dislocated joints, and bone fractures as the most common types of sports injuries (See Table 8.2.) According to Dunkin, the knee is the most commonly injured joint, largely because of its complexity and its role in bearing weight. Every year, knee problems send over 5.5 million people to orthopedic surgeons. Knee injuries can result from twisting the knee awkwardly, a direct blow, landing badly after a jump, or overuse. Injuries can range in severity from a minor bruise to serious damage to one or more of the four ligaments—the anterior cruciate, posterior cruciate, medial collateral, and lateral collateral—that stabilize the joint.

The Achilles tendon, which connects the calf muscle to the back of the heel, is another common site of sports injuries. Achilles tendon injures are especially common in people who do not exercise regularly and may not bother to stretch adequately before a game or session. This makes middle-aged "weekend warriors" particularly susceptible, according to Dunkin.

TABLE 8.2

Common types of sports injuries

- Muscle sprains and strains
- Tears of the ligaments that hold joints together
- Tears of the tendons that support joints and allow them to move
- Dislocated joints
- Fractured bones, including vertebrae.

SOURCE: Mary Anne Dunkin, "Common Types of Sports Injuries," in *Sports Injuries*, U.S. Department of Health and Human Services, National Institutes of Health, National Institute of Arthritis and Musculoskeletal and Skin Diseases, April 2004, http://www.niams.nih.gov/Health_Info/Sports_Injuries/ sports_injuries_hoh.pdf

A fracture is a break in a bone. It can come from a single event, in which case it is called an acute fracture; or it can be caused by repetitive impact, which is called a stress fracture. Stress fractures usually occur in the feet or legs, the result of the pounding these bones take from long periods of running and jumping. When the bones that come together to form a joint get separated, it is called a dislocation. Dunkin notes that the joints of the hand are the most common points of dislocation, followed by the shoulder.

Dunkin divides all sports injuries into two broad categories: acute and chronic. Acute injuries are those that occur suddenly during an activity. They are characterized by severe pain, swelling, and inability to use the injured body part. Chronic injuries usually occur through overuse over a long period. They usually result in pain when engaging in the activity, and a dull ache when at rest. There may also be swelling.

According to Maureen Haggerty, Teresa G. Odle, and Rebecca J. Frey in "Sports Injuries" (Jacqueline L. Longe, ed., *Gale Encyclopedia of Medicine*, 2006), the vast majority (95%) of sports injuries are minor soft-tissue traumas. These include bruises (or contusions), which occur when blood collects at the point of the injury, causing a discoloration of the skin. Sprains, which account for about one-third of sports injuries, are partial or complete tears of a ligament. Strains are similar to sprains. The difference is that in a strain the torn tissue is a muscle or tendon rather than a ligament. Other soft-tissue sports injuries include tendonitis (inflammation of a tendon) and bursitis (inflammation of the fluid-filled sacs that allow tendons to glide over bones). These two injuries usually result from repeated stress on the tissue involved rather than from a single event. The kinds of sports injuries that result from overuse appear to be on the rise among young people. Mark Hyman notes in "Young Athletes, Big League Pain" (*Business Week*, June 7, 2004) that in 1989 overuse injuries accounted for 20% of patients visiting the sports medicine clinic of Children's Hospital Boston. By 2004 the percentage was 70% and on the rise. Hyman blames increased pressure to perform from parents and coaches, who seek to turn every promising young athlete into a scholarship recipient and, eventually, a superstar.

Skeletal injuries from sports are less common than soft-tissue injuries. Haggerty, Odle, and Frey indicate that fractures account for 5% to 6% of sports injuries, with arms and legs being the most common sites of a break. Fractures of the skull or spine are rare in sports. Repeated foot pounding associated with such sports as long-distance running, basketball, and volleyball, and the stress fractures that can result, sometimes cause an injury called shin splints. Shin splints, according to Haggerty, Odle, and Frey, "are characterized by soreness and slight swelling of the front, inside, and back of the lower leg,

TABLE 8.3

Top injury-causing sports, 2005

Recreational activity	Number of injuries
Basketball	512,213
Bicycles	485,669
Football	418,260
Soccer	174,686
Baseball	155,898
Skateboards	112,544
Trampolines	108,029
Softball	106,884
Swimming/diving	82,354
Horseback	73,576
Weightlifting	65,716
Volleyball	52,091
Golf	47,360
Roller-skating	35,003
Wrestling	33,734
Gymnastics	27,821
In-line skating	26,935
Tennis	19,487
Track & field	17,306

SOURCE: "Basketball Tops List of Sports with Most Injuries," Loyola University Health System, June 2006, http://www.luhs.org/feature cfm?featureid=509 (accessed July 30, 2007)

and by sharp pain that develops while exercising and gradually intensifies."

The most dangerous class of sports injuries are those to the brain. A violent jarring of the brain from a blow to the head is called a concussion. Concussions often cause loss of consciousness and may also affect balance, coordination, hearing, memory, and vision.

STATISTICS ON FREQUENCY AND INJURY RATES. The article "Basketball Tops List of Sports with Most Injuries" (2006, http://www.luhs.org/feature.cfm?featureid=509) analyzes the prevalence of sports injuries using data from the U.S. Consumer Product Safety Commission. It indicates that of all sports injuries that were treated in hospital emergency rooms in 2005, basketball was the leading culprit, causing 512,213 of those injuries. (See Table 8.3.) Bicycling (485,669) and football (418,260) were close behind with injuries that required emergency room treatment. Soccer and baseball, the next two sports on the list, were far behind, causing 174,686 and 155,898 injuries, respectively.

Because they are still growing, and because their motor and cognitive skills are still developing, children and adolescents are particularly vulnerable to sports injuries. In "Facts about Childhood Sports Injuries" (2004, http://www.usa.safekids.org/content_documents/Sports _facts.pdf), Safe Kids Worldwide, a nonprofit network of organizations devoted to reducing accidental injuries of all kinds among children, reports that 3.5 million American children under the age of fourteen receive medical treatment for sports injuries every year. Sports participation in 2003 accounted for 55% of all nonfatal injuries at school and 21% of all traumatic brain injuries among children. In

2003, 205,400 kids between the ages of five and fourteen were treated in emergency rooms for basketball-related injuries. Football was close behind with 185,700 injuries. Even though baseball was the cause of fewer injuries treated in emergency rooms (108,300), it had the highest fatality rate among all sports, causing three to four childhood deaths each year.

FACTORS AFFECTING INJURY RATES. Besides children and adolescents, Dunkin notes that middle-aged people and women of all ages are also particularly vulnerable to sports injuries. Middle-aged people are susceptible to injury because they are not as agile and resilient as when they were younger. Some people expect their bodies to perform as well at the age of fifty as they remember their bodies performing at age twenty or thirty. As a result, they put themselves at risk of injury. The risk is highest when an individual tries to make too quick a transition from an inactive lifestyle to an active one. As women's sports become faster paced and more physical, injuries among female athletes are increasing. The American Sports Data press release "New National Study Is First since 1970's to Document Full Range of Sports Injuries" (May 15, 2003, http://www.americansportsdata .com/pr-sportsinjuries.asp) notes that in 2002 women were the recipients of 40% of all sports injuries and 37% of emergency room admissions.

PSYCHOLOGICAL IMPACT OF YOUTH SPORTS PARTICIPATION. Frank Brady states in "Children's Organized Sports: A Developmental Perspective" (*Journal of Physical Education, Recreation, and Dance*, February 2004) that the "positive effect of sports participation for some youths appears to be offset by the negative experiences of others." He quotes Arthur J. Pearl and Bernard R. Cahill in *Intensive Participation in Children's Sports* (1993), who state that "sports are like a double-edged sword. Swung in the right direction, the sword can have tremendously positive effects, but swung in the wrong direction it can be devastating. Adults who supervise children's sports hold the sword. Whether sport is constructive or destructive in the psychological development of young children greatly depends on the values, education and skills of those adults."

The biggest culprit in the negative psychological impact of youth sports participation is an overemphasis on competition, which Brady attributes to misplaced priorities on the part of the adults in supervisory roles.

As a result, there is a high rate of burnout and subsequent dropout in youth sports. Brady explains that sports participation peaks at age eleven and steadily declines through the teenage years. He singles out a subset of the dropout group under the category of "burnout." Burnout refers to young athletes who have been successful in their sport(s) and have participated intensively over a number of years; concentrated training at the expense of other activities can result in diminished enjoyment, competitive anxiety, and ultimately real psychological and emotional damage.

Brady also points to conflicts between heavy sports participation and cognitive development in young children. Most children are not capable of fully grasping the competitive process until about age twelve and have trouble understanding the complex interrelationships that form a team. Some adult coaches get angry and frustrated when, for example, young soccer players swarm to the ball rather than play their positions properly, when in fact many players at age seven or eight are physically incapable of absorbing the concept of a position.

The American Psychological Association (APA) argues that whether youths benefit from sports participation may depend to a large degree on their environment. The APA news release "Environment May Play a Role in Whether Youth Benefit from Sports Participation, According to Two Studies" (August 25, 2001, http://www.apa.org/releases/sportinvolvement.html) describes two studies with seemingly contradictory messages. A Clark University study of seventh graders from inner-city neighborhoods in central Massachusetts finds that boys and girls who participated in organized sports had higher self-esteem and were perceived by their teachers as having better social skills. Boys involved in sports were less likely to have experimented with marijuana. These positive traits were not accompanied by measurable negative behavior, such as increased aggression. However, the Clark University researchers explicitly caution against making "sweeping pronouncements about benefits or risks of sports involvement."

A larger study of female African-American students in rural high schools tells a different story. This study by Matthew J. Taylor of the University of Wisconsin, LaCrosse, finds that sports participation may actually increase the likelihood of substance use and other undesirable behaviors. Participation in sports did not appear to have a deterrent effect on gang involvement or other forms of delinquency. Taylor explains that the reason for conflicting results is that there are so many other variables involved, such as peer groups and community attitudes toward sports.

PHYSICAL INJURIES AMONG YOUNG ATHLETES. Even though much of the attention to the hazards of youth sports focuses on the mental and emotional pitfalls, physical injuries are a major concern as well. As noted earlier, children as a group are particularly vulnerable to sports injuries. Bill Hewitt, in "Wearing out Their Bodies?" (*People Weekly*, June 13, 2005), elaborates on the theme of youth sports and their connection to increased injury risks. He cites many examples of young athletes pushed into extremely vigorous regimens at early ages and who end up damaging their bodies. One sports surgeon is quoted as saying that ten years ago, he had never seen a baseball pitcher under nineteen years old who needed the elbow ligament replacement

operation known as "Tommy John surgery," whereas in 2004 he performed fifty-one such operations on teenage pitchers. Jeré Longman notes in "Fit Young Pitchers See Elbow Repair as Cure-All" (*New York Times*, July 20, 2007) that some young athletes are now opting to have this surgery even in the absence of an injury, in hopes that it will enhance their capabilities. Hewitt takes parents to task for pressuring their children into trying to become the next Michael Jordan (1963–), when the odds of even the most talented young athlete ever making the big leagues, much less excelling there, are microscopic. He notes that about nine million boys play in organized baseball leagues, but that there are only about 9,700 players on Division I college teams, 7,500 minor leaguers, and 829 players in Major League Baseball. Hewitt advises parents and coaches that children need at least three months off each year from sports that involve throwing. He also urges them not to ignore discomfort, because pain is an indication of an injury that must be addressed.

According to the National Alliance for Youth Sports (NAYS), parents and coaches can play a big role in helping kids avoid injuries. NAYS points to three overarching strategies for minimizing the risk of sports injuries: wearing appropriate, sport-specific, properly fitting protective gear, including helmets and goggles; protecting the skin from damaging solar rays by wearing hats and sunglasses and applying sun block when playing sports in the sun; and keeping adequately hydrated by consuming sports drinks to replace lost fluids and electrolytes lost through sweat.

SPORTS AND HEALTH: THE OUTLOOK

Are Americans heeding all the advice coming from their doctors and their government about the importance of physical activity? Data from the *Early Release of Selected Estimates Based on Data from the 2006 National Health Interview Survey* (June 25, 2007, http://www.cdc.gov/nchs/data/nhis/earlyrelease/200706_07.pdf) by the U.S. Department of Health and Human Services indicate that, in general, the answer seems to be "not really." Figure 8.1 shows that the percentage of adults who engaged in regular leisure-time physical activity between 1997 and 2006 hovered at around 31%, in spite of the aggressive promotion of exercise by the federal government and others. As shown in Figure 8.2, people tend to exercise less as they age, and this pattern holds true for both genders, with men more likely to be physically active than women in every age category. White adults, at 34%, were more likely to engage in regular leisure-time physical activity than either Hispanics (23%) or non-Hispanic African-Americans (25%). (See Figure 8.3.)

Another survey, *Physical Activity Survey, 2006* (April 2006, http://assets.aarp.org/rgcenter/health/fitness_06.pdf), by Teresa A. Keenan, finds that in 2006, 49% of adults had

FIGURE 8.1

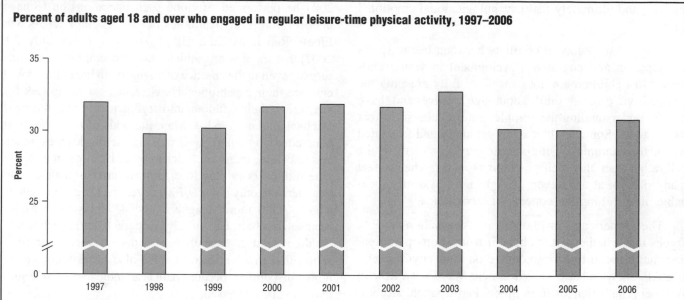

Percent of adults aged 18 and over who engaged in regular leisure-time physical activity, 1997–2006

Notes: This measure reflects the definition used for the physical activity leading health indicator (Healthy People 2010, (14)). Regular leisure-time physical activity is defined as engaging in light-moderate leisure-time physical activity for greater than or equal to 30 minutes at a frequency greater than or equal to five times per week or engaging in vigorous leisure-time physical activity for greater than or equal to 20 minutes at a frequency greater than or equal to three times per week. In early releases before September 2005 (based on the 2004 National Health Interview Survey (NHIS)), regular physical activity was calculated slightly differently than that of Healthy People 2010. The earlier early release estimates excluded from the analysis persons with unknown duration of light-moderate or vigorous leisure-time physical activity who were known to have not met the frequency recommendations for light-moderate or vigorous leisure-time physical activity (i.e., partial unknowns). With the current release, persons who were known to have not met the frequency recommendations are classified as "not regular," regardless of duration. All estimates have been rerun using the revised denominator. The impact of the change on the estimates was minimal (typically 0.1 percentage points or less). The analyses excluded persons with unknown physical activity participation (about 3% of respondents each year). Beginning with the 2003 data, NHIS transitioned to weights derived from the 2000 census. In this early release, estimates for 2000–2002 were recalculated using weights derived from the 2000 census.

SOURCE: P. Barnes and J. S. Schiller, "Figure 7.1. Percentage of Adults Aged 18 Years and Over Who Engaged in Regular Leisure-Time Physical Activity: United States, 1997–2006," in *Early Release of Selected Estimates Based on Data from the 2006 National Health Interview Survey,* U.S. Department of Health and Human Services, Centers for Disease Control and Prevention, National Center for Health Statistics, June 25, 2007, http://www.cdc.gov/nchs/data/nhis/earlyrelease/200706_07.pdf (accessed July 31, 2007).

been physically active for at least a year and that 36% of adults preferred walking. (See Figure 8.4 and Figure 8.5.)

By contrast, vigorous physical activity among adolescents seems to be on the rise. The nonprofit research agency Child Trends reports in *Vigorous Physical Activity by Youth* (June 2006, http://www.childtrendsdatabank.org/pdf/16_PDF.pdf) that 68.7% of students in grades nine through twelve engaged in vigorous physical activity in 2005, up from 62.6% in 2003. (See Figure 8.6.) Child Trends finds that this increase was evident among both males and females, and among white, African-American, and Hispanic subgroups. "Vigorous physical activity" is defined as physical activity for at least twenty minutes that made the person sweat and breathe hard, such as basketball, soccer, running, swimming laps, fast bicycling, fast dancing, or similar aerobic activities, on at least three of the seven days preceding the interview. As shown in Figure 8.7, 78% of ninth-grade boys in 2005 reported doing vigorous physical activity, whereas 68% of ninth-grade girls reported such activity. Even though the percentages for both genders declined from ninth to twelfth grade, boys were consistently more active than girls, with the gap between the genders the widest in twelfth grade. White and Hispanic students were about

equally likely to have engaged in vigorous physical activity, at 70% and 69%, respectively; African-American students, at 62%, were somewhat less likely to be physically active. (See Figure 8.8.)

In the face of an obesity epidemic in the United States, the federal government has in recent years taken an active role in promoting fitness among Americans. In 1996 the National Center for Chronic Disease Prevention and Health Promotion published *Physical Activity and Health: A Report of the Surgeon General* (http://www.cdc.gov/nccdphp/sgr/pdf/sgrfull.pdf), a blueprint for improving the physical condition of the U.S. population. Among the report's major conclusions were that people of all ages and genders benefit from regular physical activity and that significant health benefits can be obtained by engaging in a moderate amount of physical activity, such as forty-five minutes of volleyball, thirty minutes of brisk walking, or fifteen minutes of running. The report noted that additional benefits can be gained through more vigorous and greater amounts of activity. Since then, the federal government has continued its efforts to promote physical fitness through a variety of programs, including Healthy People 2010 and the HealthierUS initiative (http://www.healthierus.gov/), promoted by President George W. Bush (1946–).

FIGURE 8.2

Percent of adults who engaged in regular leisure-time physical activity, by age group and sex, 2006

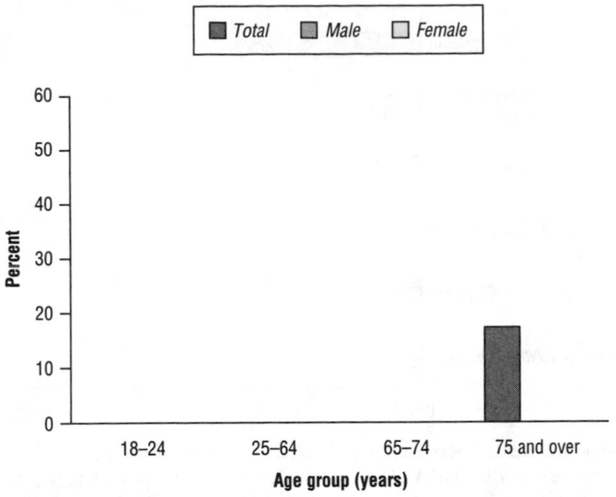
Total
Male
Female
60
50
40
30
20
10
0
Percent
18–24
25–64
65–74
75 and over
Age group (years)

Notes: This measure reflects the definition used for the physical activity leading health indicator (Healthy People 2010, (14)). Regular leisure-time physical activity is defined as engaging in light-moderate leisure-time physical activity for greater than or equal to 30 minutes at a frequency greater than or equal to five times per week or engaging in vigorous leisure-time physical activity for greater than or equal to 20 minutes at a frequency greater than or equal to three times per week. In early releases before September 2005 (based on the 2004 National Health Interview Survey (NHIS)), regular physical activity was calculated slightly differently than that of Healthy People 2010. The earlier early release estimates excluded from the analysis persons with unknown duration of light-moderate or vigorous leisure-time physical activity who were known to have not met the frequency recommendations for light-moderate or vigorous leisure-time physical activity (i.e., partial unknowns). With the current release, persons who were known to have not met the frequency recommendations are classified as "not regular," regardless of duration. The analyses excluded 742 persons (3.1%) with unknown physical activity participation.

SOURCE: P. Barnes and J. S. Schiller, "Figure 7.2. Percent of Adults Aged 18 Years and Over Who Engaged in Regular Leisure-Time Physical Activity, by Age Group and Sex: United States, 2006," in *Early Release of Selected Estimates Based on Data from the 2006 National Health Interview Survey*, U.S. Department of Health and Human Services, Centers for Disease Control and Prevention, National Center for Health Statistics, June 25, 2007, http://www.cdc.gov/nchs/data/nhis/earlyrelease/200706_07.pdf (accessed July 31, 2007)

FIGURE 8.3

Percent of adults who engaged in regular leisure-time physical activity, by race/ethnicity, 2006

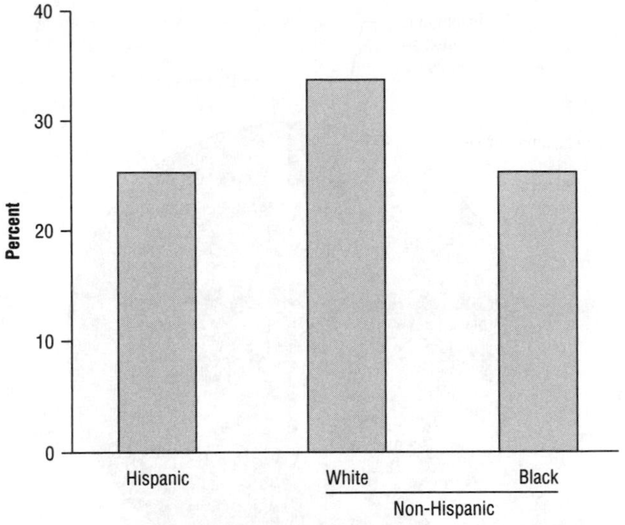
40
30
20
10
0
Percent
Hispanic
White
Black
Non-Hispanic

Notes: This measure reflects the definition used for the physical activity leading health indicator (Healthy People 2010, (14)). Regular leisure-time physical activity is defined as engaging in light-moderate leisure-time physical activity for greater than or equal to 30 minutes at a frequency greater than or equal to five times per week or engaging in vigorous leisure-time physical activity for greater than or equal to 20 minutes at a frequency greater than or equal to three times per week. In early releases before September 2005 (based on the 2004 National Health Interview Survey (NHIS)), regular physical activity was calculated slightly differently than that of Healthy People 2010. The earlier early release estimates excluded from the analysis persons with unknown duration of light-moderate or vigorus leisure-time physical activity who were known to have not met the frequency recommendations for light-moderate or vigorous leisure-time physical activity (i.e., partial unknowns). With the current release, persons who were known to have not met the frequency recommendations are classified "as not regular," regardless of duration. The analyses excluded 742 persons (3.1%) with unknown physical activity participation. Estimates are age-sex adjusted using the projected 2000 U.S. population as the standard population and using five age groups: 18–24 years, 25–34 years, 35–44 years, 45–64 years, and 65 years and over.

SOURCE: P. Barnes and J. S. Schiller, "Figure 7.3. Age-Sex-Adjusted Percentage of Adults Aged 18 Years and Over Who Engaged in Regular Leisure-Time Physical Activity, by Race/Ethnicity: United States, 2006," in *Early Release of Selected Estimates Based on Data from the 2006 National Health Interview Survey*, U.S. Department of Health and Human Services, Centers for Disease Control and Prevention, National Center for Health Statistics, June 25, 2007, http://www.cdc.gov/nchs/data/nhis/earlyrelease/200706_07.pdf (accessed July 31, 2007)

In recent years network television has taken on the obesity epidemic as well. The National Broadcasting Corporation's *The Biggest Loser* is a reality show in which eighteen obese contestants compete in various contests designed to help them slim down. The contestant who sheds the most weight (the "biggest loser") is the winner at the end of the season. The American Broadcasting Company counters with *Shaq's Big Challenge*, in which the National Basketball Association star Shaquille O'Neal (1972–) encourages a group of overweight youths to adopt a healthier lifestyle, including a better diet and more physical activity.

FIGURE 8.4

Level of physical activity, 2006

[Sample size=1,011]

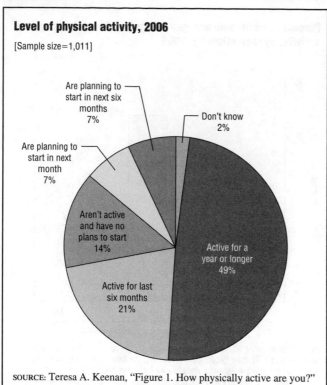

SOURCE: Teresa A. Keenan, "Figure 1. How physically active are you?" in *Physical Activity Survey, 2006*, AARP, April 2006, http://assets.aarp .org/rgcenter/health/fitness_06.pdf (accessed July 31, 2007)

FIGURE 8.5

Preferred type of exercise, 2006

[Sample size=698]

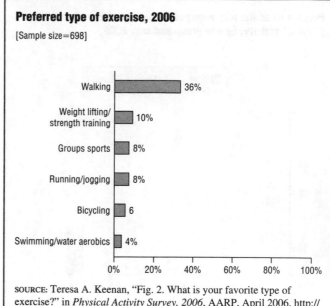

SOURCE: Teresa A. Keenan, "Fig. 2. What is your favorite type of exercise?" in *Physical Activity Survey, 2006*, AARP, April 2006, http:// assets.aarp.org/rgcenter/health/fitness_06.pdf (accessed July 31, 2007)

FIGURE 8.6

Vigorous physical activity among adolescents, 1993–2005

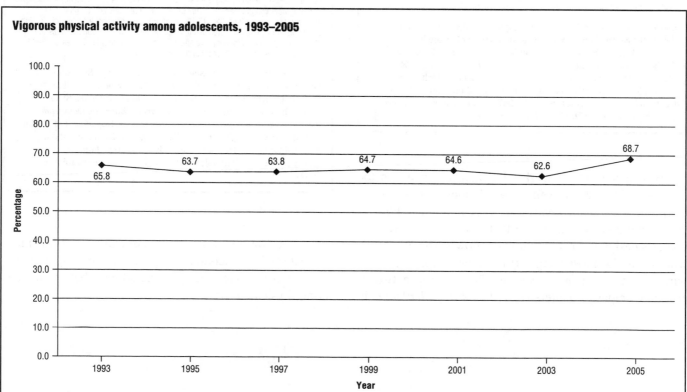

Note: Vigorous physical activities are those that caused sweating and hard breathing for at least 20 minutes on 3 or more of the 7 days preceding the survey.

SOURCE: "Figure 1. Physical Activity: The Percentage of Students in Grades 9 through 12 Who Participated in Vigorous Physical Activity, 1993–2005," in *Vigorous Physical Activity by Youth*, Child Trends, June 2006, http://www.childtrendsdatabank.org/pdf/16_PDF.pdf (accessed July 31, 2007)

FIGURE 8.7

Vigorous physical activity among adolescents, by grade and gender, 2005

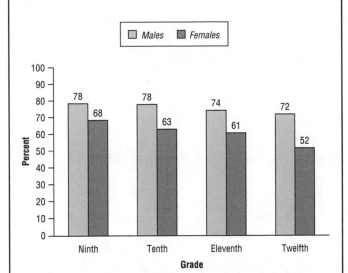

Note: Vigorous physical activities are those that caused sweating and hard breathing for at least 20 minutes on 3 or more of the 7 days preceding the survey.

SOURCE: "Figure 2. Physical Activity: The Percentage of Students in Grades 9 through 12 Who Participated in Regular Vigorous Physical Activity, by Grade and Gender, 2005," in *Vigorous Physical Activity by Youth*, Child Trends, June 2006, http://www.childtrendsdatebank.org/pdf/16_PDF.pdf (accessed July 31, 2007)

FIGURE 8.8

Vigorous physical activity among adolescents, by race/ethnicity, 2005

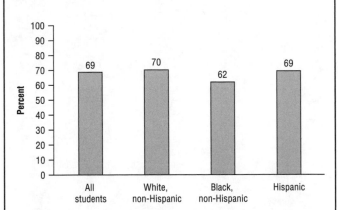

Notes: Vigorous physical activities are those that caused sweating and hard breathing for at least 20 minutes on 3 or more of the 7 days preceding the survey. Estimates reported here only include respondents who selected one race category.

SOURCE: "Figure 3. Physical Activity: The Percentage of Students in Grades 9 through 12 Who participated in Vigorous Physical Activity, by Race and Hispanic Origin, 2005," in *Vigorous Physical Activity by Youth*, Child Trends, June 2006, http://www.childtrendsdatabank.org/pdf/16_PDF.pdf (accessed July 31, 2007)

CHAPTER 9
PERFORMANCE-ENHANCING DRUGS

The spirit of sport is the celebration of the human spirit, the body and the mind. Doping is contrary to the spirit of sport, erodes public confidence and jeopardises the health and well-being of athletes.

—World Anti-Doping Agency

The word *doping* is often used to refer to any practice involving prohibited substances or other methods to give an athlete an unfair advantage over other competitors. The article "Doping in Sports: Steroids and Supplements" (*World Almanac and Book of Facts*, 2007) notes that the word *dope* probably comes from the Dutch word *dop*, an alcoholic beverage made from grape skins that traditional Zulu warriors believed enhanced their fighting ability.

A BRIEF HISTORY OF DOPING

For as long as people have been engaging in athletic competition, they have been seeking ways to gain an edge on their opponents. There is evidence that doping took place in the ancient Olympics, which lasted from 776 BC until AD 393. For example, Will Carroll notes in *The Juice: The Real Story of Baseball's Drug Problems* (2005) that Spartan coaches fed their athletes special herb and mushroom concoctions—during a period in which they were supposed to be consuming nothing but cheese and water—believed to render them oblivious to pain.

The first known case of an athlete dying as a result of doping occurred in 1886, when the Welsh cyclist Andrew Linton died during a race from Paris to Bordeaux. The substance he ingested was thought to be trimethyl, an alcohol-based product used by distance racers to ease pain and increase stamina.

According to Carroll, the modern era of doping began with the development of injectable testosterone in 1935. Testosterone is a male hormone produced naturally by the body. Injecting additional testosterone into the system increases muscle mass and strength. Originally introduced by Nazi doctors to make soldiers more aggressive, it did not take long for laboratory-produced testosterone to make its way from the battlefield to the athletic field. German athletes dominated the medals in the 1936 Olympics, probably with the assistance of these newly developed synthetic drugs.

The father of anabolic steroids—chemical variants of testosterone—in the United States was John Ziegler (1917–2000), a physician for the U.S. weightlifting team in the mid-twentieth century. Ziegler learned from his Russian counterparts that the Soviet weightlifting team's success was in part attributable to their use of performance-enhancing drugs, the formulas for which had been brought east by German scientists defecting to the Soviet Union after World War II (1939–1945). Deciding that U.S. athletes needed chemical assistance to remain competitive, Ziegler worked with the CIBA Pharmaceutical Company to develop an oral anabolic steroid. These efforts resulted in the creation of methandrostenolone, which appeared on the market in 1960. During the Olympics that year, the Danish cyclist Knut Jensen collapsed and died while competing in the 100-kilometer (62-mile) race. An autopsy revealed the presence of amphetamines and a drug called nicotinyl tartrade in his system.

Drug testing was introduced at the Olympics in 1968. By this time the International Olympic Committee (IOC) had developed a list of officially banned substances; however, because no test had yet been invented that could distinguish between anabolic steroids and naturally occurring testosterone in the body, the testing was largely ineffective. Only one athlete was found to be in violation of the new drug policy in 1968: the Swedish pentathlete Hans-Gunnar Liljenwall, who was found to have too much alcohol in his blood after drinking a few beers before the shooting portion of his event.

Steroids found their way into professional football in the late 1960s, as teams began hiring strength and conditioning coaches, who were charged with the task of growing a new breed of bigger, bulkier players. Taking their cue from the weightlifting world, these coaches turned to steroids as the fastest way of accomplishing this goal. During the 1970s performance-enhance-enhancing supplements were still way ahead of the dope detectors in the scientific arena. The East Germans showed up at the 1976 Olympics in Montreal with a team of women swimmers sporting man-sized muscles and deep voices. They won most of the medals. However, even though there was much talk about the likelihood that they were using banned substances, not a single one of these athletes tested positive. It later became clear that the athletes themselves were the victims of a mandatory doping program overseen by East German Olympic officials, who injected the swimmers with steroids without their informed consent. Several East German swimmers of that era have reported that they began receiving steroid injections at age thirteen and have suffered serious long-term health consequences—ranging from liver damage to infertility—as a result of doping (January 19, 2003, http://www.cbc.ca/sports/indepth/drugs/stories/top10.html#1).

Doping in sports has increased dramatically since then. As the practice has grown, so have the methods for detecting it and for keeping it from being detected. By the 1970s the use of performance-enhancing drugs had reached epidemic proportions among elite athletes. It was widely known that there were whole national sports programs whose success was based largely on sophisticated doping techniques, but scientists lacked the tools to prove what was going on. A breakthrough took place in 1983, when newly developed technology for analyzing blood for the presence of banned substances was deployed at the Pan Am Games in Caracas, Venezuela. The Associated Press reports in "Inquiry Set on Pan Am" (*New York Times*, September 14, 1983) that sixteen athletes from several countries were caught with performance-enhancing drugs in their system. Many other athletes, including twelve members of the U.S. track and field squad, withdrew from the event rather than risk the embarrassment of being caught cheating.

The first big-time Olympic disqualification due to steroids occurred in 1988, when the Canadian sprinter Ben Johnson (1961–) was stripped of both his gold medal and his world record in the 100-meter (109-yard) dash after testing positive for the banned steroid stanozolol. Years later, it was revealed that a number of U.S. track competitors had tested positive for illicit drugs before the 1988 Olympics in Seoul, South Korea.

THE BALCO SCANDAL

The cat-and-mouse game of doping and detection methods went on for more than two decades. A major turning point came in June 2003, when the track and field coach Trevor Graham turned over to authorities a syringe containing what turned out to be tetrahydrogestrinone

(THG), a previously unknown anabolic steroid. THG was considered a designer steroid, in that it was manufactured to be undetectable by the existing methods. Lab testing methods were quickly adjusted to detect THG. U.S. government investigators soon turned their attention to the Bay Area Laboratory Co-Operative (BALCO), the California-based distributor of the drug.

On September 3, 2003, agents of the Internal Revenue Service, the U.S. Food and Drug Administration (FDA), the San Mateo County Narcotics Task Force, and the U.S. Anti-Doping Agency raided BALCO facilities and seized containers of steroids, human growth hormone, and testosterone. Two days later officials searched the home of Greg Anderson (1964–), the personal weight trainer of the baseball star Barry Bonds (1964–), and seized more steroids, as well as documents thought to implicate a number of high-profile athletes. Over the next few months urine samples from the U.S. Track and Field Championships were retested for THG, and several came up positive. One of those athletes was Kelli White (1977–), who had won both the 100- and 200-meter (109- and 218-yard) world championships in 2003. White was stripped of her titles and banned from competition for two years. Evidence was collected from computers and documents connecting a number of other athletes to BALCO.

Victor Conte Jr., the BALCO founder and owner; James Valente, a BALCO executive; Anderson; and the track coach Remi Korchemny were indicted in February 2004 for distributing steroids. Later that year, Conte described on the December 3, 2004, broadcast of American Broadcasting Company's *20/20* how he provided performance-enhancing drugs to many elite athletes, including the sprinters Tim Montgomery (1975–) and Marion Jones (1975–). Dick Patrick, in "Doping Test Criticized, Defended after Jones Cleared" (*USA Today*, September 8, 2006), reports that Jones proclaimed her innocence throughout the scandal and sued Conte for defamation of character. She settled the suit out of court in 2006, and later that year she was cleared after her alternate blood sample tested negative for banned substances. However, the cost of defending herself was steep; according to the article "Marion Jones Running Out of Money" (*Boston Globe*, June 25, 2007), the affair cost Jones hundreds of thousands of dollars in endorsements and appearance fees, which coupled with legal fees brought her to the brink of financial ruin. In October 2007 Jones admitted to having used illegal performance-enhancing drugs during the period surrounding the 2000 Olympics in Sydney, Australia, in which she won three gold medals and two bronze. Under pressure from the U.S. Olympic Committee she surrendered her Olympic medals, and was retroactively disqualified from all events dating back to September 1, 2000. Several other high-profile track and field athletes received bans in the wake of the BALCO scandal, including the sprinters White, Montgomery, and Chrystie Gaines.

The BALCO scandal also brought fines and suspensions for a handful of professional football players: Chris Cooper (1977–), Barrett Robbins (1973–), and Dana Stubblefield (1970–). Elliot Almond and Peter Carey note in "Bonds, Marion Jones Alleged to Have Received Steroids" (Knight-Ridder/Tribune News Service, April 25, 2004) that Bill Romanowski (1966–) was reported by the *San Jose Mercury News* to have been implicated by Conte, but Romanowski retired before the National Football League (NFL) could take any formal action against him. Romanowski later admitted to having used steroids during his playing career.

In March 2005 a congressional committee held hearings on the issue of steroids in baseball. A number of legislators mocked Major League officials for the sport's weak policy and feeble efforts to deal with the problem. Many of those who testified came out looking bad, including the former home run champion Mark McGwire (1963–), who was evasive when asked whether his power-hitting abilities were chemically aided. Other current and former baseball players who testified included Jose Canseco (1964–), Curt Schilling (1966–), Sammy Sosa (1968–), Rafael Palmeiro (1964–), and Frank Thomas (1968–).

In October 2005 Conte was sentenced to four months in prison and another four months of house arrest. Anderson received three months each of prison time and home confinement. Valente and Korchemny were given probation, Valente for three years, and Korchemny one year.

WHAT ARE PERFORMANCE-ENHANCING DRUGS?
Anabolic Steroids

When people speak of performance-enhancing drugs, more often than not they are referring to anabolic steroids. In *Steroid Abuse in Today's Society* (March 2004, http://www.deadiversion.usdoj.gov/pubs/brochures/steroids/professionals/), the U.S. Drug Enforcement Administration (DEA) defines anabolic steroids as "synthetically produced variants of the naturally occurring male hormone testosterone." The full name of this class of drugs is androgenic anabolic steroids. The term *androgenic* means that the drugs promote masculine physical characteristics, and *anabolic* means tissue building. According to the DEA, the list of commonly abused steroids commercially available in the United States includes:

- Fluxoymesterone
- Methyltestosterone
- Nandrolone
- Oxandrolone
- Oxymetholone
- Stanozolol
- Boldenone

Others that are not approved for use in the United States include ethylestrenol, methandriol, methenolone, and methandrostenolone.

The main users of anabolic steroids are athletes seeking to add bulk and strength to their bodies. Besides building lean body mass, another way steroids are purported to help athletes get stronger is by reducing the amount of recovery time needed between workouts, allowing them to train harder. Anabolic steroids are currently banned by most sports organizations, including the IOC, the NFL, the National Basketball Association (NBA), the National Collegiate Athletic Association (NCAA), the National Hockey League (NHL), and Major League Baseball (MLB).

The only way to get steroids legally is through a doctor's prescription, and there are many legitimate medical uses for which a doctor might recommend them, including growth deficiencies, muscle-wasting diseases, loss of testicular function, breast cancer, low red blood cell count, or debilitated states resulting from surgery or illness. Steroids are also widely used in veterinary medicine to promote weight gain, to treat anemia, or to counteract tissue breakdown from illness or trauma. Most illicit steroids come from one of two sources. Some are diverted from the legitimate market, often through stolen or fraudulent prescriptions. The largest share, however, is smuggled into the United States from Mexico or from European countries where a prescription is not required to obtain steroids. Michael Ormsbee and Matt Vukovich report in "Performance-Enhancing Drugs: Who's Taking Them, and What Are the Benefits and Risks?" (*IDEA Fitness Journal*, May 1, 2005) that the black market sales of steroids exceed $100 million per year.

Steroids are available in several different forms, including tablets, liquids, gels, and creams. Typically, users ingest the drugs orally, inject them into muscle, or rub them on their skin. The doses taken by people who abuse steroids can be ten to one hundred times stronger than those recommended for medical conditions. Many steroid abusers engage in what is called stacking, which means mixing oral steroids with injectable ones, often taking multiple forms of the drug. Another common practice among steroid abusers is pyramiding, which means administering doses in cycles of six to twelve weeks where the dose is slowly increased to a peak midway through the cycle, then tapered back down toward the end. There is a widespread belief among steroid users that stacking and pyramiding maximize the benefits of the drugs while reducing their harmful effects, though there is no scientific evidence to support these contentions.

Other Substances and Supplements

There are a number of performance-enhancing substances besides anabolic steroids, some of which have until recently escaped the scrutiny of those in the business of regulating sports. As a result, these substances, often billed as dietary supplements, have been readily available, usually as nearby as the nutrition and vitamin store in a local mall.

ERYTHROPOIETIN. Erythropoietin (EPO) is a hormone produced naturally by the kidneys. It plays a role in regulating the number of red blood cells in the blood stream. A synthetic version of EPO was developed in the 1980s, and it quickly became popular as a performance-enhancing drug, particularly among athletes involved in endurance sports such as cycling. When used excessively, EPO can increase the number of red blood cells to such a degree that the blood becomes too thick to flow properly, potentially leading to heart attacks and strokes. According to the 2007 *World Almanac and Book of Facts*, in the late 1980s, shortly after the appearance of synthetic EPO, thirty top endurance athletes, mainly cyclists, in Belgium, the Netherlands, Denmark, and Sweden died; the likely cause of their deaths was EPO.

CREATINE. One of the most popular supplements used by athletes at all levels is creatine. Creatine is available over the counter (without a prescription) and is reputed to help improve performance in sports that involve short bursts of power, such as weightlifting, wrestling, and sprinting. Even though reliable research has not yet established a connection between creatine and serious health problems, there is some evidence that heavy use may cause kidney, liver, and heart problems. Known side effects of creatine include muscle cramps and digestive problems such as stomach pain, diarrhea, and nausea. In "Taking Performance-Enhancing Drugs: Are You Risking Your Health?" (December 26, 2006, http://www.mayoclinic.com/health/performance-enhancing-drugs/HQ01105), the Mayo Clinic explains that what actually happens when people take creatine is that their muscles draw water away from the rest of the body, creating the illusion of added muscle mass. The increased bulk is really just extra water stored in the muscles.

ANDROSTENEDIONE. Androstenedione (or andro) enjoyed a huge burst of popularity in the late 1990s, as McGwire chased, and eventually shattered, the old record for number of home runs in a single season. McGwire admittedly used andro, which was perfectly legal and within the rules of MLB at the time. Countless young aspiring power hitters followed his lead. Whether andro really helped McGwire hit seventy home runs in 1998 is not known.

Andro is a direct precursor to testosterone—meaning it turns into testosterone in the body—and is found naturally in humans. It is also found naturally in Scotch pine trees, which is why manufacturers were allowed to sell it as a dietary supplement. Andro was discovered in the 1930s, but it was not until the 1950s that scientists became aware that it turned into testosterone in the body. Andro is widely believed to boost testosterone production, which in turn increases muscle mass, energy, and

strength. The Mayo Clinic disputes these claims, though proponents of andro—including companies that make money selling it—cite research supporting andro's effectiveness as a performance enhancer. Andro is now classified as a controlled substance. The Anabolic Steroid Control Act of 2004 essentially reclassified andro as an anabolic steroid, making it illegal for use as a performance enhancer.

Heavy use of andro can produce side effects similar to those associated with other anabolic steroids. Andro can actually decrease testosterone production in men and increase production of the female hormone estrogen. It can also cause acne, shrinking of the testicles, and reduced sperm count. In women side effects of andro can include acne as well as the onset of masculine characteristics such as deepening of the voice and male-pattern baldness.

EPHEDRA. Ephedra is an herb that has been used in Chinese medicine—where it is known as *ma huang*—for thousands of years. An American version widely used by early settlers in the Southwest was called Mormon or Squaw tea. The main chemical constituent in ephedra is ephedrine, which is a powerful stimulant, similar to amphetamines. It also contains another chemical called pseudoephedrine, which has long been used as a nasal decongestant but has recently come under tighter regulation because of its role in manufacturing illegal methamphetamine. Besides its use by athletes as an energy booster, ephedra has been used as an ingredient in popular over-the-counter weight loss pills. It has also been used by people seeking to stay alert for late-night studying or socializing activities; until recently, it was an ingredient in many popular energy drinks.

Ephedra has been linked to serious side effects, such as strokes, seizures, and heart attacks, and many people have died as a direct result of its use. Ephedra can also cause elevated blood sugar levels and irregular heartbeats. It may be addictive when used over time. In February 2003 the Baltimore Orioles pitcher Steve Bechler (1979–2003) died of heatstroke after a spring training workout. Ephedra toxicity was identified as a contributing factor in his death. Bechler's death sparked renewed efforts by the FDA to take action on ephedra. In December 2003 the FDA banned ephedra from being sold over the counter as a dietary supplement. However, in April 2005 a federal judge overturned the FDA's ban on procedural grounds. The Combat Methamphetamine Epidemic Act of 2005, signed into law in March 2006, placed strict regulations on the sale of ephedrine-containing products, including record-keeping, sale from locked cabinets behind the counter, and positive identification for purchasers.

HEALTH RISKS OF STEROID USE

Steroid abuse has been linked with a wide range of health hazards, both physical and mental. Among the

TABLE 9.1

Drug use among college athletes, by division, selected years, 1993–2005

Drug	Division I				Division II				Division III			
	1993 (n=1,422)	1997 (n=6,123)	2001 (n=8,776)	2005 (n=8,543)	1993 (n=681)	1997 (n=3,254)	2001 (n=4,867)	2005 (n=4,341)	1993 (n=409)	1997 (n=4,537)	2001 (n=7,520)	2005 (n=6,493)
Amphetamines	2.1%	2.5%	3.2%	4.0%	2.0%	3.3%	3.3%	3.8%	1.9%	3.7%	3.7%	4.6%
Anabolic steroids	1.9%	1.2%	1.6%	1.2%	4.3%	1.1%	2.5%	1.2%	1.9%	1.3%	1.4%	1.0%
Ephedrine	N/A	3.0%	2.4%	2.4%	N/A	4.2%	4.1%	2.6%	N/A	3.8%	2.5%	2.6%
Nutritional supplements	N/A	N/A	46.0%	33.4%	N/A	N/A	41.5%	27.9%	N/A	N/A	39.8%	28.1%

Note: All N/A's reflect that questions regarding that drug were not asked in that particular year.
n=sample size.

SOURCE: "Table 2. Ergogenic Drug Use by NCAA Division," in *NCAA 2004–05 Drug Testing Results*, National Collegiate Athletic Association, July 6, 2006, http://www1.ncaa.org/membership/ed_outreach/health-safety/drug_ed_progs/2005/DrugStudy2005_Tables.pdf (accessed July 31, 2007)

physical problems are liver and kidney tumors, high blood pressure, elevated cholesterol levels, fluid retention, and severe acne. Ormsbee and Vukovich note that some studies associate steroid use with serious cardiovascular problems, including cardiomyopathies (inflammation of the heart muscle), irregular heart rhythm, development of embolisms (blockage of an artery by a clot or particle carried in the bloodstream), and heart failure. Men sometimes experience symptoms such as shrunken testicles, reduced sperm count, baldness, breast development, and increased risk of prostate cancer. Among women, growth of facial hair, male-pattern baldness, menstrual cycle disruptions, and deepening of the voice have all been reported. Adolescents who use steroids run the risk of halting their growth prematurely, as their bones fuse ahead of schedule. Another problem for teenagers is that steroids cause muscles to grow but do not strengthen the tendons that connect these muscles to bones. This can increase the risk of injury.

Emotional/psychological problems stemming from abuse of steroids include extreme mood swings, depression, paranoid jealousy, irritability, delusions, and impaired judgment. Sometimes these steroid-induced mood swings lead to violent behavior, a condition popularly referred to as "'roid rage."

STEROID USE AND YOUTH

Data from Lloyd D. Johnston et al.'s *Monitoring the Future, National Results on Adolescent Drug Use: Overview of Key Findings, 2006* (May 2007, http://www.monitoringthefuture.org/pubs/monographs/overview2006.pdf), an ongoing study of behavior among secondary school students, college students, and young adults, suggest that steroid use among young people peaked in the early part of the twenty-first century and has been tapering off since then. (See Figure 1.1 in Chapter 1.) According to Johnston and his colleagues, 2.7% of twelfth graders in 2006 had used steroids at some time, whereas 1.8% of tenth graders and 1.6% of eighth graders had done so. Among twelfth

graders, 1.8% reported having used steroids in the past year. Less than 1% of eighth graders had done so.

PERFORMANCE-ENHANCING DRUGS IN COLLEGE SPORTS

The NCAA Committee on Competitive Safeguards and Medical Aspects of Sports regularly compiles the results of the association's drug-testing program. The most recent available data was published in *NCAA Drug-Testing Results 2004–05* (July 6, 2006, http://www1.ncaa.org/membership/ed_outreach/health-safety/NCAA_DT_0405report.pdf). According to the NCAA, positive steroid tests among intercollegiate athletes have declined steeply in recent years. Forty-nine student-athletes tested positive for steroids in year-round testing in 2004–05, compared with ninety-three positive tests in 2000–01. Table 9.1 shows drug testing results by division since 1993. This table shows that even though steroid use has declined dramatically, dropping by nearly half in Divisions I and III and nearly three-quarters in Division II, amphetamine use has increased just as sharply, more than doubling in Division III and nearly doubling in Divisions I and II. Table 9.2 indicates that the decrease in steroid use has been most evident among white athletes, dropping from 2.6% to 1% between 1993 and 2005 among that group. Table 9.3 and Table 9.4 break the results down by gender and sport. Table 9.3 shows that the pattern of increased amphetamine use held across each of the sports listed (with baseball, football, and tennis the highest at 3.9% in 2005), whereas steroid use declined among male basketball, football, tennis, and track and field participants. As shown in Table 9.4, the pattern of increasing amphetamine use and decreasing steroid use among female college athletes held across all sports listed, with 2005 amphetamine use highest among softball players at 5.2%.

STEROIDS IN PROFESSIONAL SPORTS

Every sport has its own way of testing for performance-enhancing drugs and its own policy for dealing with

TABLE 9.2

Drug use among college athletes, by ethnic group, selected years, 1993–2005

Drug	White				African-American				Other			
	1993 (n=1,968)	1997 (n=10,850)	2001 (n=16,706)	2005 (n=14,629)	1993 (n=408)	1997 (n=1,883)	2001 (n=2,908)	2005 (n=2,765)	1993 (n=116)	1997 (n=903)	2001 (n=1,611)	2005 (n=1,954)
Amphetamines	2.1%	3.2%	3.6%	4.5%	1.8%	1.3%	1.7%	2.4 %	1.8%	3.2%	4.0%	3.4%
Anabolic steroids	2.6%	1.1%	1.3%	1.0%	2.2%	1.1%	1.5%	1.6%	1.7%	2.1%	2.2%	1.6%
Ephedrine	N/A	3.8%	2.7%	2.5%	N/A	1.2%	0.9%	2.2%	N/A	3.5%	2.4%	1.6%

Note: All N/A's reflect that questions regarding that drug were not asked in that particular year.
n=sample size.

SOURCE: "Table 4. Ergogenic Drug Use by Ethnic Group," in *NCAA 2004–05 Drug Testing Results*, National Collegiate Athletic Association, July 6, 2006, http://www1.ncaa.org/membership/ed_outreach/health-safety/drug_ed_progs/2005/DrugStudy2005_Tables.pdf (accessed July 31, 2007)

players who use them. The NFL requires its players to take year-round drug tests. The penalty for those caught using banned substances for the first time is a suspension that lasts four games, which amounts to a quarter of a season. The second offense results in a year-long suspension. MLB, which has the most widely publicized steroid problem among the major sports, implemented a new, much harsher drug policy in 2006. Under the new policy, a player's first positive test results in a fifty-game suspension without pay. A second failed test brings a one-hundred-game suspension. A player who tests positive three times is banned for life. In the NBA first-time offenders are suspended for five games. The NHL implemented random drug testing at the beginning of the 2005–06 season.

Football

About seven players per year fail the NFL steroid test, but there is reason to believe that many more steroid users are getting away with it. In 2005 Onterrio Smith (1980–) of the Minnesota Vikings was suspended for a year after being caught with a device called a Whizzinator, which is designed to undermine the accuracy of a urine test. In "Steroids Prescribed to NFL Players" (March 30, 2005, http://www.cbsnews.com/stories/2005/03/29/60II/main683747.shtml), *60 Minutes Wednesday* reveals that three players on the Carolina Panthers had filled prescriptions for steroids before the 2004 Super Bowl. None of these players failed a drug test, but the league has indicated that they will be monitored closely.

Baseball

For the last several years, MLB has suffered from a serious steroid-induced public relations problem. Baseball had no official steroid policy before 2002. That year, as part of the collective bargaining agreement between players and owners, a plan was put in place to hold survey testing in 2003; if more than 5% of players came up positive in anonymous tests, a formal testing policy, with accompanying penalties, would be implemented the following year. When the results of the survey showed a positive rate of between 5% and 7%, the policy development process was triggered. Beginning in 2004 every player was to be tested once per year during the season. The first time a player tested positive, he was to be placed in treatment; a second positive test would result in a fifteen-day suspension. A fifth positive test could result in a suspension lasting up to a year.

Under the policy, not a single player was suspended. However, it was clear that performance-enhancing drugs were still being used on a large scale, and pressure mounted to toughen the policy. The 2005 season brought a new policy in which steroids, steroid precursors (such as andro), designer steroids, masking agents, and diuretics were all banned. All players would be subject to unannounced mandatory testing during the season. In addition, there would be testing of randomly selected players, with no maximum number, and random testing during the off-season. The penalties for a positive result were a ten-day suspension for the first offense, thirty days for a second, sixty days for the third, and one year for the fourth. All these suspensions were without pay. The following season, the penalties were stiffened to those noted earlier.

The question of steroid use in baseball began to arise more frequently as long-standing home run records began to topple in quick succession. In 1998 McGwire and Sosa both passed the single-season home run record of sixty-one set by Roger Maris (1934–1985) in 1961, hitting seventy and sixty-six, respectively. Both players were dogged by rumors that they were assisted by performance-enhancing drugs. In 2001 Bonds extended the record to seventy-three. In 2005 Canseco published *Juiced: Wild Times, Rampant 'Roids, Smash Hits, and How Baseball Got Big*. In it, Canseco paints a lurid picture of rampant steroid use throughout the sport and names a number of players as steroid users.

Amid the furor created by Canseco's book, Congress convened in March 2005 a series of hearings on steroid use in baseball. Several prominent players were called to testify, including Canseco, McGwire, Palmeiro, Sosa, and

TABLE 9.3

Drug use in selected men's college sports, selected years, 1993–2005

Drug	Baseball				Basketball				Football				Tennis				Track/field			
	1993	1997	2001	2005	1993	1997	2001	2005	1993	1997	2001	2005	1993	1997	2001	2005	1993	1997	2001	2005
Amphetamines	1.7%	1.9%	2.7%	3.9%	0.7%	1.3%	1.5%	1.2%	2.9%	2.1%	4.3%	3.9%	0.0%	3.0%	2.2%	3.9%	1.1%	1.6%	1.4%	3.1%
Anabolic steroids	0.7%	1.9%	2.3%	2.3%	2.6%	0.6%	1.4%	1.5%	5.0%	2.2%	3.0%	2.3%	0.0%	0.5%	0.6%	0.3%	0.0%	1.3%	1.3%	0.8%
Ephedrine	N/A	3.3%	3.2%	3.3%	N/A	1.4%	1.9%	1.0%	N/A	5.3%	3.8%	4.2%	N/A	2.9%	1.6%	1.1%	N/A	2.4%	1.8%	1.8%

SOURCE: "Table 6. Ergogenic Drug Use in Men's Sports," in *NCAA 2004–05 Drug Testing Results*, National Collegiate Athletic Association, July 6, 2006, http://www1.ncaa.org/membership/ed_outreach/health-safety/drug_ed_progs/2005/DrugStudy2005_Tables.pdf (accessed July 31, 2007)

TABLE 9.4

Drug use in selected women's college sports, selected years, 1993–2005

Drug	Basketball				Softball				Swimming				Tennis				Track/field			
	1993	1997	2001	2005	1993	1997	2001	2005	1993	1997	2001	2005	1993	1997	2001	2005	1993	1997	2001	2005
Amphetamines	1.5%	1.0%	2.0%	2.9%	4.0%	4.7%	3.9%	5.2%	2.2%	4.7%	3.3%	4.4%	0.0%	2.5%	2.7%	2.6%	1.4%	2.1%	1.7%	1.9%
Anabolic steroids	1.5%	0.4%	0.7%	0.3%	1.7%	0.9%	0.8%	0.4%	0.6%	0.8%	1.3%	0.1%	2.7%	0.3%	0.0%	0.2%	2.7%	0.6%	0.6%	0.1%
Ephedrine	N/A	1.8%	1.3%	1.5%	N/A	1.1%	2.3%	2.9%	N/A	0.5%	2.2%	1.7%	N/A	1.9%	1.2%	1.2%	N/A	0.9%	1.3%	1.1%

SOURCE: "Table 7. Ergogenic Drug Use in Women's Sports," in *NCAA 2004–05 Drug Testing Results*, National Collegiate Athletic Association, July 6, 2006, http://www1.ncaa.org/membership/ed_outreach/health-safety/drug_ed_progs/2005/DrugStudy2005_Tables.pdf (accessed July 31, 2007)

TABLE 9.5

Major League Baseball players suspended for using performance enhancing drugs, April 2005–July 2007

Player	Team	Date announced
Alex Sanchez	Tampa Bay	April 2005
Jorge Piedra	Colorado	April 2005
Agustin Montero	Texas	April 2005
Jamal Strong	Seattle	April 2005
Juan Rincón	Minnesota	May 2005
Rafael Betancourt	Cleveland	July 2005
Rafael Palmeiro	Baltimore	August 2005
Ryan Franklin	Seattle	August 2005
Mike Morse	Seattle	September 2005
Carlos Almanzar	Texas	October 2005
Felix Heredia	NY Mets	October 2005
Matt Lawton	NY Yankees	November 2005
Yasaku Iriki	NY Mets	April 2006
Jason Grimsley	Arizona	June 2006
Guillermo Mota	NY Mets	November 2006
Juan Salas	Tampa Bay	May 2007
Neifi Perez	Detroit	July 2007
Donnie Sadler	Arizona	July 2007

SOURCE: Created by Robert Jacobson for The Gale Group, 2007

Schilling. Canseco reiterated his claims before the congressional panel. McGwire was elusive, saying, "I'm not here to talk about the past," whereas Palmeiro denied all wrongdoing. Palmeiro, after testifying under oath that he had "never used steroids," tested positive for the drug in July 2005. Bob Hohler notes in "Palmeiro Remains on Sideline" (*Boston Globe*, August 12, 2005) that Palmeiro was suspended for ten games and fined $164,000.

Palmeiro was not the first high-profile baseball player to get caught using steroids. As the BALCO scandal continued to unfold, Bonds admitted during grand jury testimony in 2004 to having used steroids, though he claimed that he had done so unknowingly via an arthritis cream he thought was steroid-free. Even though baseball players test positive regularly—Palmeiro was the seventh to do so in 2005—most of them are lesser known, and their stories do not make the headlines. The only prominent baseball player to publicly admit to intentionally using steroids is Jason Giambi (1971–), who confessed that he had used performance-enhancing drugs during his stellar 2003 season, in which he hit forty-one home runs. Table 9.5 contains a list of MLB players who have been suspended for using performance-enhancing drugs as of July 2007.

Another book sparked a further investigation in 2006. In *Game of Shadows: Barry Bonds, BALCO, and the Steroids Scandal That Rocked Professional Sports* (2006), Mark Fainaru-Wada and Lance Williams outline a series of damaging accusations associated with the BALCO affair. Fainaru-Wada and Williams focus most of their attention on Bonds, but they also implicate several other athletes, including Jones and Montgomery. Shortly after the

book came out, it was announced that Allan H. Selig (1934–), the baseball commissioner, had engaged the former U.S. senator George Mitchell (1933–) to head an independent investigation into steroid use in baseball, in an effort to stave off further intervention by Congress. As Bonds was surpassing Hank Aaron's (1934–) all-time home run record in the summer of 2007, a feat he accomplished on August 7, Mitchell announced that his investigation was in its final phase and that a report would be released in the coming months.

Steroid use in baseball appears to be particularly widespread among players from Latin American countries. Joseph Contreras, in "Too Intense?" (*Newsweek*, May 27, 2006), notes that a majority of players who tested positive during MLB's first year of mandatory testing were from Latin America. Contreras quotes some insiders as pointing to the increased pressure on young players from poor countries to do well, as baseball presents one of the few potential paths out of poverty for these individuals. In "Caught Looking" (*ESPN Magazine*, May 28, 2007), Ian Gordon points to a language barrier as part of the problem, suggesting that some Spanish-speaking players may not be getting the message about banned substances in spite of the league's best outreach efforts.

Basketball

Rookie NBA players are tested up to four times per season, and veterans are subject to one random test during training camp. Prohibited substances include amphetamines, cocaine, opiates, marijuana, and steroids. Penalties range from suspensions for a number of games to a lifetime ban. As of 2007, basketball had largely avoided the kind of scandals involving performance-enhancing drugs that plagued the baseball world.

Hockey

Until 2005 the NHL had no formal antidoping policy. However, in the wake of scandals that dogged other major sports in recent years, the league unveiled its first such policy in September 2005 at a congressional hearing on drug use in professional sports. Under the new policy, NHL players are subject to a maximum of two random tests with no advance notice during the NHL season for the performance-enhancing drugs designated on the World Anti-Doping Agency's (WADA) "Prohibited List" (2007, http://www.wada-ama.org/en/prohibitedlist.ch2). A first-time positive test will result in a twenty-game suspension. The suspension increases to sixty games for a second offense, and a third positive test can result in permanent suspension from the league.

Cycling

Perhaps no other sport has been tainted by doping scandals more than professional bicycle racing, particularly the sport's most illustrious event: the Tour de

France. During the 1967 Tour, the British cyclist Tom Simpson (1937–1967) died on one of the climbs in the race after using large amounts of amphetamines. The first major drug scandal in cycling took place in 1998, when the Festina cycling team was thrown out of the competition after the team masseur Willy Voet (1945–) was caught in possession of various narcotics and other banned substances, including EPO, growth hormones, testosterone, and amphetamines. In 2004 David Millar (1977–), a time-trial world champion, was banned from the tour following the discovery of banned drugs at the offices of his cycling team, Cofidis. Doping allegations have plagued the career of the American cyclist Lance Armstrong (1972–), who won his seventh consecutive Tour de France in 2005 before announcing his retirement. In 2002 Armstrong was linked to the sports physician Michele Ferrari (1953–), who was reputed to have developed a system for taking EPO without detection. In 2005 EPO was found in Armstrong's old laboratory samples from the 1999 Tour de France. Armstrong vehemently denied ever using banned drugs and questioned the validity of such old samples that had passed through so many hands over the years. In 2006 investigators cleared Armstrong of the charges and criticized antidoping authorities for mishandling evidence and making irresponsible accusations.

Armstrong's exoneration notwithstanding, the situation only became worse for the Tour de France. On the eve of the 2006 race, several top riders, including the contenders Jan Ullrich (1973–) and Ivan Basso (1977–), were banned from competing as a result of accusations made by Spanish police after a long investigation called Operacion Puerto. The 2006 Tour was won by the American cyclist Floyd Landis (1975–). However, shortly after the conclusion of the race, it was revealed that Landis had failed a drug test at the seventeenth stage of the race, with tests showing an abnormally high level of testosterone in his blood. Landis maintained his innocence, but he was nevertheless stripped of his title and fired from his racing team.

The doping situation at the tour continued its downward spiral in 2007. Several prominent riders either tested positive for banned substances before or during the race, or were punished for avoiding testing. They included the German cyclist Patrik Sinkewitz (1980–), who tested positive at a pre-tour training camp; Alexander Vinokourov (1973–) of Russia, who was pulled after the fifteenth stage for receiving an illicit blood transfusion; and the Danish racer Michael Rasmussen (1974–), who was withdrawn from the tour for intentionally avoiding a required blood test.

STEROIDS AND THE LAW

Anabolic steroids are Schedule III–controlled substances in the United States. In October 2004 the federal Anabolic Steroids Act was signed into law. The act updated the Anabolic Steroid Control Act of 1990 in a number of ways. It amended the definition of anabolic steroids, adding THG, androstenedione, and certain related chemicals to the list of substances the law covered. The act also directed the U.S. Sentencing Commission to review federal sentencing guidelines for offenses related to steroids and provided for increased penalties for committing these offenses. It authorized the U.S. attorney general to exempt from regulation steroid-containing drugs that do not pose a drug abuse threat. Finally, the law directed the U.S. secretary of health and human services to provide grants for the development of science-based educational programs for elementary and secondary schools on the hazards of anabolic steroid use. A number of states have passed their own laws targeted specifically at curbing steroid use among youths.

Antidoping Agencies

By the end of the twentieth century the global sports community recognized that it would take a coordinated international effort to bring the problem of performance-enhancing drugs under control. WADA was created in 1999 as a collaborative initiative between sports agencies and governments across the globe. WADA's role is to lead international efforts against doping in sports through public education, advocacy, research, and drug testing and to provide leadership for the efforts of agencies working against doping in individual countries. Table 9.6 shows a list of organizations that have signed on to the WADA code. The U.S. Anti-Doping Agency (USADA), an independent nonprofit organization, was launched in October 2000 to lead this work at the national level. The USADA oversees testing, education, research, and adjudication on drug issues for U.S. athletes competing in the Olympic, Pan Am, and Paralympic games.

TABLE 9.6

Organizations that have signed on to WADA (World Anti-Doping Agency) Code

All Olympic events
All Paralympic events
Commonwealth Games
World Cup
Tennis Grand Slam events
Davis Cup (tennis)
Tour de France
U.S. Tennis Association
International Association of Athletics Federations (track & field)
International Basketball Federation
International Gymnastics Federation
International Hockey Federation
International Triathlon Union
International Swimming Federation
International Table Tennis Federation
World Taekwondo Federation
World Bridge Federation
International Chess Federation

List of notable organizations not covered by WADA rules

Major League Baseball
NFL
NBA
NHL
Major League Soccer
NCAA
PGA
LPGA
U.S. Golf Association (U.S. Open)
British Open (golf)

SOURCE: Created by Robert Jacobson for The Gale Group, 2007

CHAPTER 10
SPORTS AND GAMBLING

The drive in humans to gamble on sports seems to be almost as strong as the drive to participate in them. People have been betting on the outcome of sporting events since ancient times. In ancient Rome the wealthy class wagered on chariot races, animal fights, and gladiator battles. The Romans spread their penchant for gambling across the breadth of their empire, including Britain. In the sixteenth and seventeenth centuries people throughout Europe enjoyed betting on cockfights, wrestling, and footraces. In the eighteenth century horse racing and boxing rose to prominence as spectator sports on which the public enjoyed gambling. The nineteenth and twentieth centuries brought a new emphasis on team sports, and Europeans began risking their wages on rugby, soccer, and cricket games.

Colonists brought their yen for gambling on sports with them to North America. Horse racing was a particularly popular sport among those inclined toward gambling. Most forms of gambling, including sports gambling, became illegal in the United States during the nineteenth century, as laws changed to conform to the morals of the time. Nevertheless, it remained legal to bet on horse racing, and other sports gambling continued to flourish underground. The state of Nevada legalized gambling in 1931, but after a couple of decades it was so tainted by organized crime and other scandals that it was the subject of government crackdowns during the 1950s. A new, highly regulated version of sports betting returned to Nevada in 1975; centered in Las Vegas, this segment of the gambling industry continues to thrive in the twenty-first century.

Modern sports gambling in the United States can be roughly divided into three categories: pari-mutuel gambling on horse racing, dog racing, and jai alai games; legal sports betting through a licensed bookmaker; and illegal sports gambling. The third category makes up the biggest portion of sports gambling in the nation.

PARI-MUTUEL GAMBLING

Pari-mutuel betting was invented in late nineteenth-century France by Pierre Oller. *Pari-mutuel* is a French term that means "mutual stake." In this kind of betting all the money bet on an event is combined into a single pool, which is then split among the winning bettors, with management first taking some share off the top before distribution. The share management receives is called the takeout; the takeout rate, which in the United States is set by state law, is usually about 20% of the total betting pool. Unlike placing a bet with a bookmaker, an individual betting on a pari-mutuel event is betting against other gamblers rather than against the house. The house keeps the same percentage of the total bets regardless of the outcome of the event. Another source of revenue from pari-mutuel gambling is breakage. Winning bettors are not usually paid out to the exact penny total; rather, payouts are rounded down. The leftover money, or breakage, is usually only a few cents per bet, but it adds up to a substantial sum over the course of thousands of transactions. Breakage may be split in various ways. For example, breakage generated by California horse tracks is split among the state, the track operators, and the horse owners.

In pari-mutuel betting the total pool in a race depends on how much is bet on that race. Every bet that is placed on a particular horse or player affects the odds; as a result, the more people who bet on a particular outcome, the lower the payout is for those who bet on that outcome. Betting on a long shot offers a potentially better payout, but a lower likelihood of winning anything.

The pari-mutuel system has been used in horse racing since about 1875, but it did not become widespread until the 1920s and '30s, with the introduction of the totalizor, a special calculator that could automatically calculate the odds for each horse in a race based on the bets that had been placed. Before the 1930s most betting on horse races was done through bookmakers. Corruption was widespread. In 1933 California, Michigan, Ohio, and New Hampshire legalized pari-mutuel gambling on horse racing mainly as a way to regulate the industry, decrease corruption, and generate revenue for the state. Many other states followed their lead over the next several years.

Historically, most pari-mutuel betting has taken place in person at the location where the event is happening. However, in recent years bets have been placed at off-track betting facilities, which were first approved by the New York legislature in 1970. Wagering via telephone or the Internet is also available in some states. Many races are simulcast to in-state and out-of-state locations, including off-track betting sites. This allows bettors to engage in intertrack wagering, which means one can bet on a race at one track while being physically present at a completely different track.

The American Gaming Association (AGA) estimates in the fact sheet "Gaming Revenue: Current-Year Data" (October 2006, http://www.americangaming.org/Industry/factsheets/statistics_detail.cfv?id=7) that the total gross revenue from pari-mutuel gambling in the United States in 2005 was $3.7 billion, the vast majority of which came from horse racing.

An increasing share of pari-mutuel wagering has been taking place at racinos. Racinos, a growing phenomenon in the gaming industry, are horse- or greyhound-racing tracks that also offer casino gaming on site. According to Gaming and Resort Development, in "U.S. Casino & Racino Revenue Analysis 2006" (2007, http://casinodev.com/revised sitework/Articles/National2006Report.pdf), 10.3% of all casino gambling in 2006 took place at racinos.

Thoroughbred Horse Racing

People have been betting on horse races for thousands of years. Horse racing was a popular spectator sport among wealthy Greeks and Romans. Later, knights returning to Western Europe from the Crusades brought with them speedy Arabian stallions, which were bred with English mares to create the line now called Thoroughbred. Thoroughbreds are fast, graceful runners and are identified by their height and long, slim legs. Thoroughbred racing quickly caught on among the British aristocracy, and it was soon dubbed the "Sport of Kings." The sport came to North America with the colonists; there are records of horse racing taking place in the New York area as early as 1665.

Thoroughbred racing remained popular in the United States throughout the eighteenth and nineteenth centuries. The sport was scaled back significantly during World War II (1939–1945), and after the war it remained in steep decline. The reasons for horse racing's loss of popularity in the postwar years include competition from the rise of amusement parks and malls; the failure of the

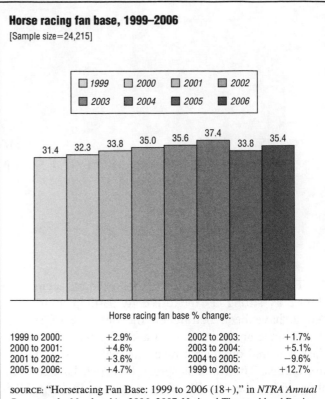

FIGURE 10.1

Horse racing fan base, 1999–2006
[Sample size=24,215]

Legend: 1999, 2000, 2001, 2002, 2003, 2004, 2005, 2006

31.4 32.3 33.8 35.0 35.6 37.4 33.8 35.4

Horse racing fan base % change:

1999 to 2000:	+2.9%	2002 to 2003:	+1.7%
2000 to 2001:	+4.6%	2003 to 2004:	+5.1%
2001 to 2002:	+3.6%	2004 to 2005:	−9.6%
2005 to 2006:	+4.7%	1999 to 2006:	+12.7%

SOURCE: "Horseracing Fan Base: 1999 to 2006 (18+)," in *NTRA Annual Report to the Membership, 2006–2007*, National Thoroughbred Racing Association, 2007, http://www.ntra.com/content/NTRAAnnualReport 2007.pdf (accessed July 31, 2007)

racing industry to embrace television; and the rise of other gambling opportunities, such as casinos and lotteries. However, even though attendance at horse races has declined substantially, the money continues to flow, and has actually increased since the 1990s. Gary Rotstein reports in "How Slot Machines Have Saved Racetracks" (*Pittsburgh Post-Gazette*, February 25, 2007) that in 1990 the total amount bet (handle) on Thoroughbred races in the United States was $9.4 billion. In "Total Handle, Purses up for 2006" (January 16, 2007, http://www.ntra.com/content.aspx?type=pr&id=22765), the National Thoroughbred Racing Association indicates that in 2006 the total waging on U.S. races was $14.8 billion. According to Figure 10.1, the self-described fan base for horse racing has hovered between a low of 31.4% in 1999 to a high of 37.4% in 2004.

Bill Toland indicates in "Horse Racing Has Grim Underside" (*Pittsburgh Post-Gazette*, June 10, 2006) that in 2006 there were about ninety Thoroughbred racetracks in the United States. The racetracks in warm parts of the country are open throughout the year, whereas others are active only during the warm months. Some are government owned, whereas others are privately held. The Thoroughbred gambling business is dominated by a handful of companies, the largest being two publicly traded firms: Churchill Downs and Magna Entertainment.

The three most prestigious Thoroughbred races together make up the Triple Crown of horse racing. These races, which take place over a five-week period during May and June each year, are the Kentucky Derby at Churchill Downs in Louisville, Kentucky; the Preakness Stakes at Pimlico in Baltimore, Maryland; and the Belmont Stakes at Belmont Park in Elmont, New York. According to the Kentucky Derby, in "Wagering and Attendance Results from Kentucky Derby 133" (May 6, 2007, http://www.kentuckyder by.com/2007/derby_news/wagering-and-attendance-results-kentucky-derby-133), in 2007 the betting totaled $118.3 million, a slight decline from the record set in 2006. Most of this total—$106.2 million—was bet off-track. Magna Entertainment, in "Preakness Broadcast Highest Rated Sports Program of Weekend" (May 24, 2007, http://www.preakness.com/NewsEvents/FeatureStories/ Details/Baltimore052407.htm), notes that $87.2 million was wagered on the 2007 Preakness Stakes, whereas Matt Hegarty reports in "Handle, Attendance down for Belmont Stakes" (June 12, 2007, http://sports.espn.go .com/sports/horse/triplecrown07/news/story?id=2901730) that the 2007 Belmont Stakes drew a handle of $37.8 million.

Non-Thoroughbred Horse Racing

Even though Thoroughbreds dominate the horse-racing scene in the United States, pari-mutuel gambling is available for other types of horses as well. Harness racing, in which horses trot or pace rather than gallop and pull the jockey in a two-wheeled cart called a sulky, uses a horse called a Standardbred, which is typically shorter and more muscular than a Thoroughbred. According to the U.S. Trotting Association (May 2007, http://www.us trotting.com/trackside/trackfacts/trackfacts.cfm), there were forty-six licensed harness-racing tracks around the country in 2007. Another type of horse commonly raced is the quarter horse, which gets its name from the fact that it excels at sprinting distances under a quarter of a mile. Finally, the Arabian Jockey Club (2006, http:// www.arabianracing.org/RacingStats.asp?ID=3) notes that in 2006 about twenty-three tracks around the United States featured Arabian horses, the only true purebred horses on the circuit.

Greyhound Racing

Like horses, greyhounds have been raced for amuse-ment and gambling purposes for centuries. Greyhound racing has been called the "Sport of Queens," probably because it was Queen Elizabeth I (1533–1603) of Eng-land who first standardized the rules for greyhound cours-ing (a sport in which greyhounds are used to hunt rabbits) in the sixteenth century. Greyhound racing was brought to the United States in the late nineteenth century, and the first circular greyhound track was opened in Califor-nia in 1919.

Greyhound racing is not nearly as popular as horse racing, and its popularity has been declining since the early 1990s. The sport reached its peak of popularity in 1992, when, according to the Greyhound Racing Association of America (GRA-America; September 19, 2006, http:// www.gra-america.org/the_sport/history.html), nearly 3.5 million people attended the 16,827 races that took place at more than 50 tracks. Nearly $3.5 billion was bet on greyhound races that year. Revenue has dropped by nearly half since then. The GRA-America (2007, http://www.gra-america.org/the_sport/racetracks.html) notes that there were forty-six greyhound tracks operating in fifteen states in 2007. More than a third of the tracks currently in oper-ation are located in Florida. The decline in the popularity of greyhound racing is in part due to allegations, many of them well documented, of the mistreatment of the dogs. For example, the Greyhound Protection League collects data on cruelty and deaths related to greyhound racing, and lobbies for the sport to be banned altogether.

Jai Alai

Jai alai is a sport similar to handball. Like handball, it is played on a court and involves bouncing a ball against a wall. In jai alai the ball is caught using a long, curved basket called a cesta. The Florida Gaming Corporation (February 17, 2004, http://www.fla-gaming.com/history.htm) states that the first permanent jai alai arena, or fronton, was built in Florida in 1926. Jai alai is an endangered sport in the United States. The Committee on Regulated Industries of the Florida Senate notes in *Legalized Gambling in Florida—The Competition in the Marketplace* (November 2004, http:// www.flsenate.gov/data/Publications/2005/Senate/reports/ interim_reports/pdf/2005-155ri.pdf) that $430.3 million was bet on jai alai between 1987 and 1988. By the 2003 to 2004 season the handle had decreased to $93.8 million. In the United States, jai alai is confined almost entirely to Florida, where the sport retains a sizeable following. Most of the frontons in Florida, however, rely on revenue from other forms of gambling, such as poker, to help keep them in business.

LEGAL SPORTS GAMBLING

As of 2007 gambling on sports was legal in only one state: Nevada. Nowhere else in the United States is betting allowed on big-time sports such as professional football, basketball, or baseball. In *Hidden Revenue: Regulating the Underground Economy of Sports Betting* (February 2005, http://www.pfnyc.org/publications/2005_02_hid den_revenue.pdf), Jonathan A. Schwabish and Michael R. Simas explain that this state of affairs was essentially locked into place by the passage of the Professional and Amateur Sports Protection Act of 1992, which banned sports betting everywhere except those states where it was already allowed in some form: Delaware, Montana, Nevada, and Oregon. However, aside from Nevada, the action is limited; it may be part of a lottery game, or fantasy leagues and office pools may be legal.

In Nevada legal sports gambling takes place through licensed establishments (books) that accept and pay out bets on sporting events. Sports books are legal only in Nevada. One must be at least twenty-one years old to place bets with licensed bookmakers. The AGA states in the fact sheet "Sports Wagering" (March 12, 2007, http://www .americangaming.org/industry/factsheets/issues_detail.cfv?id =16) that in 2007 there were 170 locations licensed to operate sports and/or race books, all of them in Nevada.

Bookmaking

Bookmaking is the term used for determining gambling odds and handling bets and payouts. The person doing the bookmaking is called a bookmaker or bookie. Bookmakers make their money by charging a commission on each bet; the commission is usually between 4% and 5%.

Most sports bets are based on a point spread, which is set by the bookmaker. A point spread is how much a favored team must win a game by for those betting on that team to collect. For example, if Team A is a ten-point favorite to defeat Team B, the bettor is actually betting on whether Team A will beat Team B by at least this margin. If Team A wins by nine points, then those betting on Team B are winners and those picking team A are losers. In this example, Team B has lost the game, but has "beat the spread." The point spread concept was introduced in the 1940s by the bookmaker Charles K. McNeil as a way of encouraging people to bet on underdogs. Before the point spread system, bookmakers risked losing large sums on lopsided games in which everybody bet on the favorite to win.

Nevada: The Gambling Capital of the United States

Nevada legalized gambling in the 1930s as a way of generating revenue during the Great Depression (1929–1939). The state's legislature made off-track betting on horses legal during the 1940s. Betting on sports and racing was popular in Nevada's casinos throughout that decade. At the beginning of the 1950s, however, the Nevada gambling world came under the scrutiny of Congress for its ties to organized crime. Senator Estes Kefauver (D-TN; 1903–1963) initiated hearings to investigate the matter. These nationally televised hearings drew attention to a culture of corruption and gangland activity that had settled in Las Vegas. The hearings resulted in the imposition of a 10% federal excise tax on sports betting. This tax effectively strangled casino-based sports bookmaking in Nevada.

Koleman S. Strumpf of University of North Carolina, Chapel Hill, reports in *Illegal Sports Bookmakers* (February 2003, http://www.unc.edu/~cigar/papers/Bookie4b.pdf)

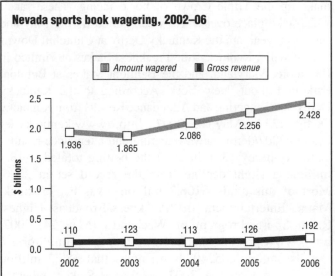
that the sports books mounted a comeback in the 1970s, after the excise tax was reduced to 2% in 1974, and by the 1980s sports and race bookmaking was a booming industry, helped along by another reduction in the excise tax, to 0.3% in 1983. Bookmakers such as Jimmy "The Greek" Snyder (1919–1996) became national celebrities by appearing regularly on television. Between 1982 and 1987 Nevada sports book betting increased by 230%. Betting volume began to taper off in the mid-1990s, in part due to the rise of online wagering, though it has rebounded somewhat in the last few years. For example, the amount of revenue rose from $1.8 billion in 2003 to $2.4 billion in bets in 2006, an increase of 33%. (See Figure 10.2.)

Football is the biggest betting draw among the major sports. According to the AGA, in 2006 football accounted for 47% of sports book wagering, followed by basketball (26%) and baseball (19%). (See Figure 10.3.) The Super Bowl alone is a gigantic gambling event. The Nevada Gaming Commission and State Gaming Control Board notes that $93.1 million was bet on the 2007 Super Bowl, the second highest total in Super Bowl history. Table 10.1 and Figure 10.4 show total Super Bowl betting with Nevada sports books, along with revenue from that betting, for the years 1998 through 2007. In "Sports Wagering," the AGA indicates that the National Collegiate Athletic Association (NCAA) basketball tournament brings in a similar sum, although it involves sixty-four teams and six rounds of games. Industrywide, the AGA notes that about one-third of the bets placed legally in Nevada sports books are on college sports. It is

FIGURE 10.3

Nevada sports book wagering, by sport, 2006

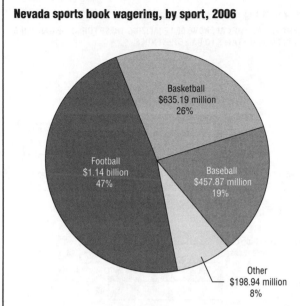

Basketball $635.19 million 26%

Football $1.14 billion 47%

Baseball $457.87 million 19%

Other $198.94 million 8%

Note: Figures represent sports betting totals from commercial casinos in Nevada, the only commercial casino state where sports books currently are operational.

SOURCE: "What Sports are the Most Popular to Bet On?" in *2007 State of the States: The AGA Survey of Casino Entertainment*, American Gaming Association, 2007, p. 34, http://www.americangaming.org/assets/files/aga_2007_sos.pdf (accessed July 31, 2007). Reprinted with permission of the American Gaming Association. All rights reserved.

TABLE 10.1

Nevada sports book wagering on Super Bowls, 1998–2007

Year	Wagers	Win/loss	Win %	Game results
2007	$93,067,358	$12,930,175	13.9%	Indianapolis 29, Chicago 17
2006	$94,534,372	$8,828,431	9.3%	Pittsburgh 21, Seattle 10
2005	$90,759,236	$15,430,138	17.0%	New England 24, Philadelphia 21
2004	$81,242,191	$12,440,698	15.3%	New England 32, Carolina 29
2003	$71,693,032	$5,264,963	7.3%	Tampa Bay 48, Oakland 21
2002	$71,513,304	$2,331,607	3.3%	New England 20, St. Louis 17
2001	$67,661,425	$11,002,636	16.3%	Baltimore 34, N.Y. Giants 7
2000	$71,046,751	$4,237,978	6.0%	St. Louis 23, Tennessee 16
1999	$75,986,520	$2,906,601	3.8%	Denver 34, Atlanta 19
1998	$77,253,246	$472,033	0.6%	Denver 31, Green Bay 24

SOURCE: "Summary of Nevada Sports Book Performance for the Last Ten Super Bowls," in *GCB Press Release: 2007 Superbowl*, Nevada Gaming Commission and State Gaming Control Board, February 6, 2007, http://gaming.nv.gov/documents/pdf/pr_2007superbowl.pdf (accessed July 31, 2007)

currently illegal to gamble on high school sports and on the Olympics.

ATTITUDES TOWARD SPORTS GAMBLING

In spite of gambling's reputation as a so-called vice, Americans are overwhelmingly comfortable with sports gambling, though a relatively small percentage actually participate. A 2006 Pew Research Center poll found that 67% of Americans had engaged in some form of gambling over the past year, but that only 14% of those

FIGURE 10.4

Super Bowl betting history, 2001–07

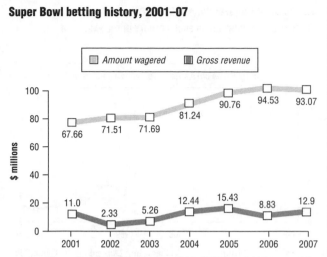

SOURCE: "Super Bowl Betting History, 2002–2007," in *2007 State of the States: The AGA Survey of Casino Entertainment*, American Gaming Association, 2007, p. 34, http://www.americangaming.org/assets/files/aga_2007_sos.pdf (accessed July 31, 2007). Reprinted with permission of the American Gaming Association. All rights reserved.

FIGURE 10.5

Participation in sports and other gambling, 2006

PERCENT SAYING THEY DID EACH ACTIVITY IN THE PAST YEAR

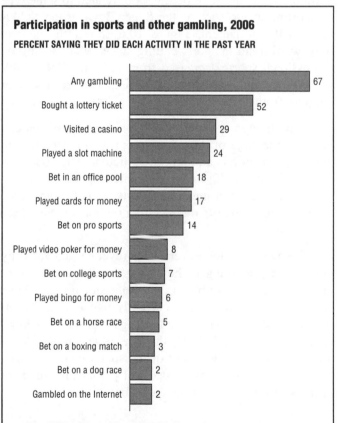

SOURCE: "What Kind of Bet Did You Place This Year?" in *Gambling: As the Take Rises, So Does Public Concern*, Pew Research Center, May 23, 2006, http://pewresearch.org/assets/social/pdf/Gambling.pdf (accessed July 31, 2007)

surveyed said they had bet on professional sports in the past year, and 7% had bet on college sports. (See Figure 10.5.) Another 5% had bet on horse racing, and 3% had

FIGURE 10.6

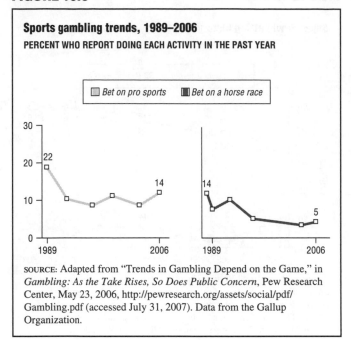

Sports gambling trends, 1989–2006

PERCENT WHO REPORT DOING EACH ACTIVITY IN THE PAST YEAR

☐ Bet on pro sports ■ Bet on a horse race

SOURCE: Adapted from "Trends in Gambling Depend on the Game," in *Gambling: As the Take Rises, So Does Public Concern*, Pew Research Center, May 23, 2006, http://pewresearch.org/assets/social/pdf/Gambling.pdf (accessed July 31, 2007). Data from the Gallup Organization.

FIGURE 10.7

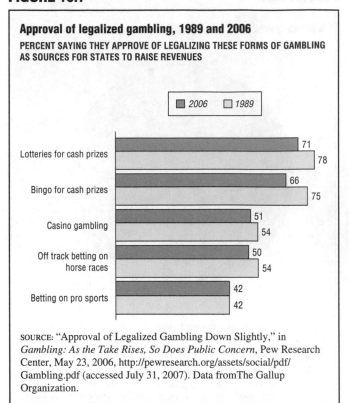

Approval of legalized gambling, 1989 and 2006

PERCENT SAYING THEY APPROVE OF LEGALIZING THESE FORMS OF GAMBLING AS SOURCES FOR STATES TO RAISE REVENUES

■ 2006 ☐ 1989

	2006	1989
Lotteries for cash prizes	71	78
Bingo for cash prizes	66	75
Casino gambling	51	54
Off track betting on horse races	50	54
Betting on pro sports	42	42

SOURCE: "Approval of Legalized Gambling Down Slightly," in *Gambling: As the Take Rises, So Does Public Concern*, Pew Research Center, May 23, 2006, http://pewresearch.org/assets/social/pdf/Gambling.pdf (accessed July 31, 2007). Data fromThe Gallup Organization.

wagered on boxing. Eighteen percent said they had participated in an office betting pool related to some type of sporting event, such as the Super Bowl or the NCAA basketball tournament. Figure 10.6 shows the general downward trend in sports betting since 1989. Betting on professional sports decreased from 22% in 1989 to 14% in 2006; betting on horse racing experienced a similar decline, from 14% in 1989 to 5% in 2006.

Even though not many people actually participate, a larger percentage of Americans approve of gambling in general, and sports gambling in particular. The 2006 Pew survey found that 42% of respondents approved of legalized gambling on professional sports, and 50% approved of states legalizing off-track betting on horse racing. (See Figure 10.7.)

The potential for government revenue generated by legal sports gambling is the strongest argument for proponents of legalizing betting on professional and college sports in states where it is currently banned. Ari Weinberg estimates in "The Case for Legal Sports Gambling" (*Forbes*, January 27, 2003) that the 1992 law that locks all states except Nevada out of the sports gambling market deprives other states of taxes of perhaps hundreds of billions of dollars in illegal sports bets each year.

ILLEGAL SPORTS GAMBLING

Even though gambling is legal in one form or another—whether in casinos, at racetracks, or on lotteries—in every state except Utah and Hawaii, illegal gambling nevertheless flourishes as well. The AGA estimates that the Nevada sports books account for less than 1% of all sports gambling in the United States. So prevalent is illicit sports gambling that it is

almost impossible to calculate the dollar amounts involved. In "Ban on College Sports Betting Could Cost State Books Millions" (*Las Vegas Review-Journal*, May 18, 1999), Robert Macy estimates that illegal sports gambling in the United States ranges from $80 billion to $380 billion per year.

Many different activities fall into the category of illegal gambling, ranging from betting on sports outside of the legitimate, licensed bookmaking system to benign office pools. Sports gambling has a long history of association with organized crime, which ran illegal bookmaking operations across the country as early as the 1920s. After Nevada legalized casino gambling in 1931, organized crime quickly took control of the industry. When the federal government made progress in driving organized crime out of the casino business in the 1950s, the mobsters focused their efforts on bookmaking, which was not yet available in the casinos. To this day, a large portion of sports gambling is believed to be controlled by organized crime figures.

FIXING, SHAVING, AND TAMPERING: SPORTS GAMBLING SCANDALS

Shady characters, including prominent organized crime figures, have always gravitated toward sports, sometimes as a means of laundering money obtained illicitly in other industries. The history of sports is rife with tales of gamblers paying off athletes to "take a dive" or miss the crucial shot. Major professional sports leagues and the NCAA have taken measures to distance themselves from sports gambling, but their efforts have not prevented a long list of sports gambling scandals from taking place in the last several decades.

Perhaps the most notorious sports gambling scandal in history was the so-called Black Sox Scandal of 1919, in which gamblers bribed several members of the Chicago White Sox to intentionally throw the World Series. A huge point-shaving scandal encompassing seven schools and thirty-two players rocked college basketball in 1951. Point shaving is a type of game fixing in which players, who are usually bribed by gamblers, conspire to avoid beating a published point spread. In 1978 associates of the Lucchese organized crime family orchestrated a point-shaving scheme with key members of the Boston College basketball team. Another point-shaving scheme involving college basketball was uncovered at Arizona State University in 1994. Lesser-known scandals have taken place in the intervening years.

Many high-profile professional athletes have gotten in trouble over the years for gambling on the sport in which they participate, which inevitably creates suspicion about game fixing. In 1963 the National Football League (NFL) players Alex Karras (1935–) of the Detroit Lions and Paul Hornung (1935–) of the Green Bay Packers were suspended for betting on their own teams' games. Denny McLain (1944–) of the Detroit Tigers, the last pitcher to win thirty games in a season, was suspended for most of the 1970 season for associating with gamblers. In 1989 the baseball player Pete Rose (1941–), who holds the record for the most career hits, was kicked out of baseball for gambling on Major League Baseball games. He denied doing so at the time but has since admitted to betting on baseball games while serving as manager of the Cincinnati Reds. Rose's lifetime suspension has kept him out of the Baseball Hall of Fame, into which he would certainly have been inducted had his gambling activities not come to light. In 1999 the former San Francisco Forty-niners owner Eddie DeBartolo (1946–) was fined $1 million and suspended by the NFL for paying a $400,000 bribe to obtain a license to operate a casino in Louisiana.

The National Basketball Association (NBA) was rocked in the summer of 2007 by revelations that the veteran referee Tim Donaghy (1967–) had been involved in gambling on NBA games, including games in which he had officiated. The NBA immediately took the position that Donaghy's activities represented an isolated case and that gambling among referees was extremely rare. In August 2007 Donaghy pleaded guilty to two felony charges stemming from evidence that he had provided betting recommendations to gamblers based on inside information about game circumstances. Just days after the NBA scandal broke, professional tennis was forced to grapple with a gambling-related scandal of its own

when suspicious betting patterns emerged on a match between the high-ranked Russian player Nikolay Davydenko (1981–) and the much lower-ranked Martin Vassallo Arguello (1980–) of Argentina at an Association of Tennis Professionals tournament in Poland.

Since the 1990s college sports have been at the center of the most visible sports gambling scandals. During the 1994–95 season two Northwestern University basketball players were caught shaving points. Two years later, thirteen football players at Boston College were suspended for gambling on college football games. Other cases have involved the University of Washington football coach Rick Neuheisel (1961–), the University of Michigan basketball player Chris Webber (1973–), the Florida State University quarterback Adrian McPherson (1983–), and the University of Florida basketball player Teddy Dupay (1979–).

After decades of taking measures to avoid even the appearance of impropriety by distancing themselves from gambling entirely, there are some signs that the major sports leagues are ready to establish a cozier relationship with the gambling industry, simply because the money in sports gambling is too good to resist. A prime example are the Maloof brothers—Joseph (1955–), Gavin (1956–), and George Jr. (1964–)—who together own both the NBA's Sacramento Kings and the Palms Casino in Las Vegas. Joseph and Gavin run the Kings, while George oversees the Palms. When the Maloofs sought to buy the Kings in 1998, the NBA was willing to give its blessing provided the Maloofs quit accepting bets on NBA games in their casino's legal bookmaking operation. Before the Maloofs, there was the ITT Corporation, a conglomerate that owned three Las Vegas casinos at the time, which was allowed to purchase half interest in two New York teams: the Knicks and the Rangers. In 2005 and 2006 the National Hockey League's Pittsburgh Penguins attempted to obtain a license for a slot machine casino to raise funds to build a new stadium; the effort failed when the Pennsylvania gaming board awarded the only available license to another entity in December 2006. One of the partners in the group that won the license was the Pittsburgh Steelers running back Jerome Bettis (1972–). Bettis's participation in a proposal to open a horse track/casino/hotel complex raised some concern around the NFL, but not as many as would have been raised a few years earlier. Of course, Bettis had a good role model: the Rooney family, owners of the Steelers, also own two horse-racing facilities.

GAMBLING IN COLLEGE SPORTS

The college sports gambling cases noted earlier are probably just the tip of the iceberg. Gambling on sports, which is technically legal only in Nevada and only by adults, is extremely common among college athletes themselves. The *2003 NCAA National Study on*

Collegiate Sports Wagering and Associated Behaviors (December 2004, http://www.ncaa.org/library/research/sports_wagering/2003/2003_sports_wagering_study.pdf) finds that in 2003 more than two-thirds (69%) of male student-athletes and nearly half (47%) of female student-athletes participated in some form of gambling in the past year; 35% of male student-athletes and 10% of female student-athletes reported having bet on sporting events in the past year, in direct violation of NCAA rules regarding sports wagering. The report includes the startling finding that 20.8% of male student-athletes and 5.7% of female student-athletes had gambled on collegiate sporting events in the past year. About 1% of football players and 0.5% of men's basketball players reported having accepted money to play poorly in a game. About 2% of men's football and basketball players said they had been asked to affect the outcome of a game.

In "A Study of Gambling Activity in a NCAA Division II Institution" (*Sports Journal*, vol. 9, no. 4, fall 2006), which focuses on gambling among students and student-athletes at the University of Western Georgia, Frank Butts finds even higher rates of gambling in general—including an astonishing 97.3% of male student-athletes having gambled in some form in the past year—but lower rates of gambling specifically on college sports.

The NCAA has long supported a complete ban on college sports gambling. Naturally, Nevada-based gambling interests strongly oppose such a measure. The gaming industry points out that the problems associated with gambling on college sports are mostly related to illegal gambling, not legitimate wagering that takes place through licensed bookmakers. For example, Brady Dennis reports in "March on Vegas Is Bettors' Ritual" (*St. Petersburg Times*, March 31, 2005) that $90 million was bet legally on the 2005 NCAA basketball tournament, an amount that represented a minute fraction of an estimated $3.5 billion that was wagered when Internet bets and informal office pools were factored in.

Since 2000 members of Congress have advocated banning college sports betting, but they have met with little success. Among the biggest proponents of banning all gambling on college sports has been Senator John McCain (R-AZ; 1936–), who first introduced the Amateur Sports Integrity Act in 2000. Initially, the bill had Nevada gambling businesses worried, but in the end it made little progress in the face of heavy lobbying on the part of the gaming industry and a lack of significant public support. McCain reintroduced the bill during the next two congressional sessions, but it met the same fate. Representative Tom Osborne (R-NE; 1937–), the U.S. House of Representatives sponsor of the bill, reintroduced a version in March 2005 (though McCain opted not to do so in the Senate at the time), just as the NCAA basketball tournament was in high

gear. Gaming industry representatives working against the bill claimed that it would have a devastating effect on their business, noting that college sports gambling accounts for a sizeable share of the total bets placed with licensed Nevada bookmakers. Tony Batt notes in "College Betting Ban Resurfaces" (*Las Vegas Review-Journal*, March 19, 2005) that Bob Scucci, the sports book director at the Stardust Casino, said, "It would be tough to put an exact dollar amount on it, but college football and basketball combine for maybe one-third of our handle." However, Batt reports in "McCain Joins in on NCAA Contest Fun" (*Las Vegas Review-Journal*, March 15, 2007) that by March 2007 McCain himself had apparently softened his stance on betting on college sports; his presidential campaign Web site invited visitors to join him in picking winners in the NCAA men's basketball tournament.

ONLINE GAMBLING

The new frontier of sports gambling is the Internet. Nobody knows exactly how much money is bet online, and the legal status of some aspects of online gambling remains ambiguous. In "Sports Wagering," the AGA indicates that online sports betting generated about $4.3 billion in revenues in 2005.

Internet gambling first became available in the late 1990s, and the Nevada sports books quickly sensed that it presented a serious challenge. Many authorities argued that, based on the federal Wire Act of 1961, which was originally enacted to get organized crime out of sports betting, online sports gambling is technically illegal in the United States; however, not everybody agreed with this analysis. Moreover, most Internet gambling operations are based offshore, which complicates legal issues. The Internet knows no geographic boundaries—an online gambling operation based in Antigua can be accessed as easily from Dubai, Saudi Arabia, as from Dubuque, Iowa. The U.S. government has attempted to take measures to curb online gambling, both sports betting and other types, but because these businesses are not based in the United States, enforcement is problematic. After all, these businesses are legal in the countries in which they are based.

The World Trade Organization has urged the United States to give up its attempts to ban Internet betting, but some members of Congress continued to champion legislation banning online gambling. The most active proponent of banning Internet gambling has been Senator Jon Kyl (R-AZ; 1942–), who first introduced the Internet Gambling Prohibition Act in 1997. Others in Congress argued that rather than trying to prohibit online gambling, it should instead be regulated and taxed, generating substantial revenue for state and federal governments. In the fall of 2006 the Unlawful Internet Gambling Enforcement

Act was passed as an amendment to an unrelated bill, and signed into law by President George W. Bush (1946–). The act does not outlaw Internet gambling, but it prohibits U.S. financial institutions from transferring funds to and from online gambling operations. The impact of the act on online sports gambling was still being assessed as of late 2007, although one immediate result was that a number of prominent online gaming establishments stopped accepting bets from U.S. customers, even though the act did not directly require them to do so.

IMPORTANT NAMES AND ADDRESSES

Amateur Athletic Union
1910 Hotel Plaza Blvd.
Lake Buena Vista, FL 32830
(407) 934-7200
FAX: (407) 934-7242
URL: http://www.aausports.org/

American Gaming Association
1299 Pennsylvania Ave. NW
Washington, DC 20004
(202) 552-2675
URL: http://www.americangaming.org/

Association of Tennis Professionals Tour
201 ATP Tour Blvd.
Ponte Vedra Beach, FL 32082
(904) 285-8000
FAX: (904) 285-5966
URL: http://www.atptennis.com/

Bowling Proprietors' Association of America
615 Six Flags Dr.
Arlington, TX 76011
1-800-343-1329
FAX: (817) 633-2940
URL: http://www.bpaa.com/

Champ Car World Series
5350 Lakeview Parkway South Dr.
Indianapolis, IN 46268
(317) 715-4100
FAX: (317) 715-4110
URL: http://
www.champcarworldseries.com/

Indy Racing League
4565 W. Sixteenth St.
Indianapolis, IN 46222
(317) 492-6526
URL: http://www.indycar.com/

International Boxing Federation
516 Main St., 2nd Fl.
East Orange, NJ 07018
(973) 414-0300
FAX: (973) 414-0307
URL: http://www.ibf-usba-boxing.com/

International Olympic Committee
Château de Vidy 1007
Lausanne, Switzerland
(41-21) 621-6111
FAX: (41-21) 621-6116
URL: http://www.olympic.org/

Ladies Professional Golf Association Tour
100 International Golf Dr.
Daytona Beach, FL 32124-1092
(386) 274-6200
FAX: (386) 274-1099
URL: http://www.lpga.com/

Major League Baseball
Office of the Commissioner
245 Park Ave., 31st Fl.
New York, NY 10167
(212) 931-7800
URL: http://www.mlb.com/

Major League Baseball Players Association
12 E. Forty-ninth St., 24th Fl.
New York, NY 10017
(212) 826-0808
FAX: (212) 752-4378
URL: http://www.mlbplayers.com/

Major League Soccer
110 E. Forty-second St., 10th Fl.
New York, NY 10017
(212) 450-1200
FAX: (212) 450-1300
URL: http://www.mlsnet.com/

National Alliance for Youth Sports
2050 Vista Pkwy.
West Palm Beach, FL 33411
(561) 684-1141
1-800-729-2057
FAX: (561) 684-2546
E-mail: nays@nays.org
URL: http://www.nays.org/

National Association for Stock Car Auto Racing
PO Box 2875
Daytona Beach, FL 32120
URL: http://www.nascar.com/

National Basketball Association
Olympic Tower
645 Fifth Ave.
New York, NY 10022
(212) 407-8000
URL: http://www.nba.com/

National Basketball Players Association
310 Lenox Ave.
New York, NY 10027
(212) 655-0880
FAX: (212) 655-0881
URL: http://www.nbpa.com/

National Collegiate Athletic Association
700 W. Washington St.
Indianapolis, IN 46206-6222
(317) 917-6222
FAX: (317) 917-6888
URL: http://www.ncaa.org/

National Football League
280 Park Ave., 15th Fl.
New York, NY 10017
(212) 450-2000
FAX: (212) 681-7599
URL: http://www.nfl.com/

National Football League Players Association
1133 Twentieth St. NW
Washington, DC 20036
(202) 463-2200
1-800-372-2000
URL: http://www.nflpa.org/main/default.aspx

National Hockey League
1251 Avenue of the Americas, 47th Fl.
New York, NY 10020
(212) 789-2000
FAX: (212) 789-2020
URL: http://www.nhl.com/

National Hockey League Players Association
20 Bay St., Ste. 1700
Toronto, ON M5J 2N8 Canada
(416) 408-4040
URL: http://www.nhlpa.com/

National Sporting Goods Association
1601 Feehanville Dr., Ste. 300
Mt. Prospect, IL 60056
(847) 296-6742
FAX: (847) 391-9827
E-mail: info@nsga.org
URL: http://www.nsga.org/

National Thoroughbred Racing Association
2525 Harrodsburg Rd.
Lexington, KY 40504
(859) 223-5444
1-800-792-6872
FAX: (859) 223-3945
E-mail: ntra@ntra.com
URL: http://www.ntra.com/

Nevada Gaming Commission and State Gaming Control Board
1919 College Pkwy.
Carson City, NV 89706
(775) 684-7750
FAX: (775) 687-5817
URL: http://gaming.nv.gov/

Professional Bowlers Association
719 Second Ave., Ste. 701
Seattle, WA 98104
(206) 332-9688
FAX: (206) 654-6030
URL: http://www.pba.com/

Professional Golfers' Association of America
100 Avenue of the Champions
Palm Beach Gardens, FL 33418
(561) 624-8400
URL: http://www.pga.com/

Sony Ericsson Women's Tennis Association Tour
One Progress Plaza, Ste. 1500
St. Petersburg, FL 33701
(727) 895-5000
FAX: (727) 894-1982
URL: http://www.sonyericssonwtatour.com/1/

Special Olympics
1133 Nineteenth St. NW
Washington, DC 20036
(202) 628-3630
FAX: (202) 824-0200
URL: http://www.specialolympics.org/

Sporting Goods Manufacturers Association
1150 Seventeenth St. NW, Ste. 850
Washington, DC 20036
(202) 775-1762
FAX: (202) 296-7462
E-mail: info@sgma.com
URL: http://www.sgma.com/

U.S. Anti-Doping Agency
1330 Quail Lake Loop, Ste. 260
Colorado Springs, CO 80906-4651
(719) 785-2000
1-866-601-2632
FAX: (719) 785-2001
URL: http://www.usantidoping.org/

U.S. Bowling Congress
5301 S. Seventy-sixth St.
Greendale, WI 53129
1-800-514-2695
FAX: (414) 421-8560
URL: http://www.bowl.com/

U.S. Golf Association
PO Box 708, Liberty Corner Rd.
Far Hills, NJ 07931
(908) 234-2300
FAX: (908) 234-9687
URL: http://www.usga.org/

U.S. Olympic Committee
One Olympic Plaza
Colorado Springs, CO 80909
(719) 632-5551
URL: http://www.usoc.org/

U.S. Tennis Association
70 W. Red Oak Lane
White Plains, NY 10604
(914) 696-7000
URL: http://www.usta.com/

Women's National Basketball Association
Olympic Tower
645 Fifth Ave.
New York, NY 10022
(212) 688-9622
FAX: (212) 750-9622
URL: http://www.wnba.com/

Women's Sports Foundation
Eisenhower Park
East Meadow, NY 11554
(516) 542-4700
1-800-227-3988
FAX: (516) 542-4716
E-mail: info@womenssportsfoundation.org
URL: http://www.womenssportsfoundation.org/

World Boxing Association
PO Box 377
Maracay, 2101-A, Estado Aragua,
Venezuela
(0244) 663-1584
FAX: (0244) 663-3177
E-mail: wbaven@wbaonline.com
URL: http://www.wbaonline.com/

World Boxing Council
Cuzco 872, Colonia Lindavista
Mexico City, C.P. 07300, D.F. Mexico
52 (55) 5119-5274
E-mail: info@wbcboxing.com
URL: http://www.wbcboxing.com/

World Boxing Organization
First Federal Bldg., Ste. 711-714
1056 Muñoz Rivera Ave.
San Juan 00927 Puerto Rico
(787) 765-4628
FAX: (787) 758-9053
URL: http://www.wbo-int.com/

RESOURCES

A substantial amount of information in this volume that pertains to sports participation originated in the *Superstudy of Sports Participation*, which is conducted annually by the independent research company American Sports Data. *Superstudy* data were interpreted and reported by industry organizations such as the Sporting Goods Manufacturing Association (SGMA), the trade association for sporting goods manufacturers, and the National Sporting Goods Association (NSGA), the trade group for sporting goods retailers. The SGMA releases the annual *Sports Participation Topline Report*, which is based on *Superstudy* data, as well as other reports on specific aspects of sports participation. Furthermore, the NSGA conducts its own survey research on participation, as well as industry research on nationwide sales of sporting goods. Another source of data on sports participation was the U.S. Census Bureau's *Statistical Abstract of the United States: 2007* (2006).

The *Statistical Abstract of the United States: 2007* also includes information on attendance at sporting events. Most of the attendance figures for the major sports were obtained from ESPN.com. This was supplemented by information from a variety of print media, including *USA Today* and *Sports Illustrated*. *USA Today*'s online database of sports salaries was also an important source of information.

Polling data provided by the Gallup Organization was key in assembling information on the preferences of sports fans, including trends related to race, gender, age, and geography.

"Sports and Television" (2004) by the Museum of Broadcast Communications provided information on the history of sports on television. Another key source on this topic, as well as other aspects of sports media, was *The Business of Sports* (2004), edited by Scott R. Rosner and Kenneth L. Shropshire. The *Business of Sports* provides comprehensive coverage of all economic aspects of the sports industry. Besides sports media, the book includes essential information on the financial structure of professional team sports, college sports, and the Olympics. Also, the *SportsBusiness Journal* provided additional information on the broadcast contracts of major sports.

Nonprofit advocacy and public education groups provided substantial information for this volume. The Center on Alcohol Marketing and Youth provided data on alcohol advertising during sports programming. The Women's Sports Foundation offered research on gender equity in sports. Another key source of information on gender equity was *Women in Intercollegiate Sport: A Longitudinal, National Study—Twenty Nine Year Update, 1977–2006* (2006) by Linda Jean Carpenter and R. Vivian Acosta.

The National Collegiate Athletic Association (NCAA) provided a wealth of data on many aspects of college sports. Key NCAA publications that contributed information include the *1981–82—2005–06 Sports Sponsorship and Participation Report* (Nicole Bracken, May 2007), the *2003–04 NCAA Gender-Equity Report* (Denise DeHass, September 2006), the *1999–00—2004–05 NCAA Student-Athlete Race and Ethnicity Report* (Roberto Vincente, June 2006), and the *2002–03 NCAA Revenues and Expenses of Divisions I and II Intercollegiate Athletics Programs Report* (Daniel L. Fulks, February 2005). Information on eligibility rules for college athletes was found in the NCAA's *Guide for the College-Bound Student-Athlete* (2007).

The independent research company Plunkett Research offered information on revenues of the major professional sports. Team-by-team revenue and valuation figures were provided by *Forbes*, and *SportsBusiness Journal* provided data on sales of licensed merchandise. Most of the information about the structure and workings of the major sports leagues came from the leagues themselves. Likewise, information about the PGA Tour, the Association of Tennis Professionals Tour, the National Association for Stock Car Auto Racing, the various boxing organizations, and other nonteam sports was obtained from the Web sites of these organizations. Revenues from Sports Venues, a company specializing in directories and other publications about the sports venue industry, also provided helpful information.

The International Olympic Committee (IOC) provided a wealth of information about the structure and workings of the Olympic movement. One important IOC report, the *2006 Marketing Fact File* (July 2005), offered detailed information on Olympic financial matters, including sources of revenue and how it is distributed.

Steroid Abuse in Today's Society (March 2004), by the U.S. Drug Enforcement Administration, provided valuable information about steroids.

The American Gaming Association and the Nevada Gaming Commission and State Gaming Control Board were useful sources of information on legal sports gambling. The Pew Research Center provided information about the prevalence of and attitudes toward gambling. Christiansen Capital Advisors provided research on Internet sports gambling.

INDEX